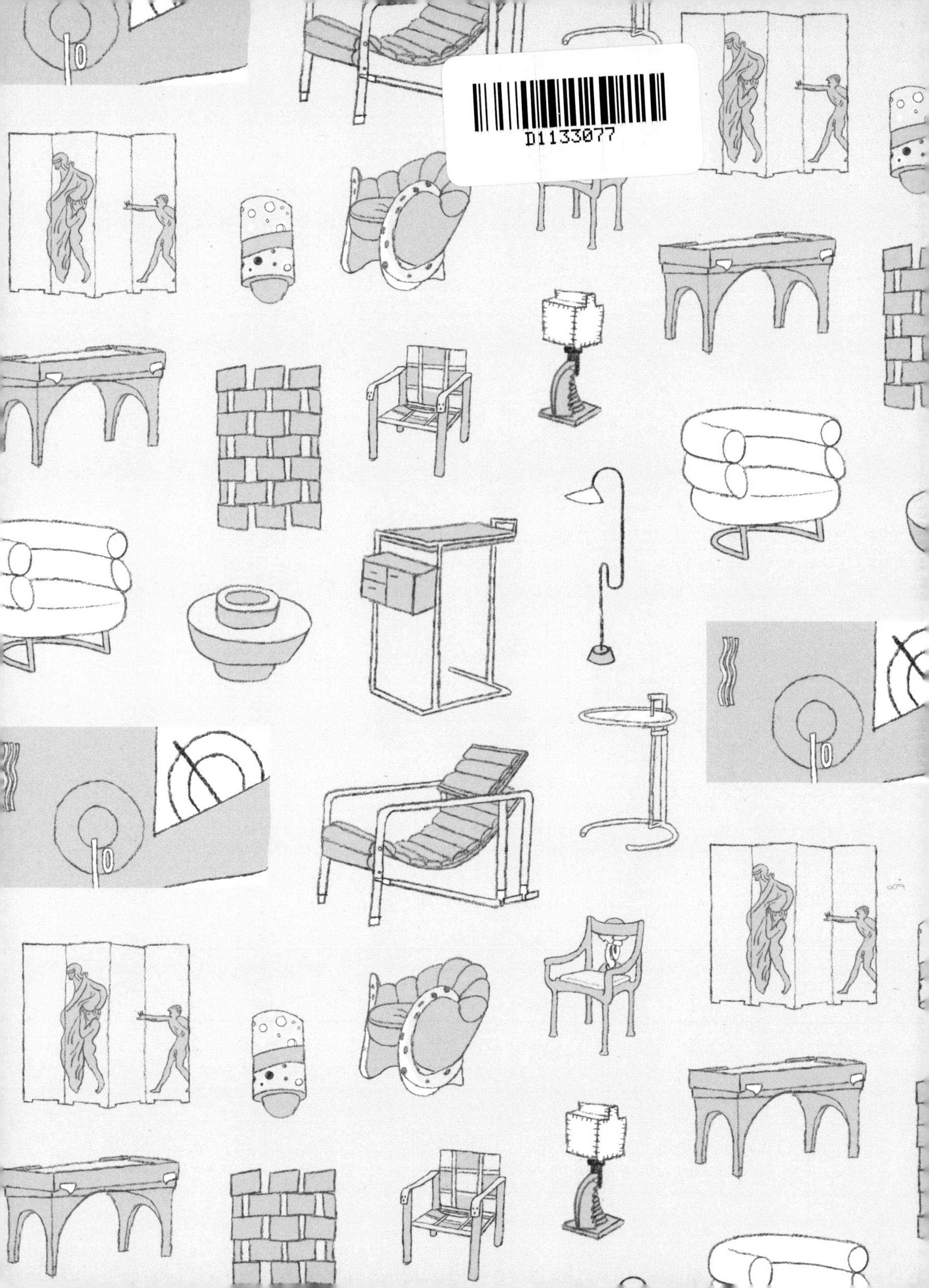

THIS ONE IS FOR THE
GIRLS, WOMEN AND GRANNIES, AND
THE MEN THAT SUPPORT THEM.

Charlotte Malterre-Barthes & Zosia Dzierżawska

EILEEN GRAY

A HOUSE UNDER THE SUN

NOBROW

LONDON I NEW YORK

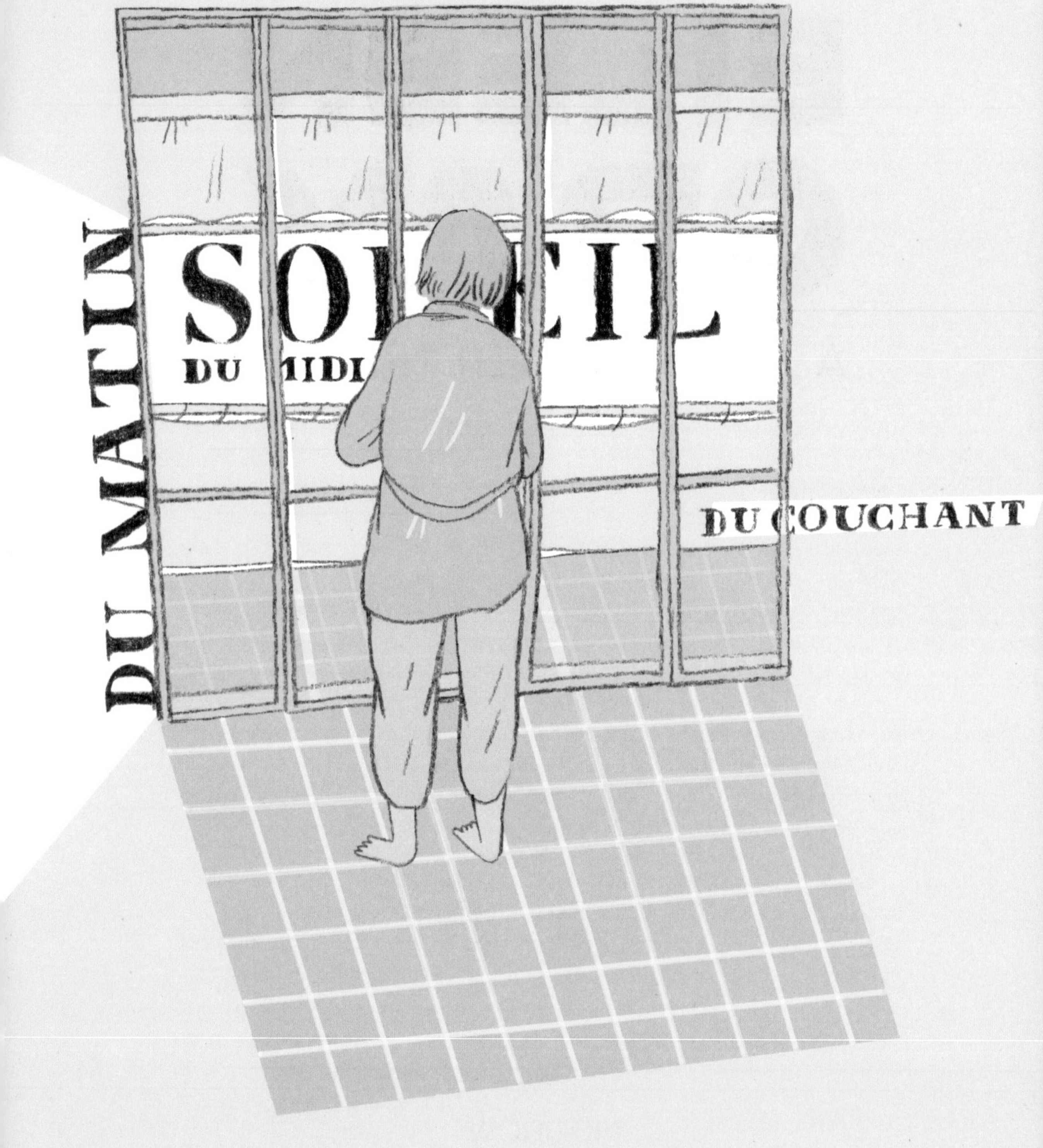
DU MATIN
DU MIDI
DU COUCHANT

FOREWORD

For much of the twentieth century, Eileen Gray remained an elusive lacquer artist, designer and self-taught architect. Though hundreds of her architectural projects exist, E-1027 – created for her lover at the time, Romanian architect Jean Badovici – and her own home, Tempe à Pailla, are the only architectural works still intact. Later in her life, Gray attempted to destroy her personal papers, wanting to be only remembered for her work.

In *Eileen Gray: A House Under the Sun*, Charlotte Malterre-Barthes and Zosia Dzierżawska illustrate the story of Gray and E-1027, which remains her most famous project. The house was a very personal statement, the sole expression of years of ideas, which then culminated in what is now considered a masterpiece of twentieth century architecture.

Through stunning, poignant illustrations, Malterre-Barthes and Dzierżawska detail Gray's life and inner circle. They exquisitely re-examine the complex situation which surrounded Badovici commissioning Le Corbusier to paint a series of murals at the house between 1938 and 1939. These pictorial interventions demonstrated Badovici's and Corbusier's lack of understanding of Gray's work and what she was attempting to achieve at E-1027. This wonderful book displays just how much the murals broke the structural integrity of the interior, compromising not just the space but the totality of the house as an ensemble. Le Corbusier published *Œuvre Complète* in 1946 and *L'Architecture d'Aujourd'hui* in 1948, where E-1027 was merely referred to as "a house in Cap Martin". Gray's name was omitted and thus began her subsequent omission from the canon of modern architecture.

Charlotte Malterre-Barthes and Zosia Dzierżawska transport the reader back to E-1027 and the way the house looked upon its completion in 1929. They leave the reader with a nostalgic image of Eileen Gray absorbing the building in its totality – enjoying her last moments in her house under the sun.

Jennifer Goff
Curator of the Eileen Gray collection,
National Museum of Ireland.

THE LAST SWIM

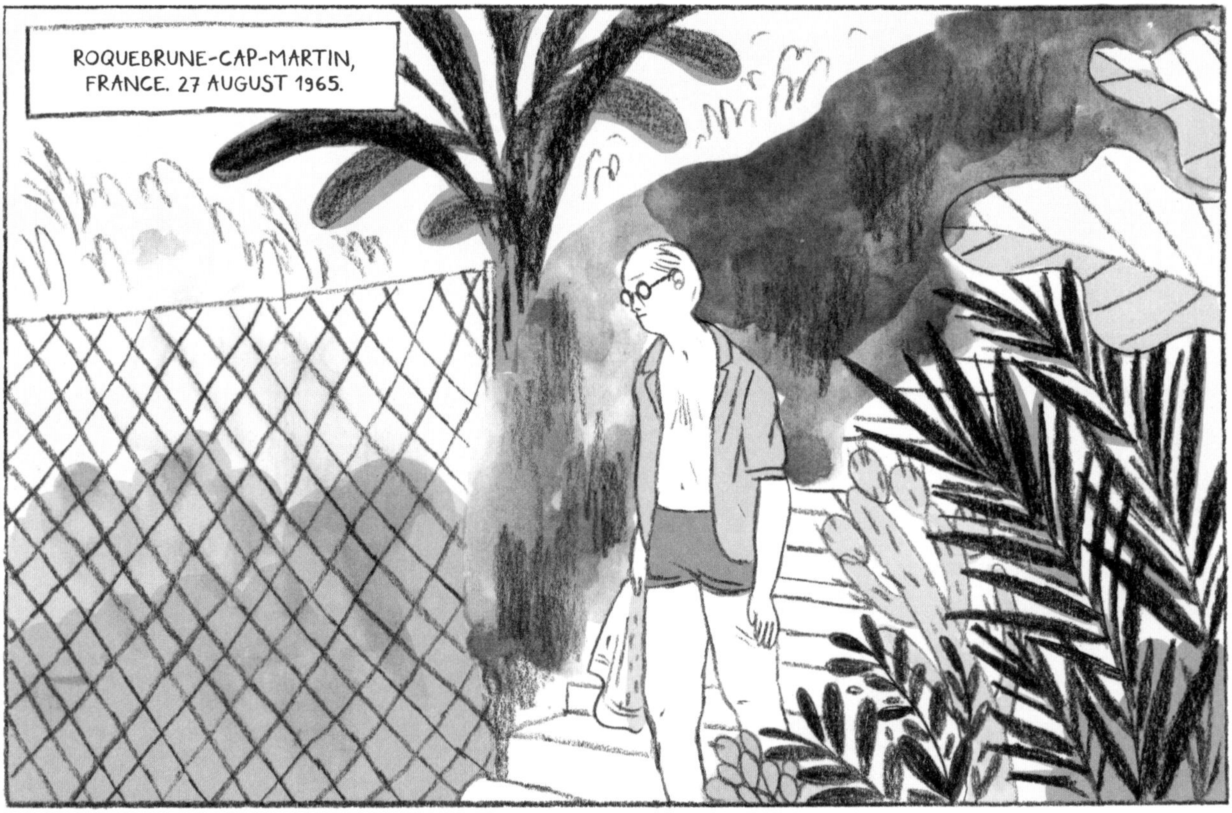
ROQUEBRUNE-CAP-MARTIN, FRANCE. 27 AUGUST 1965.

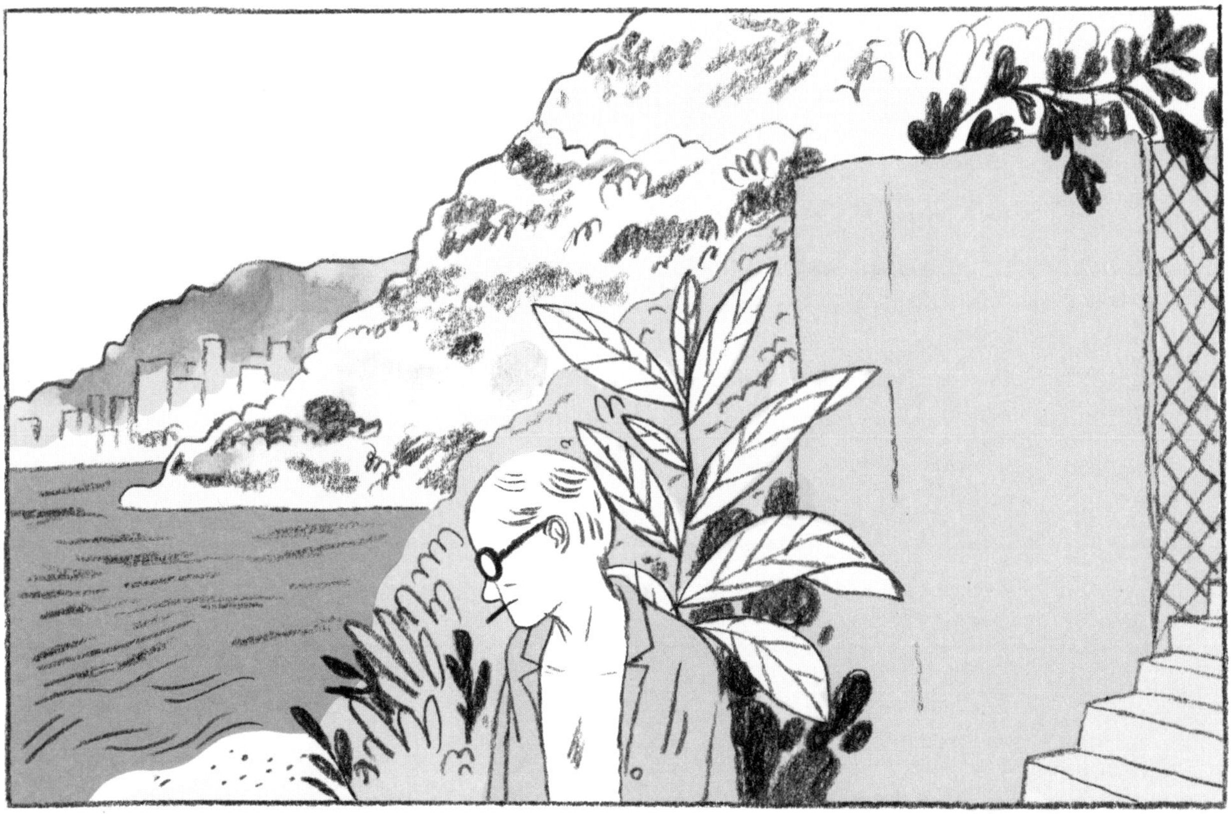

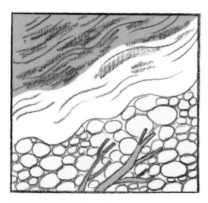
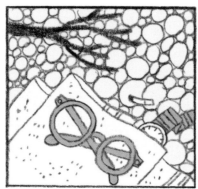

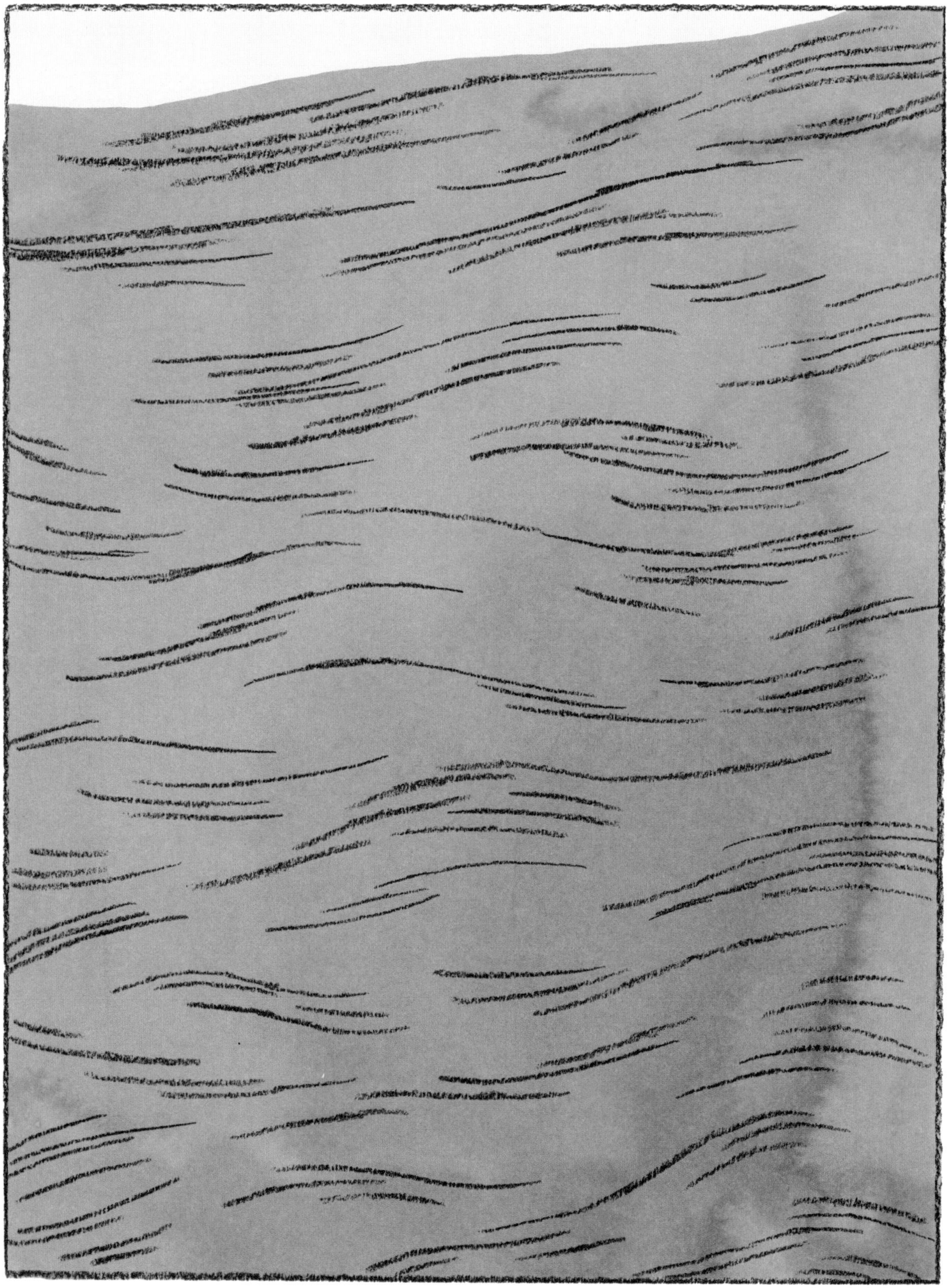

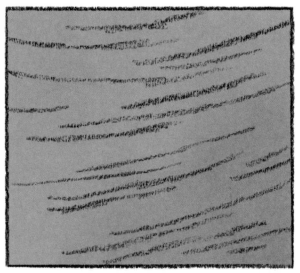

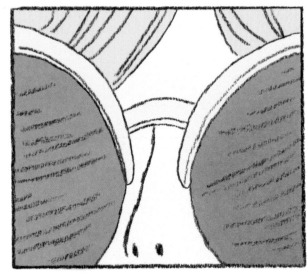

CHÉRI, I THINK THERE'S SOMETHING IN THE WATER... DRIFTWOOD MAYBE?

COULD IT BE... NOM DE DIEU! IT'S A BODY!

QUICK, WE'VE GOT TO GET THEM OUT!

GO! CALL FOR HELP!

HELP! ANYONE! SOMEONE'S DROWNED!

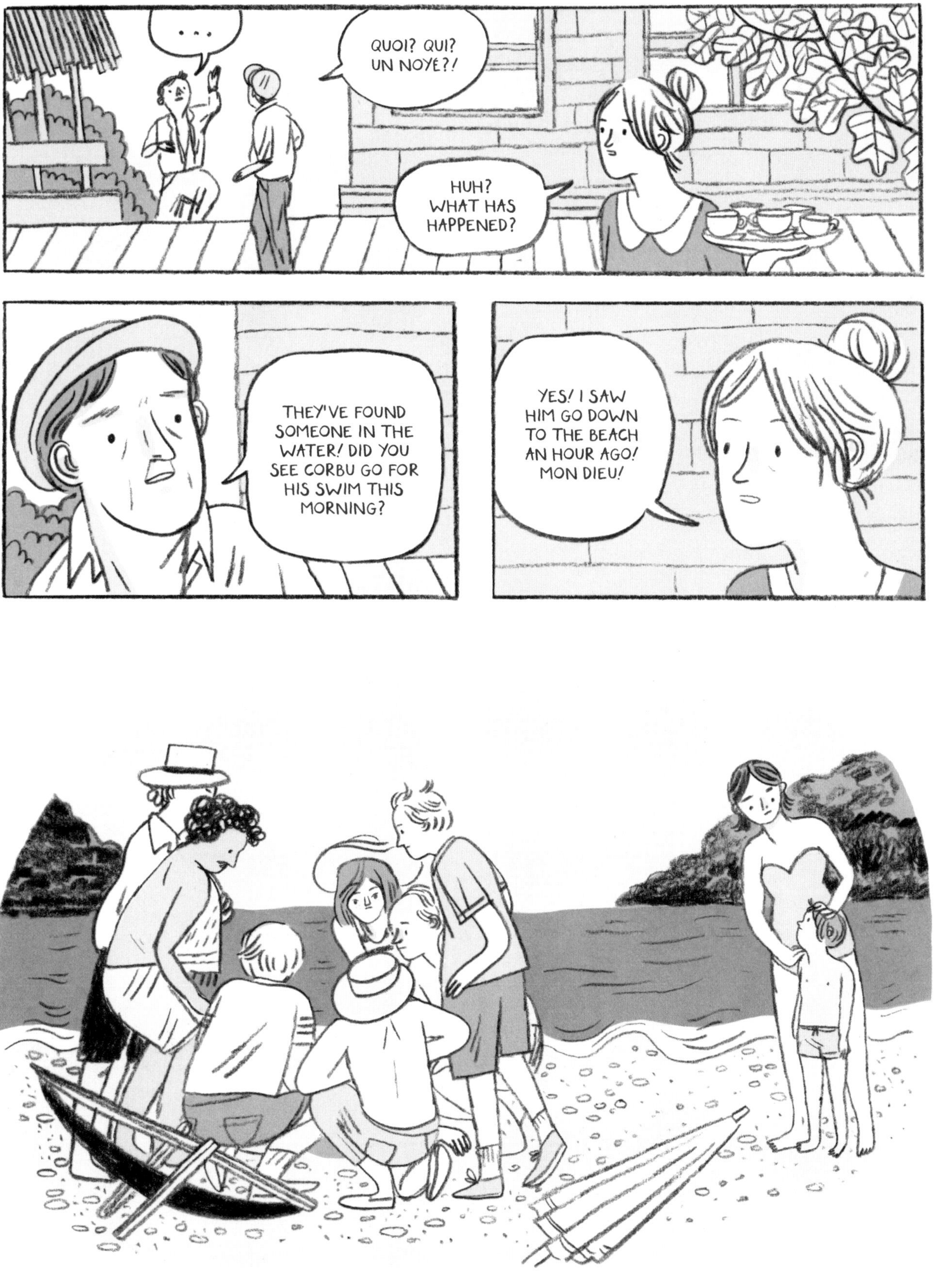
. . .
QUOI? QUI? UN NOYÉ?!
HUH? WHAT HAS HAPPENED?
THEY'VE FOUND SOMEONE IN THE WATER! DID YOU SEE CORBU GO FOR HIS SWIM THIS MORNING?
YES! I SAW HIM GO DOWN TO THE BEACH AN HOUR AGO! MON DIEU!

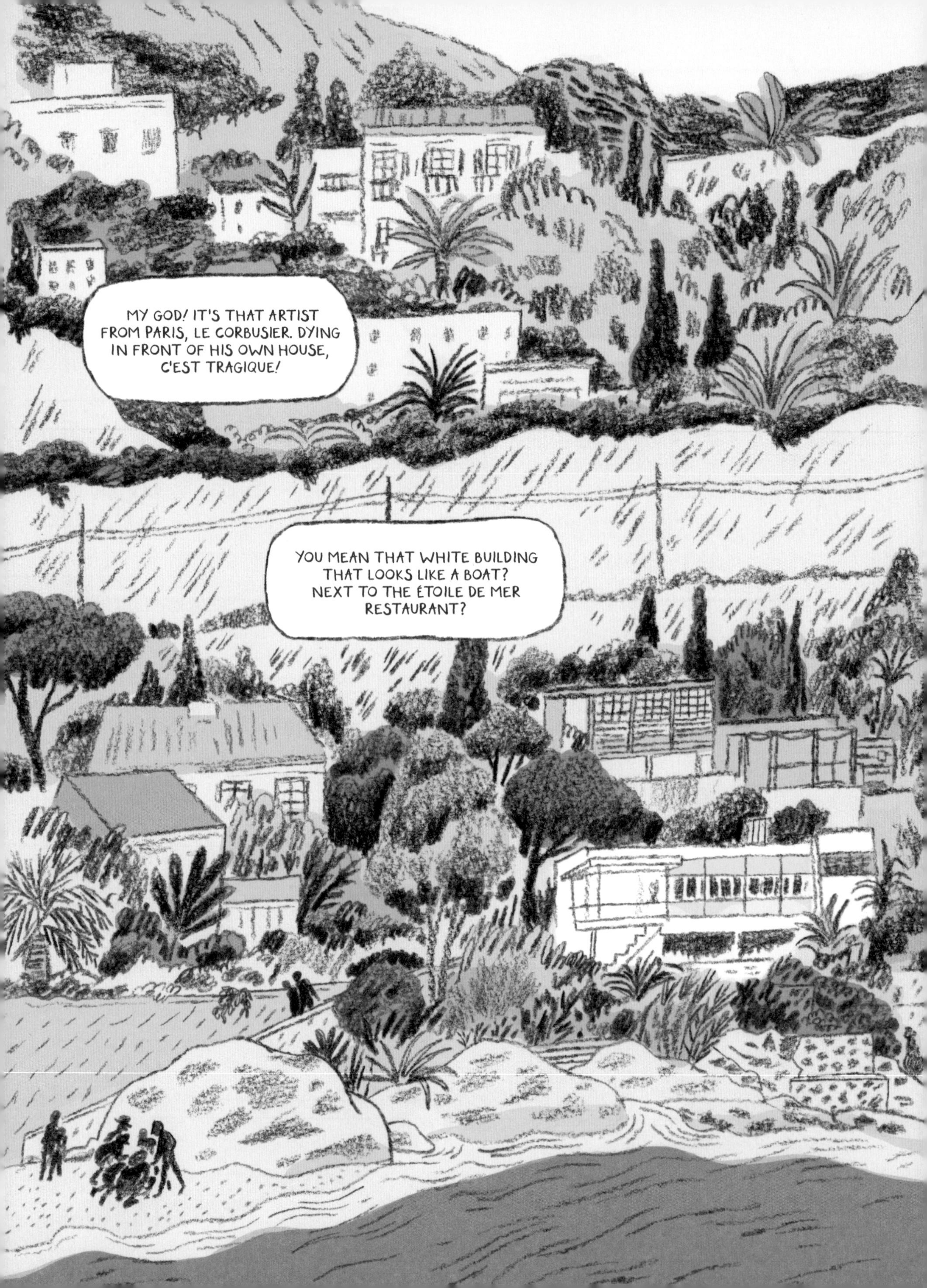
MY GOD! IT'S THAT ARTIST FROM PARIS, LE CORBUSIER. DYING IN FRONT OF HIS OWN HOUSE, C'EST TRAGIQUE!
YOU MEAN THAT WHITE BUILDING THAT LOOKS LIKE A BOAT? NEXT TO THE ÉTOILE DE MER RESTAURANT?

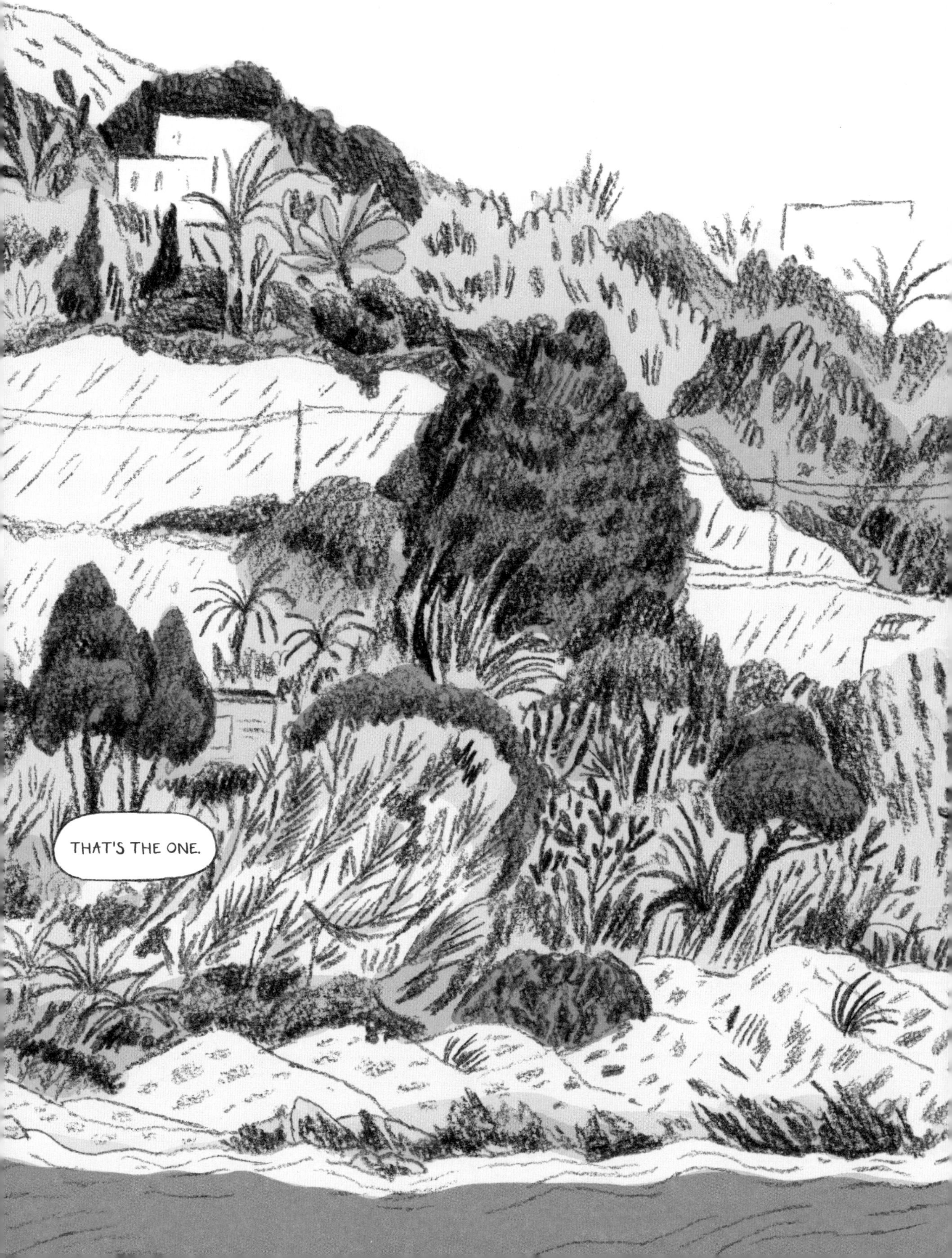
THAT'S THE ONE.

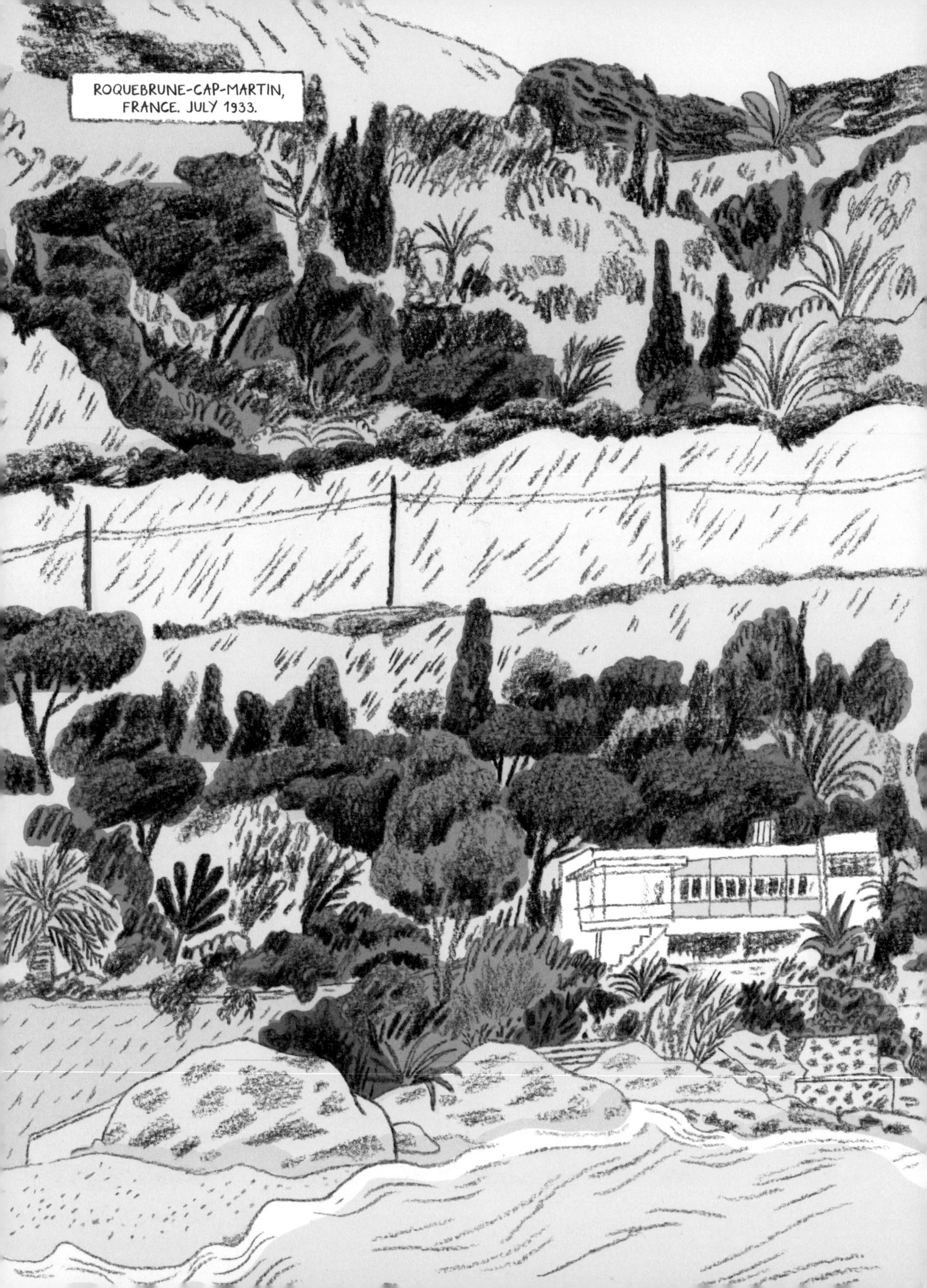
ROQUEBRUNE-CAP-MARTIN, FRANCE. JULY 1933.

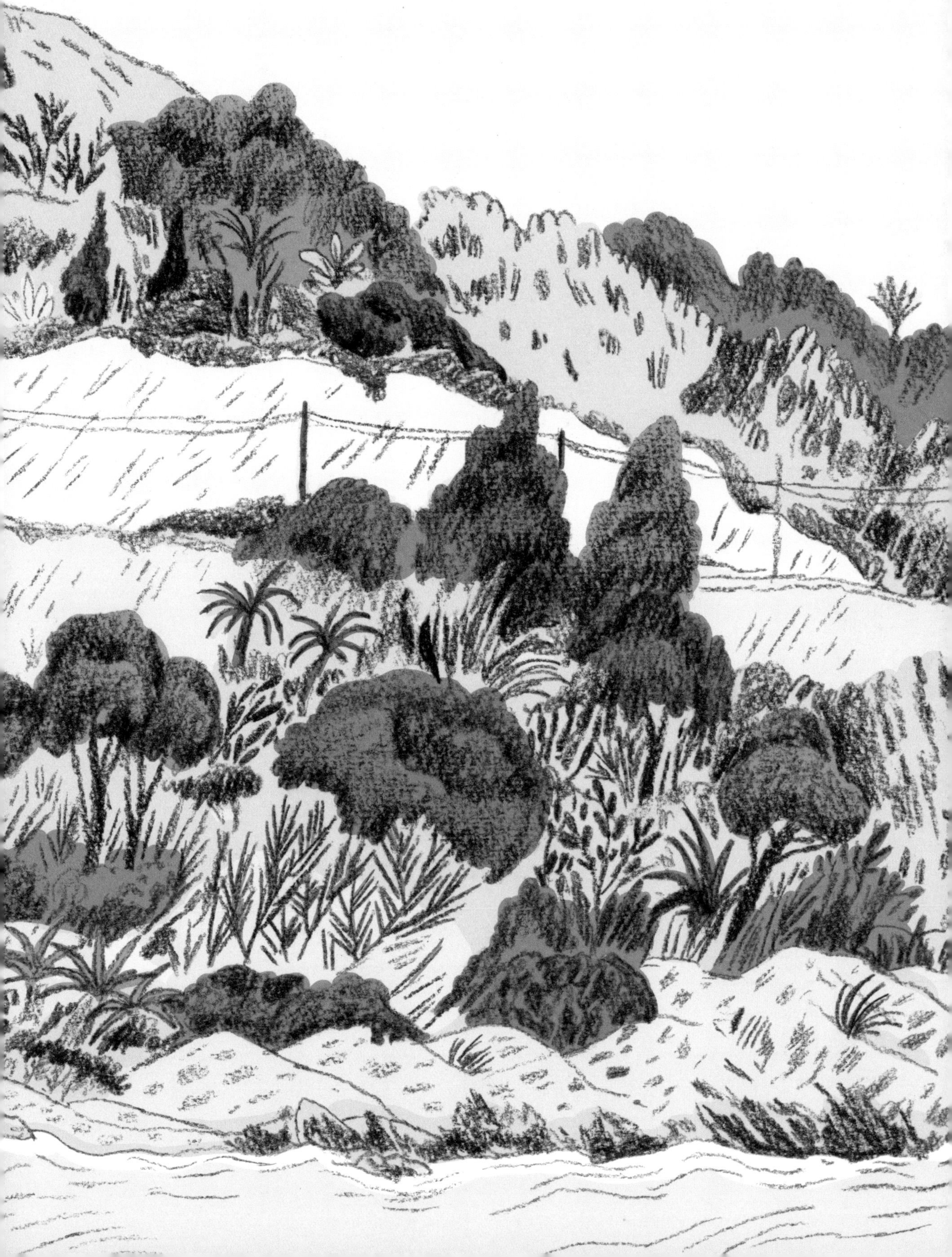

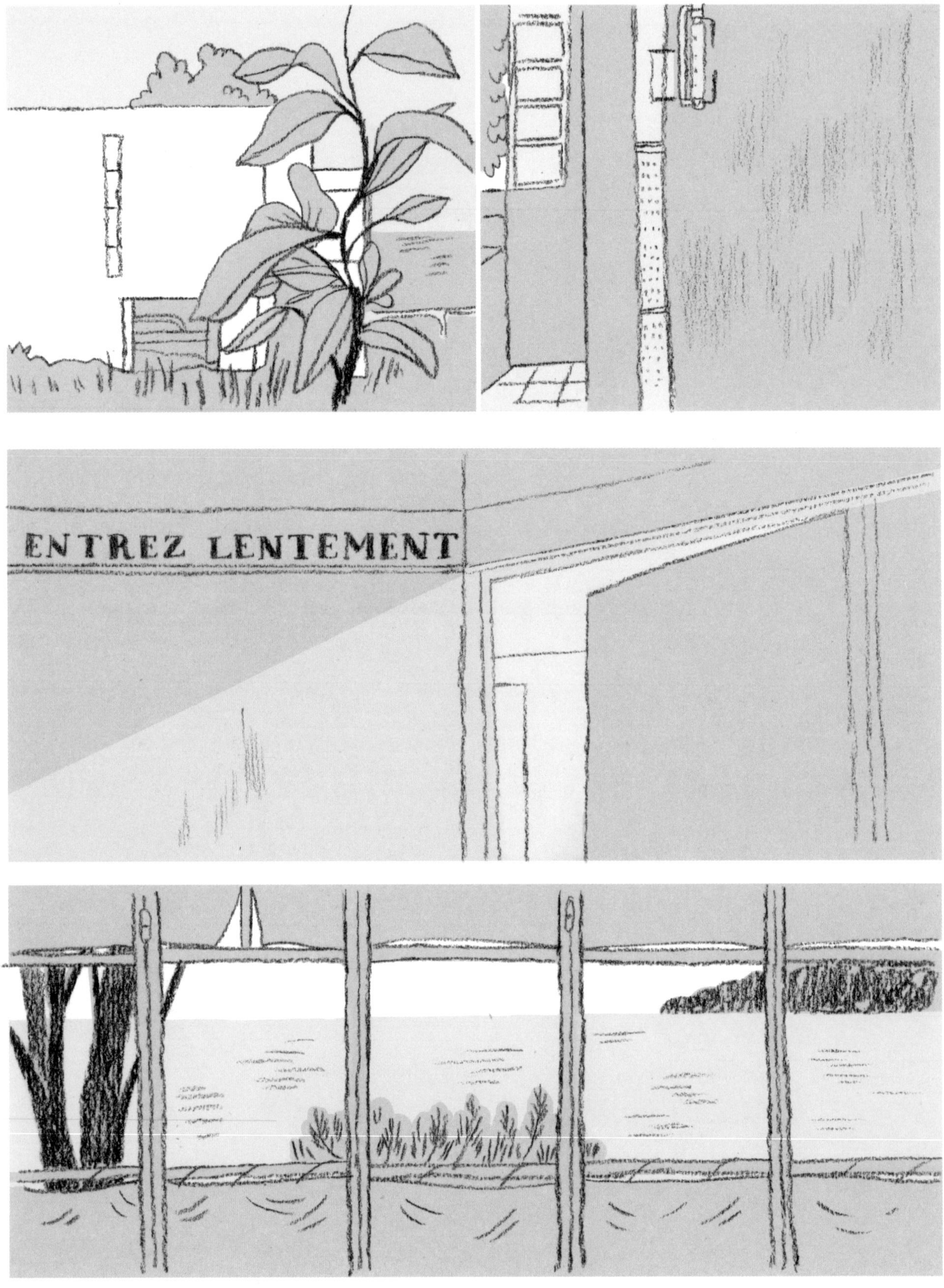
ENTREZ LENTEMENT

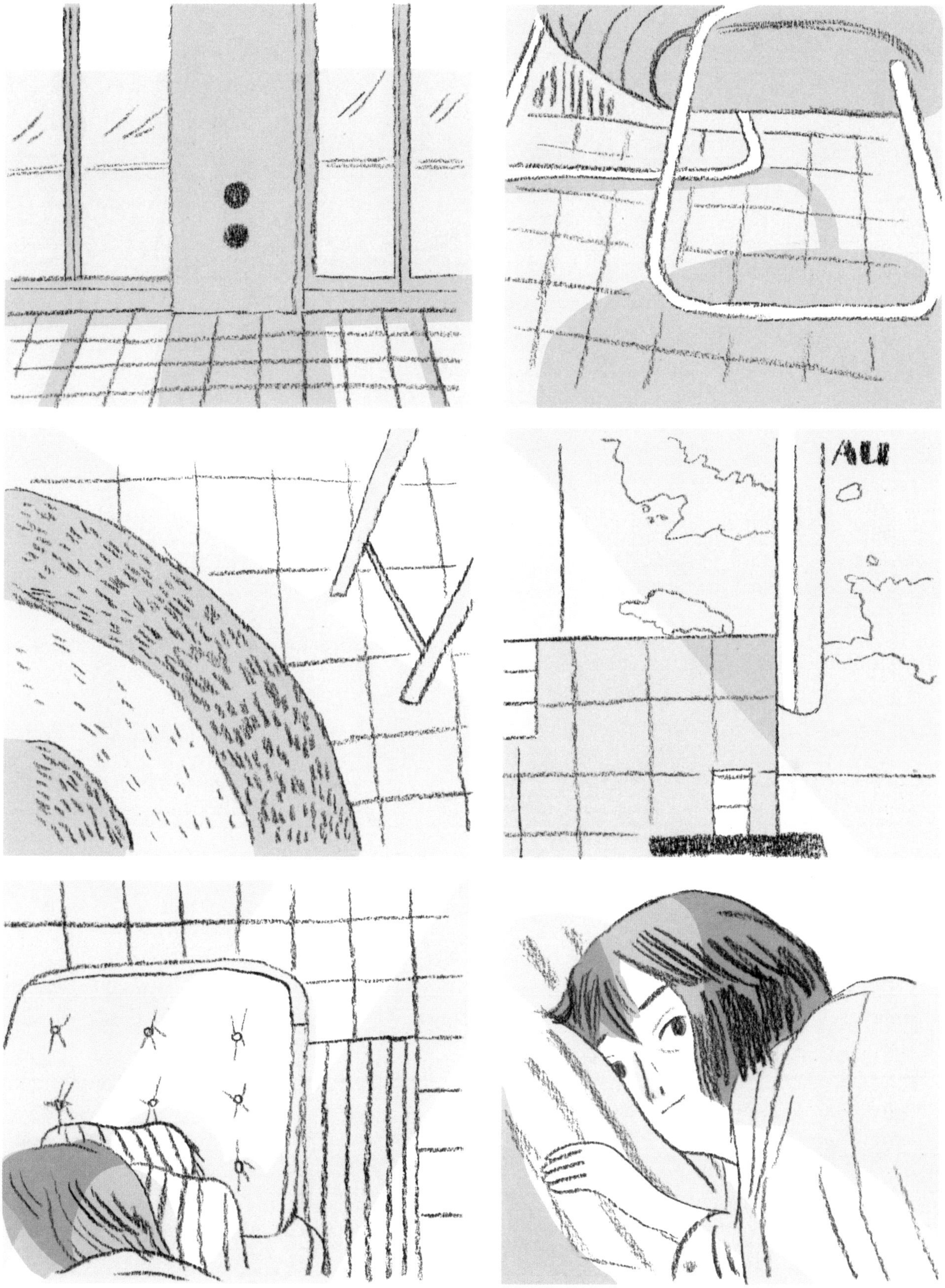

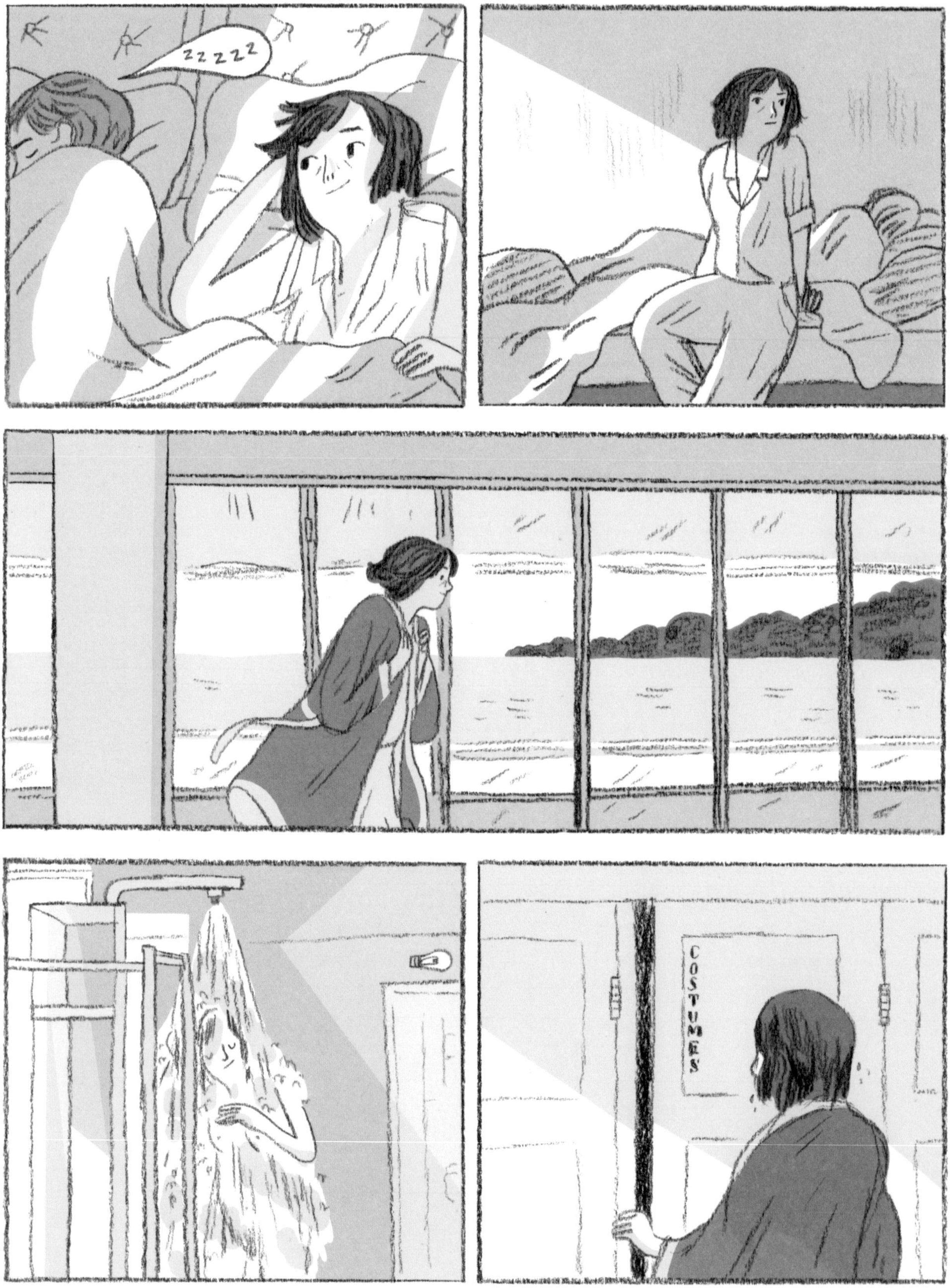
ZZZZZ
COSTUMES

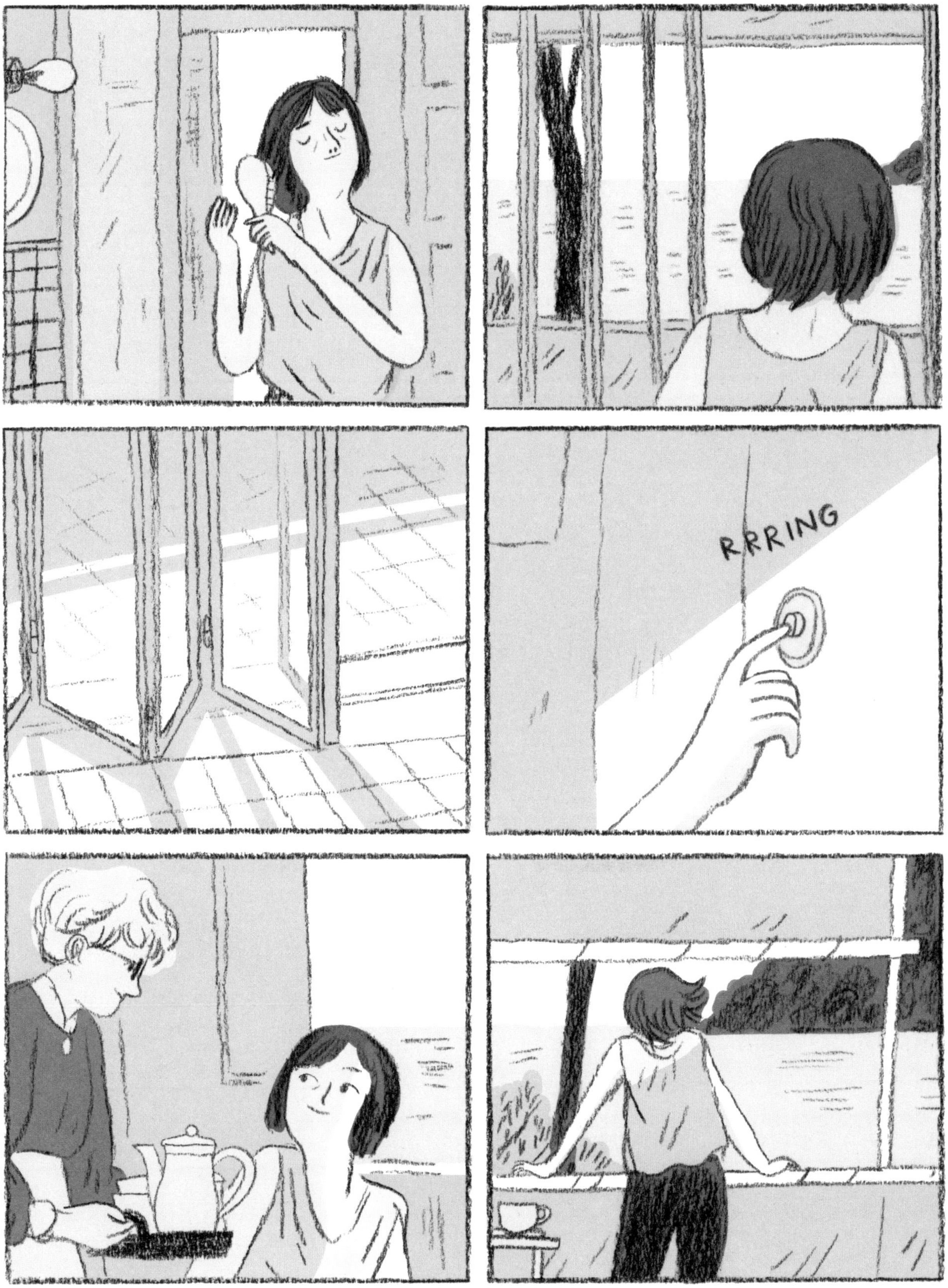
RRRING

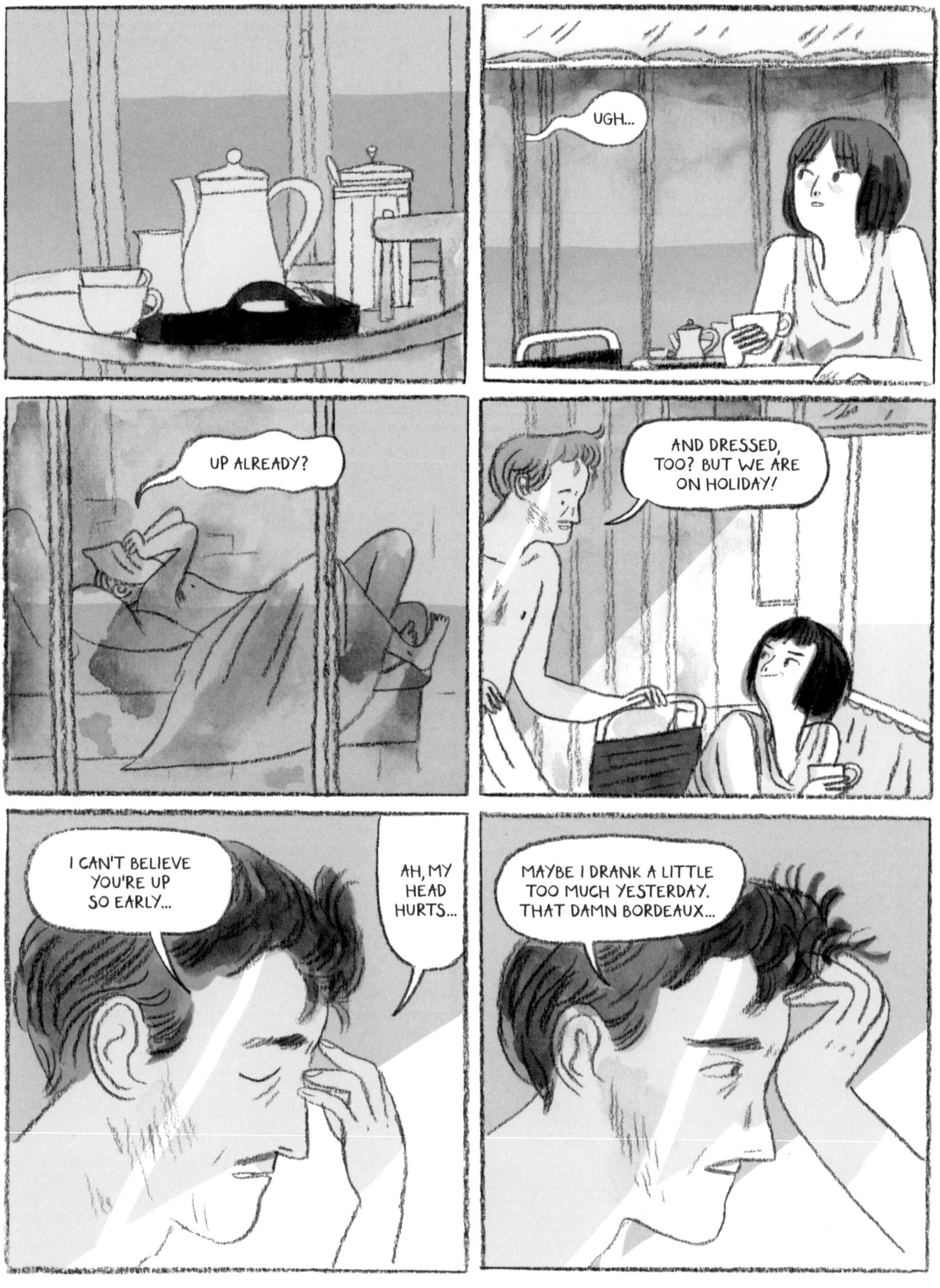
UGH...
UP ALREADY?
AND DRESSED, TOO? BUT WE ARE ON HOLIDAY!
I CAN'T BELIEVE YOU'RE UP SO EARLY...
AH, MY HEAD HURTS...
MAYBE I DRANK A LITTLE TOO MUCH YESTERDAY. THAT DAMN BORDEAUX...

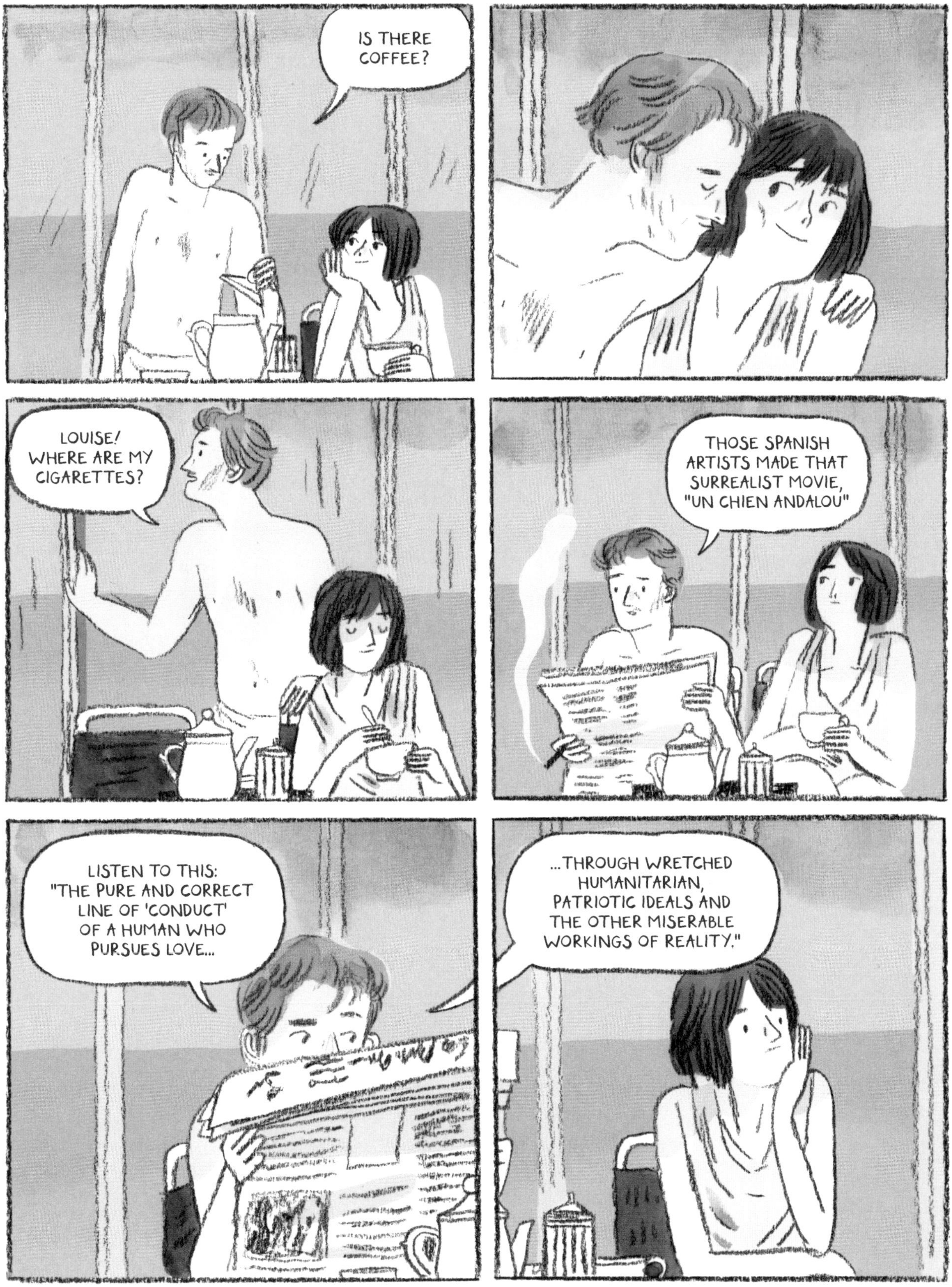
IS THERE COFFEE?
LOUISE! WHERE ARE MY CIGARETTES?
THOSE SPANISH ARTISTS MADE THAT SURREALIST MOVIE, "UN CHIEN ANDALOU"
LISTEN TO THIS: "THE PURE AND CORRECT LINE OF 'CONDUCT' OF A HUMAN WHO PURSUES LOVE...
...THROUGH WRETCHED HUMANITARIAN, PATRIOTIC IDEALS AND THE OTHER MISERABLE WORKINGS OF REALITY."

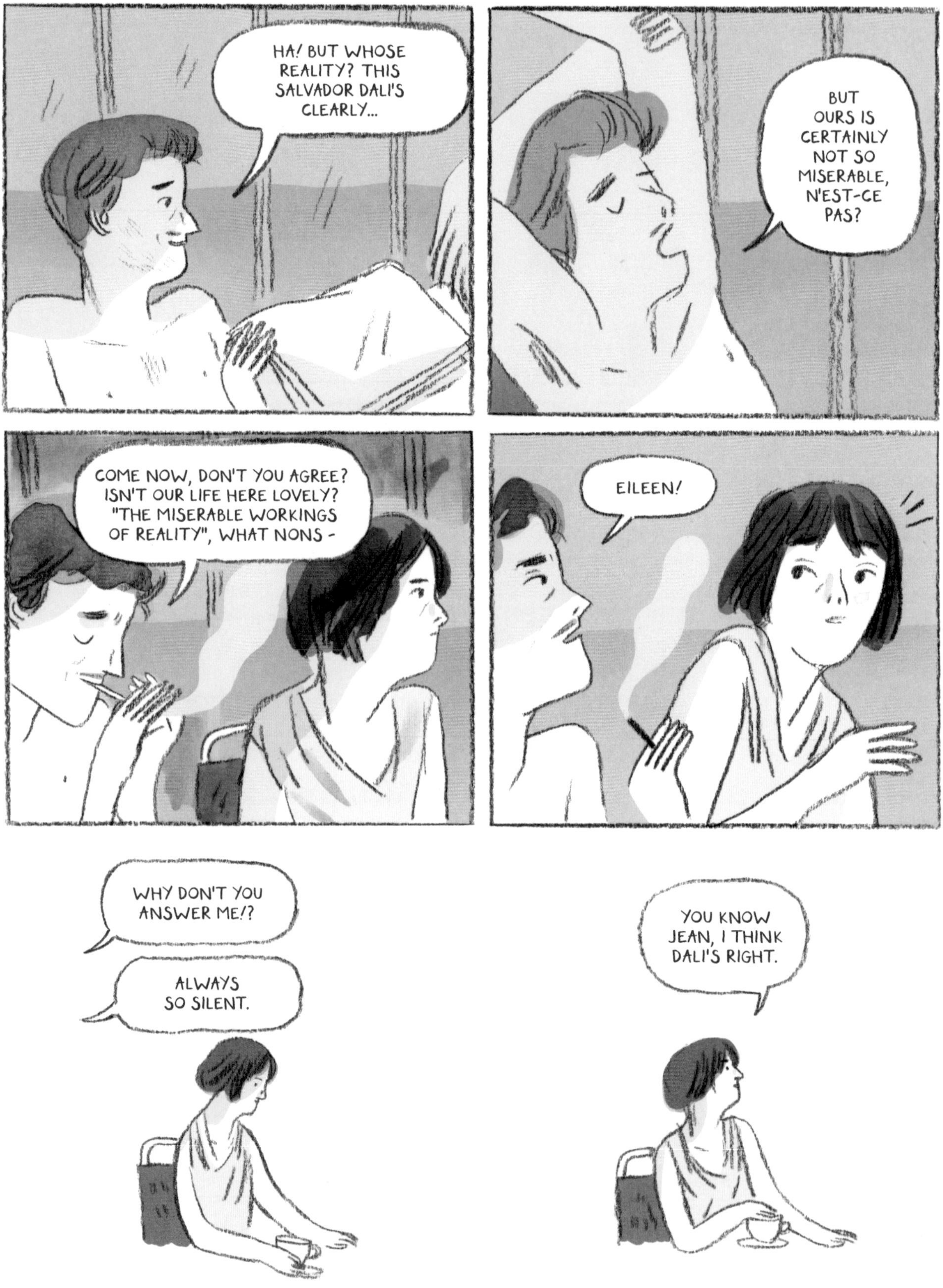

HA! BUT WHOSE REALITY? THIS SALVADOR DALI'S CLEARLY...
BUT OURS IS CERTAINLY NOT SO MISERABLE, N'EST-CE PAS?
COME NOW, DON'T YOU AGREE? ISN'T OUR LIFE HERE LOVELY? "THE MISERABLE WORKINGS OF REALITY", WHAT NONS -
EILEEN!
WHY DON'T YOU ANSWER ME!?
ALWAYS SO SILENT.
YOU KNOW JEAN, I THINK DALI'S RIGHT.

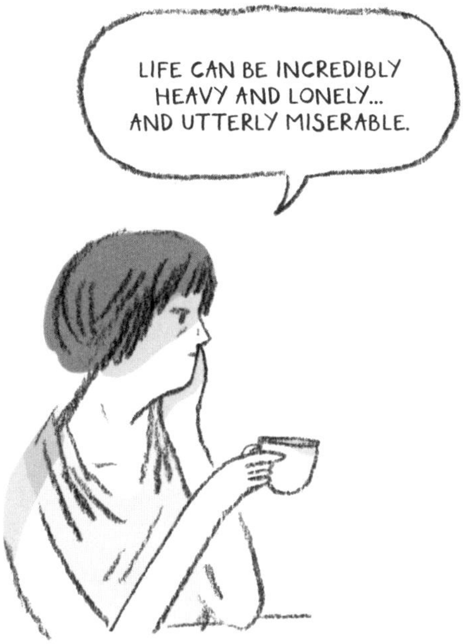
LIFE CAN BE INCREDIBLY HEAVY AND LONELY... AND UTTERLY MISERABLE.

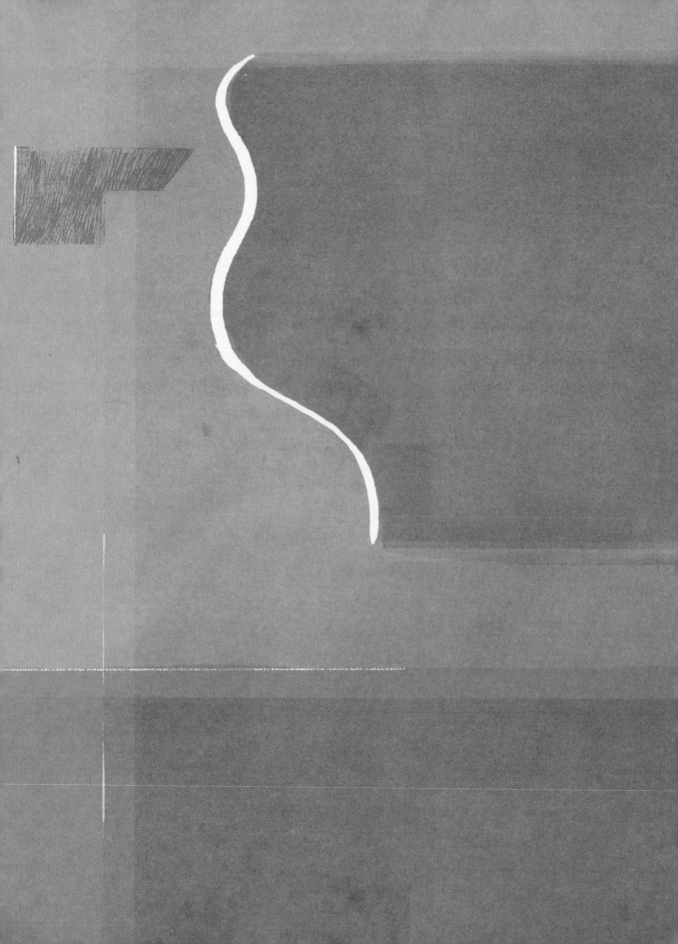

LITTLE EILEEN

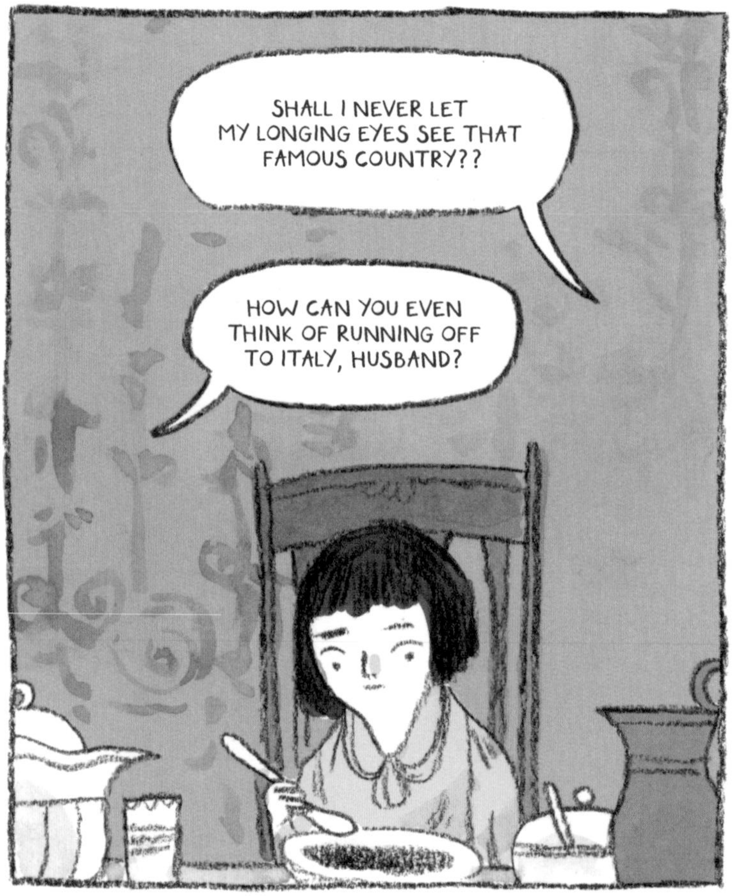
SHALL I NEVER LET MY LONGING EYES SEE THAT FAMOUS COUNTRY??
HOW CAN YOU EVEN THINK OF RUNNING OFF TO ITALY, HUSBAND?

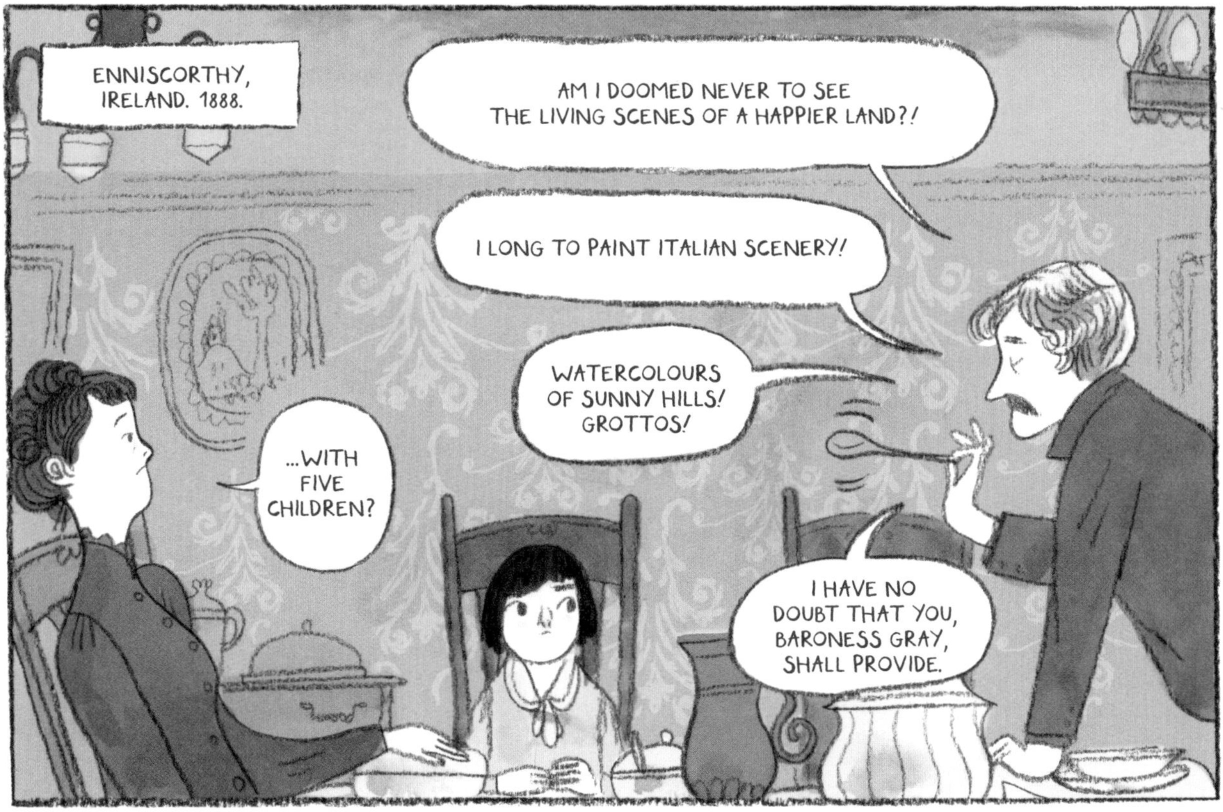
ENNISCORTHY, IRELAND. 1888.
AM I DOOMED NEVER TO SEE THE LIVING SCENES OF A HAPPIER LAND?!
I LONG TO PAINT ITALIAN SCENERY!
WATERCOLOURS OF SUNNY HILLS! GROTTOS!
...WITH FIVE CHILDREN?
I HAVE NO DOUBT THAT YOU, BARONESS GRAY, SHALL PROVIDE.

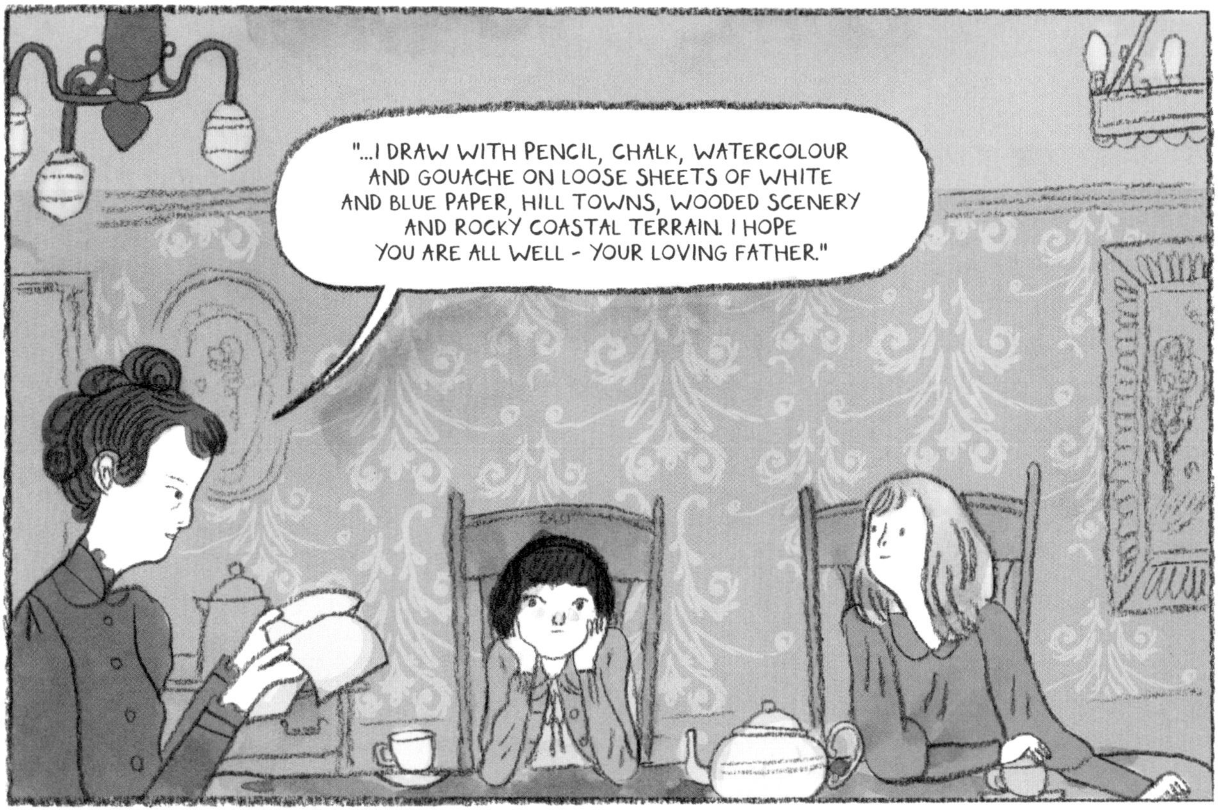
"...I DRAW WITH PENCIL, CHALK, WATERCOLOUR AND GOUACHE ON LOOSE SHEETS OF WHITE AND BLUE PAPER, HILL TOWNS, WOODED SCENERY AND ROCKY COASTAL TERRAIN. I HOPE YOU ARE ALL WELL - YOUR LOVING FATHER."

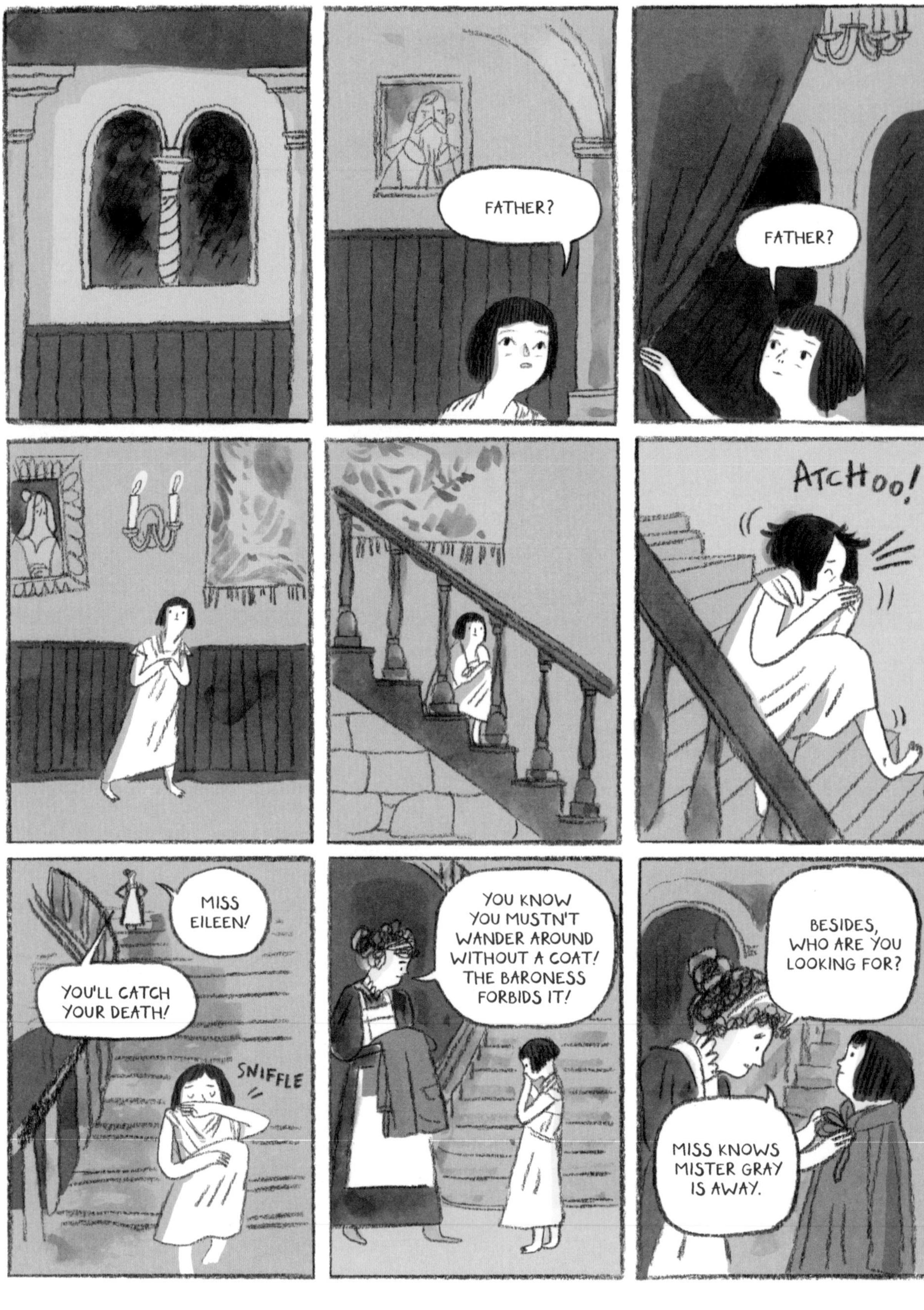
FATHER?
FATHER?
ATCHOO!
MISS EILEEN!
YOU'LL CATCH YOUR DEATH!
SNIFFLE
YOU KNOW YOU MUSTN'T WANDER AROUND WITHOUT A COAT! THE BARONESS FORBIDS IT!
BESIDES, WHO ARE YOU LOOKING FOR?
MISS KNOWS MISTER GRAY IS AWAY.

DEATH? IS IT SOMETHING YOU CAN CATCH?

MOTHER?

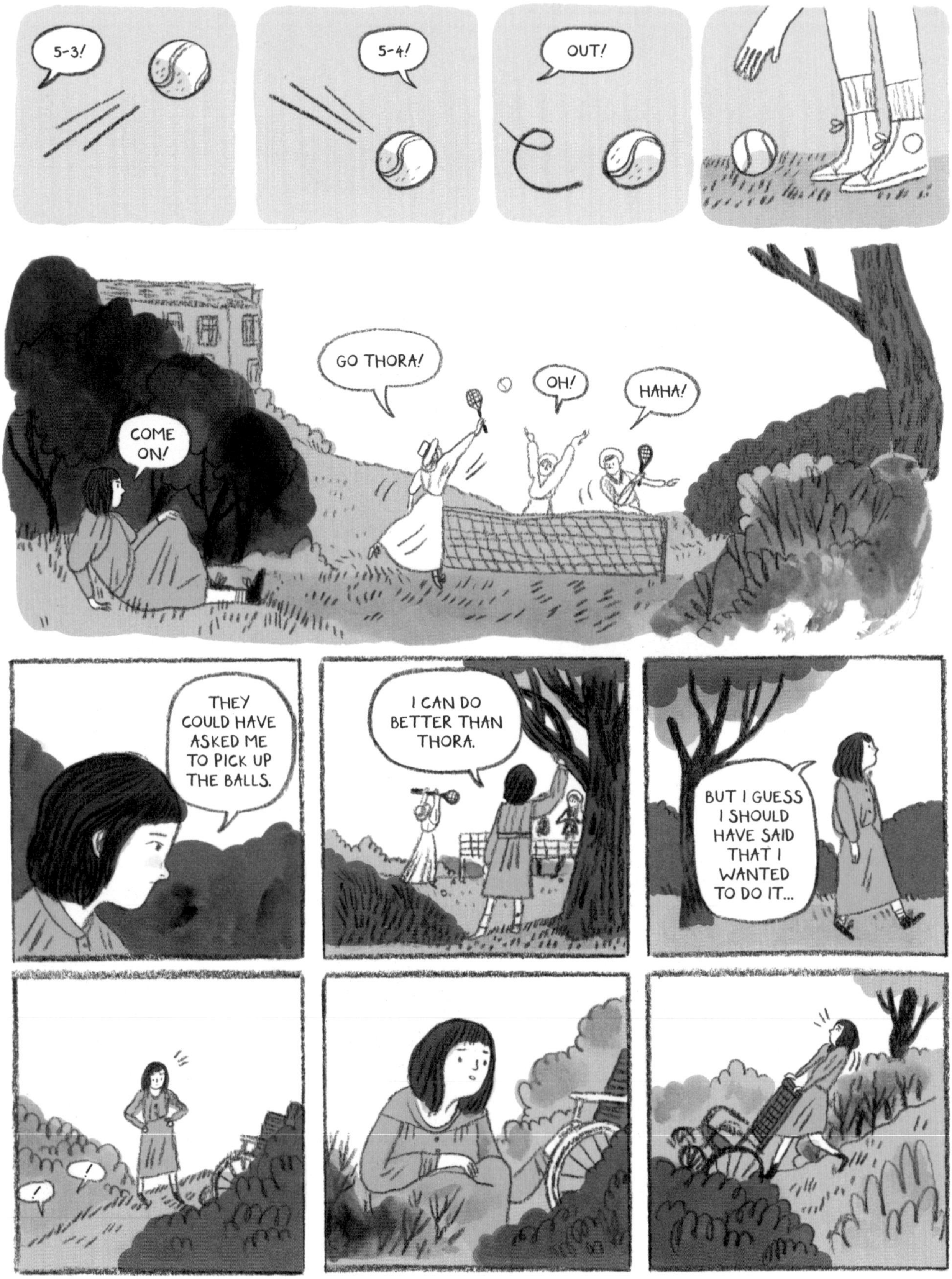
5-3!
5-4!
OUT!
COME ON!
GO THORA!
OH!
HAHA!
THEY COULD HAVE ASKED ME TO PICK UP THE BALLS.
I CAN DO BETTER THAN THORA.
BUT I GUESS I SHOULD HAVE SAID THAT I WANTED TO DO IT...
!
!

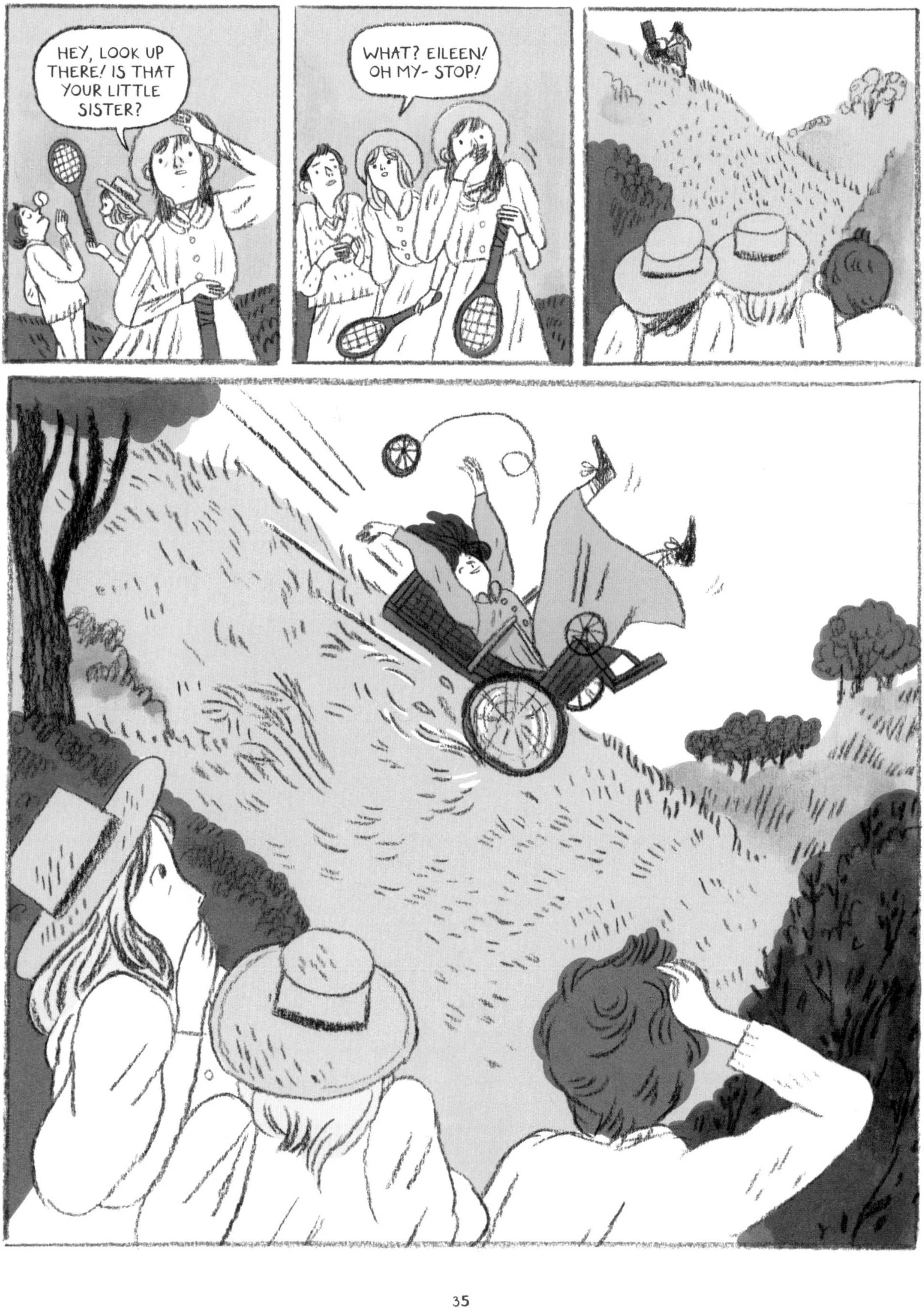
HEY, LOOK UP THERE! IS THAT YOUR LITTLE SISTER?
WHAT? EILEEN! OH MY- STOP!

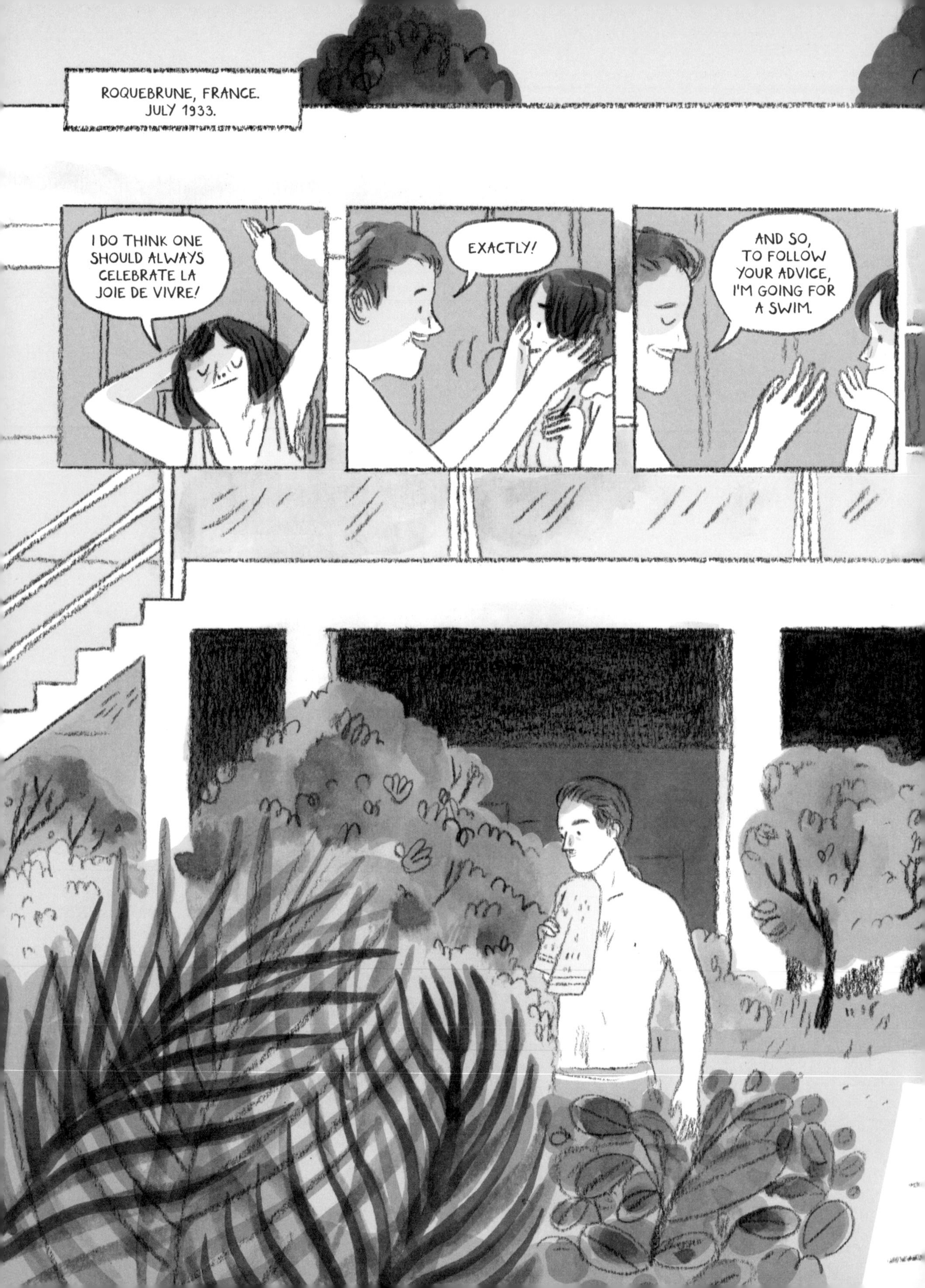
ROQUEBRUNE, FRANCE. JULY 1933.
I DO THINK ONE SHOULD ALWAYS CELEBRATE LA JOIE DE VIVRE!
EXACTLY!
AND SO, TO FOLLOW YOUR ADVICE, I'M GOING FOR A SWIM.

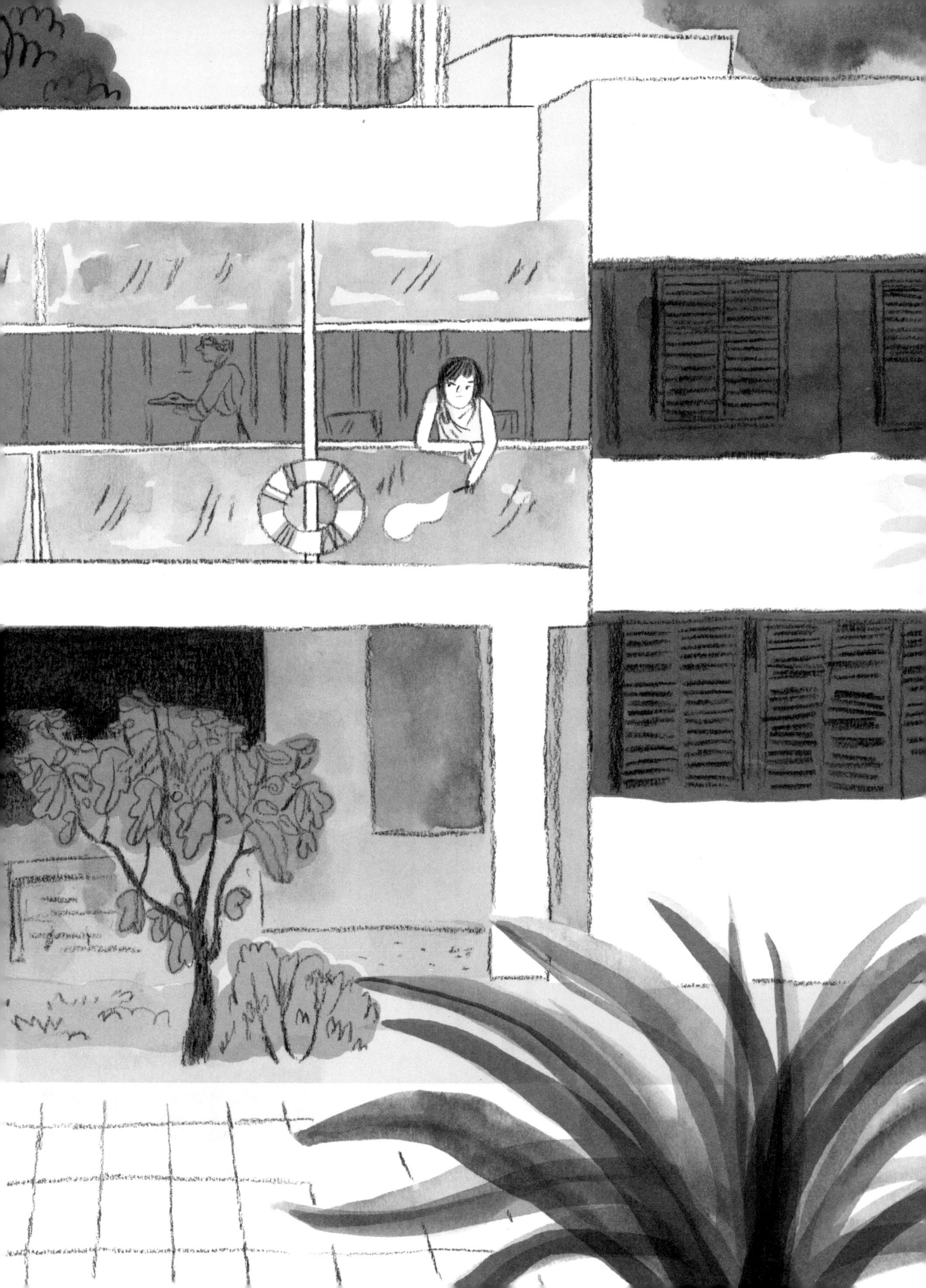

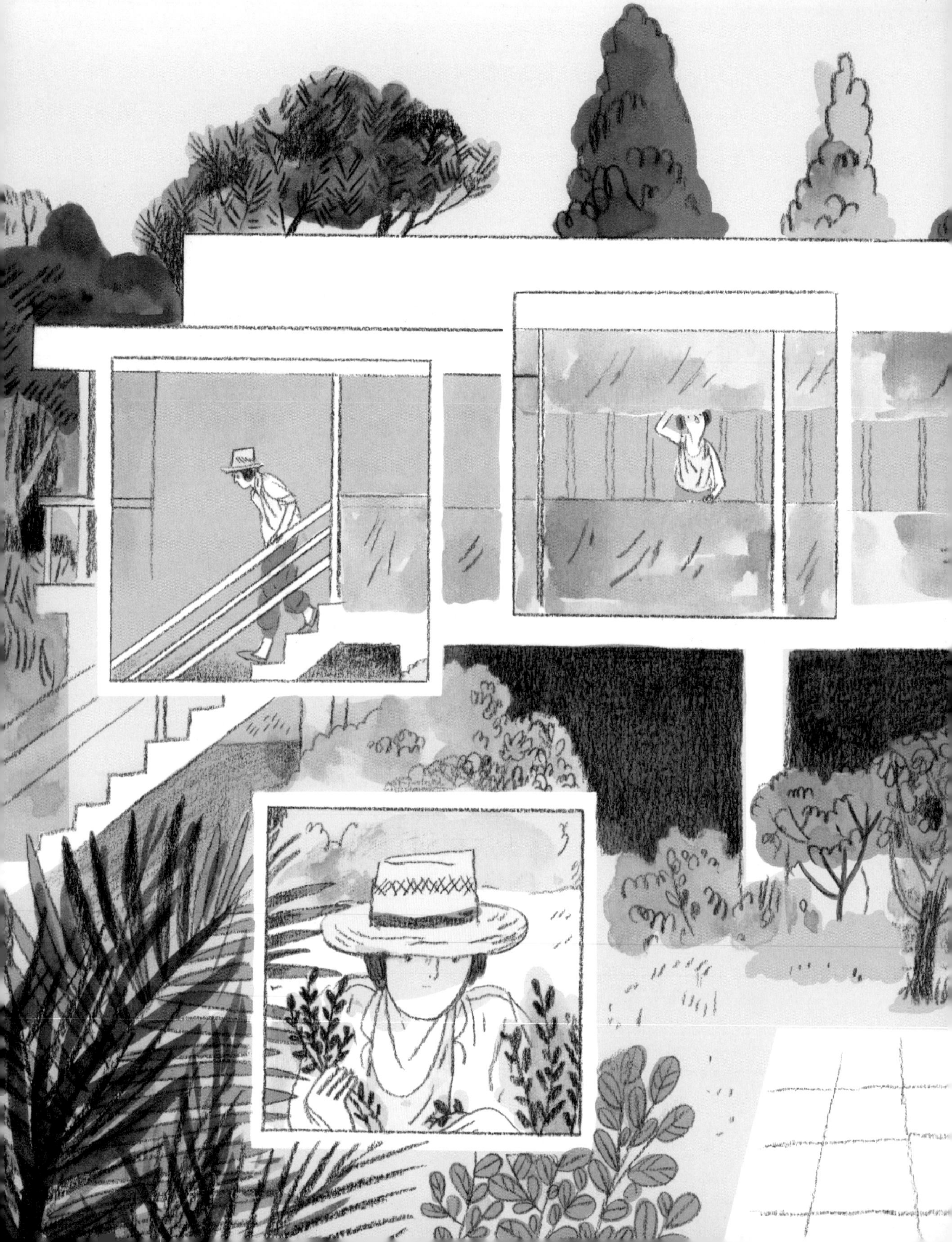

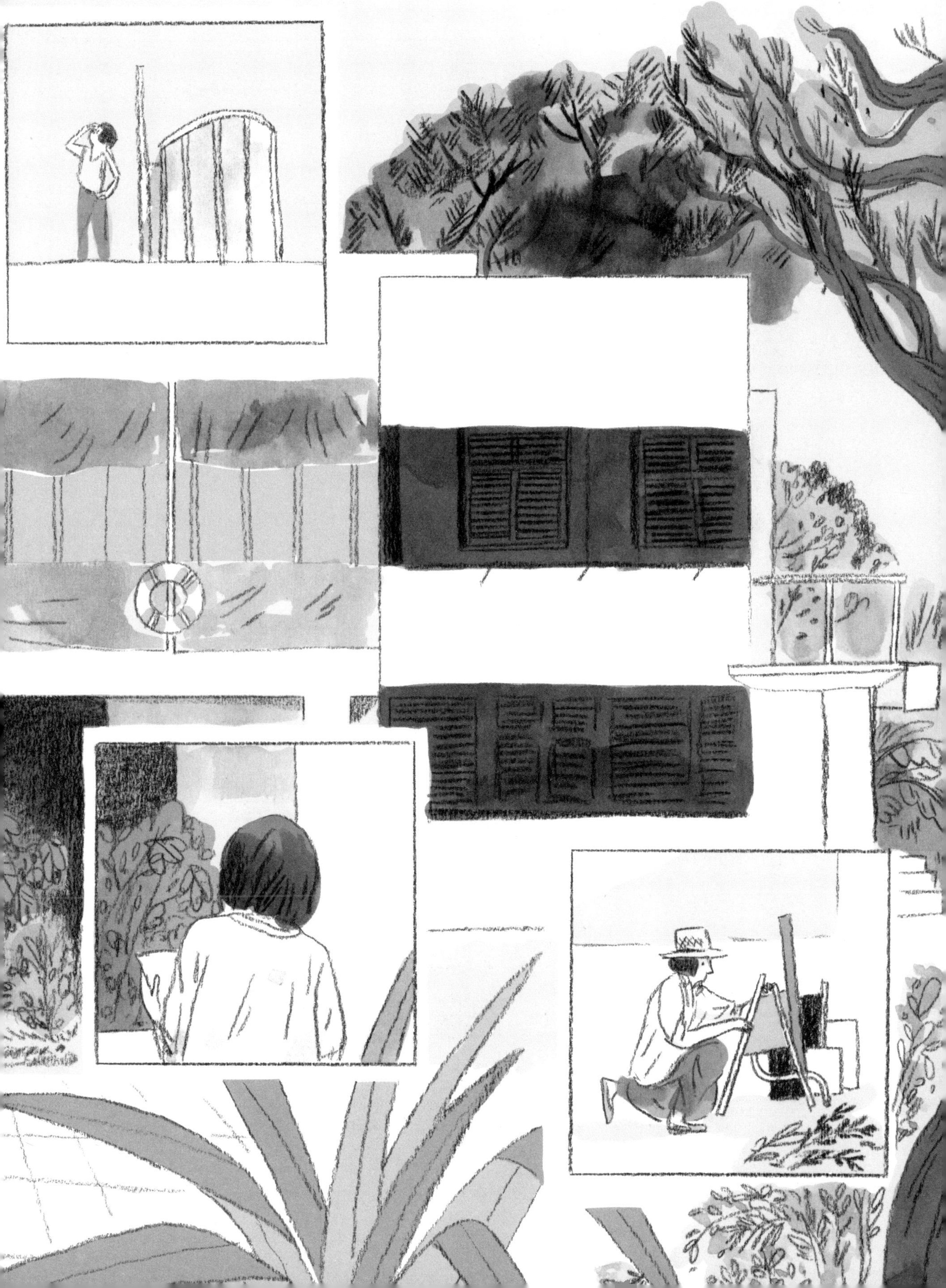

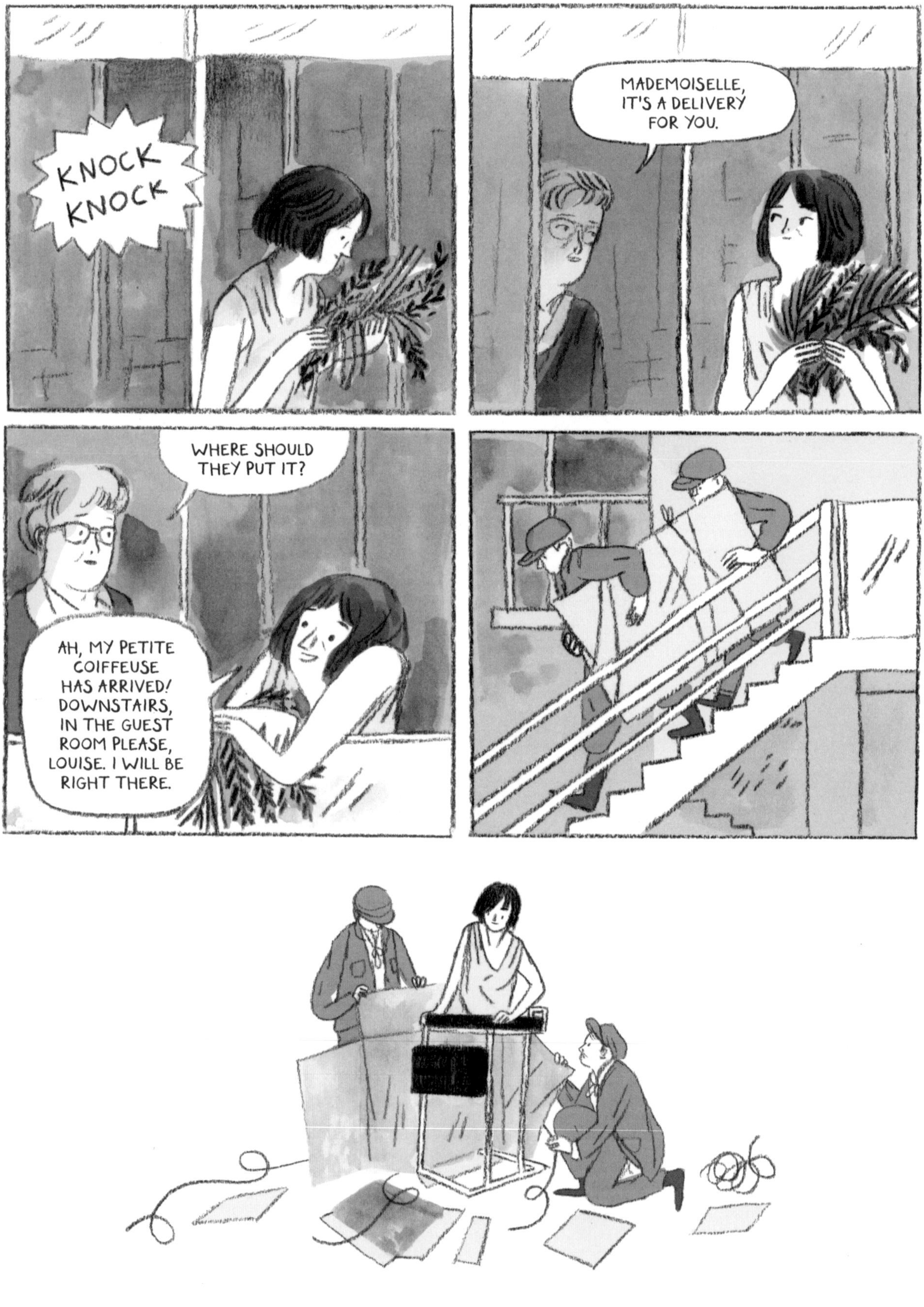
KNOCK KNOCK
MADEMOISELLE, IT'S A DELIVERY FOR YOU.
WHERE SHOULD THEY PUT IT?
AH, MY PETITE COIFFEUSE HAS ARRIVED! DOWNSTAIRS, IN THE GUEST ROOM PLEASE, LOUISE. I WILL BE RIGHT THERE.

FALLING
FOR LACQUER

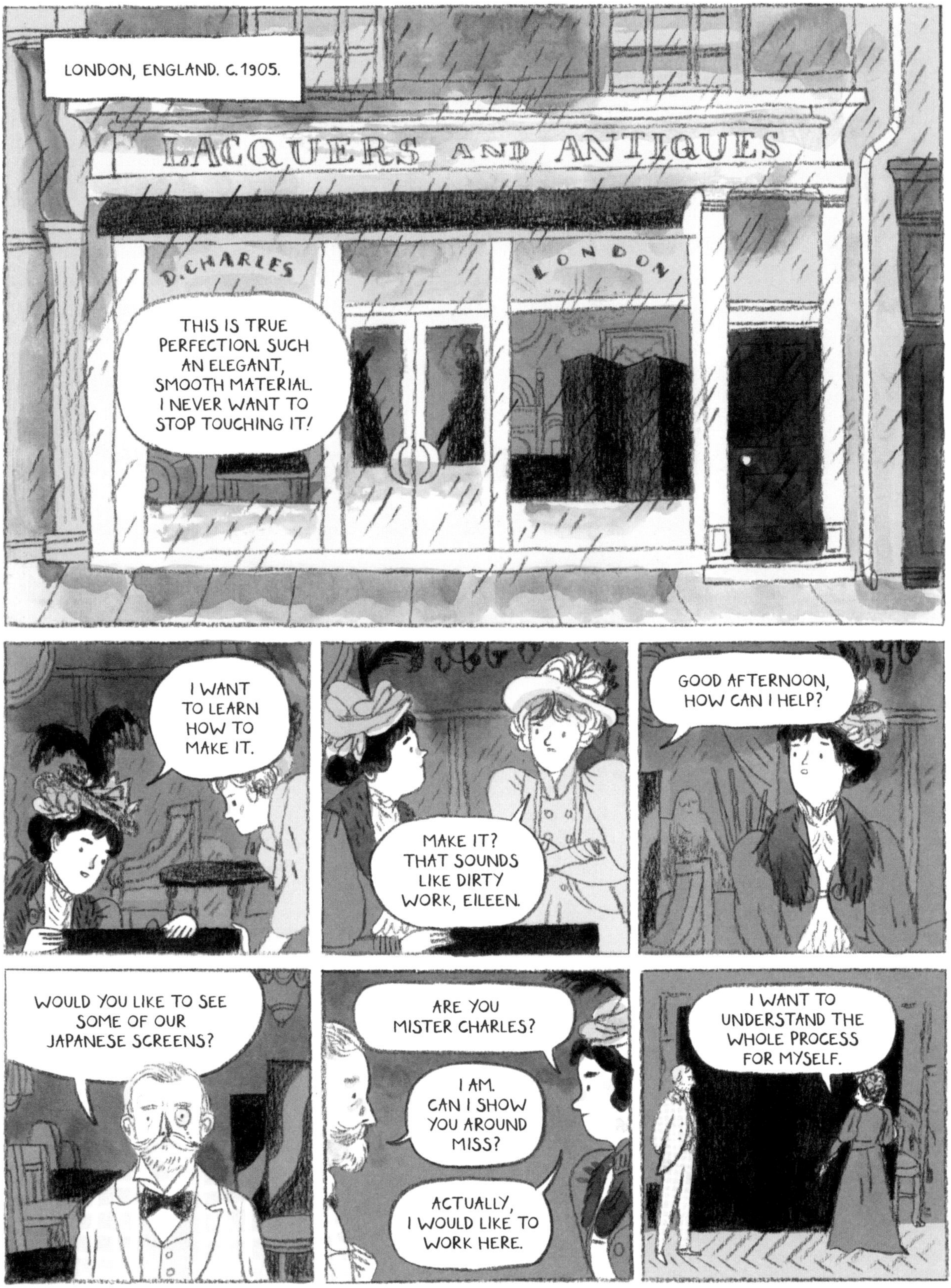
LONDON, ENGLAND. C.1905.
LACQUERS AND ANTIQUES
D.CHARLES
LONDON
THIS IS TRUE PERFECTION. SUCH AN ELEGANT, SMOOTH MATERIAL. I NEVER WANT TO STOP TOUCHING IT!
I WANT TO LEARN HOW TO MAKE IT.
MAKE IT? THAT SOUNDS LIKE DIRTY WORK, EILEEN.
GOOD AFTERNOON, HOW CAN I HELP?
WOULD YOU LIKE TO SEE SOME OF OUR JAPANESE SCREENS?
ARE YOU MISTER CHARLES?
I AM. CAN I SHOW YOU AROUND MISS?
ACTUALLY, I WOULD LIKE TO WORK HERE.
I WANT TO UNDERSTAND THE WHOLE PROCESS FOR MYSELF.

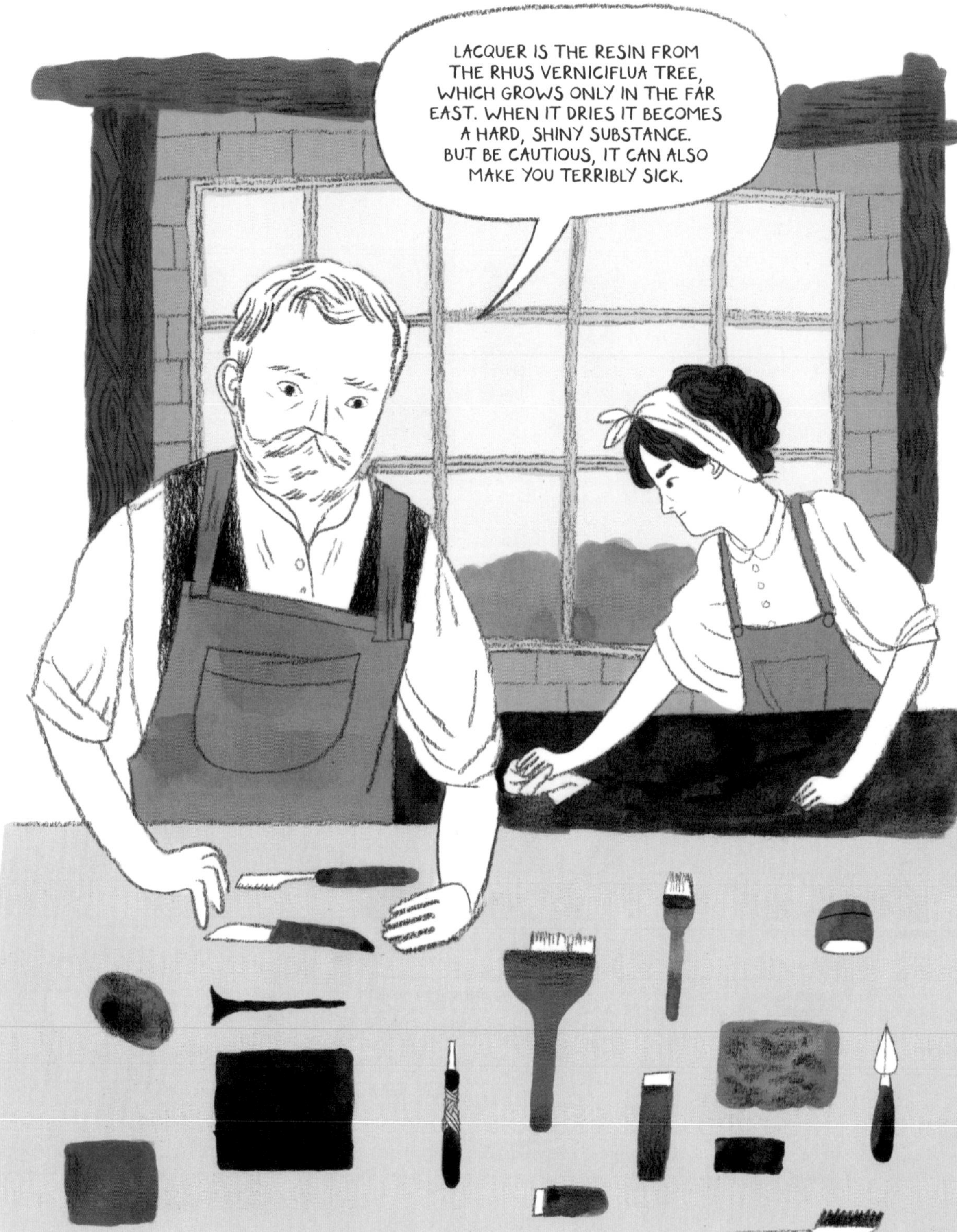
LACQUER IS THE RESIN FROM THE RHUS VERNICIFLUA TREE, WHICH GROWS ONLY IN THE FAR EAST. WHEN IT DRIES IT BECOMES A HARD, SHINY SUBSTANCE. BUT BE CAUTIOUS, IT CAN ALSO MAKE YOU TERRIBLY SICK.

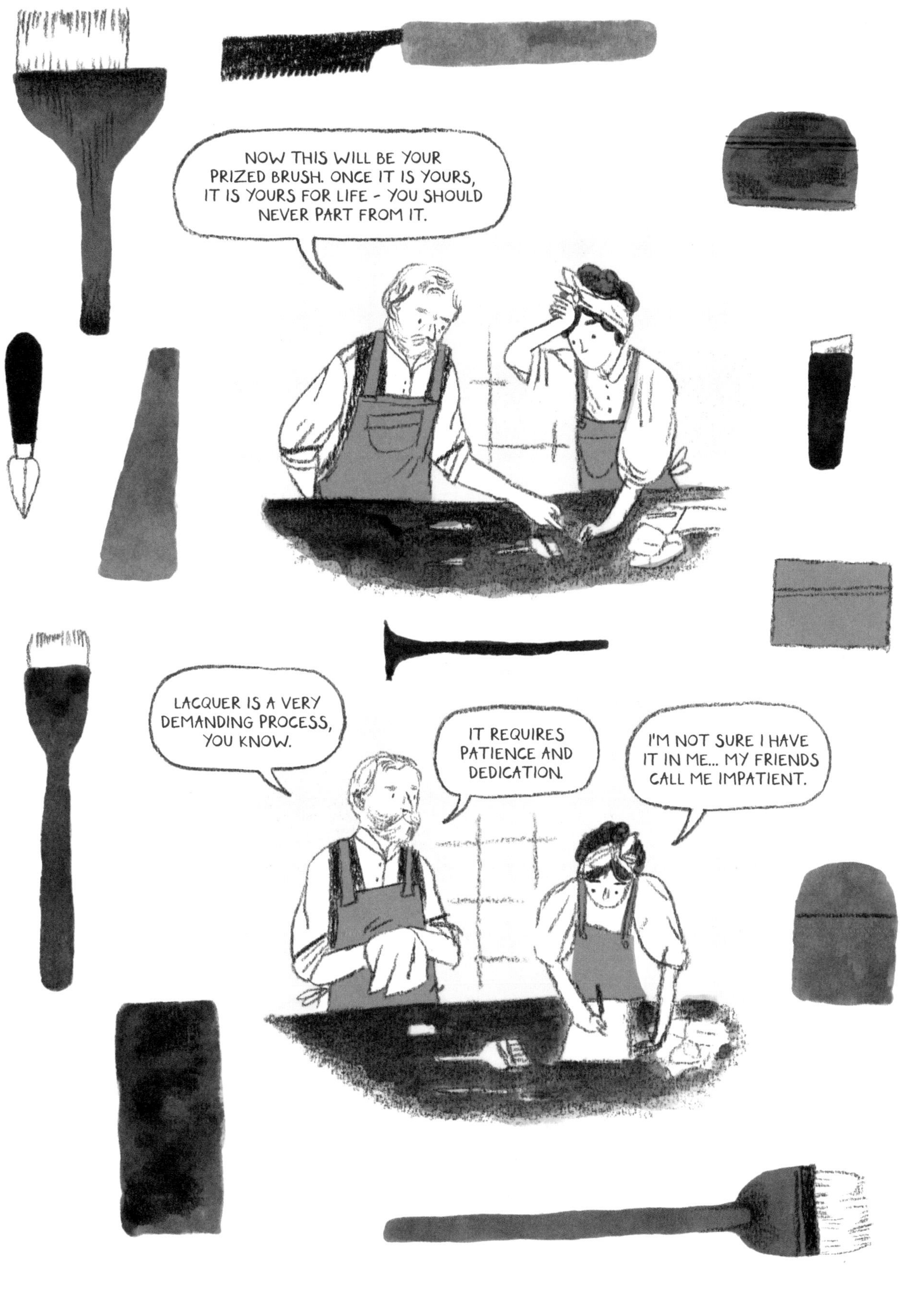
NOW THIS WILL BE YOUR PRIZED BRUSH. ONCE IT IS YOURS, IT IS YOURS FOR LIFE - YOU SHOULD NEVER PART FROM IT.
LACQUER IS A VERY DEMANDING PROCESS, YOU KNOW.
IT REQUIRES PATIENCE AND DEDICATION.
I'M NOT SURE I HAVE IT IN ME... MY FRIENDS CALL ME IMPATIENT.

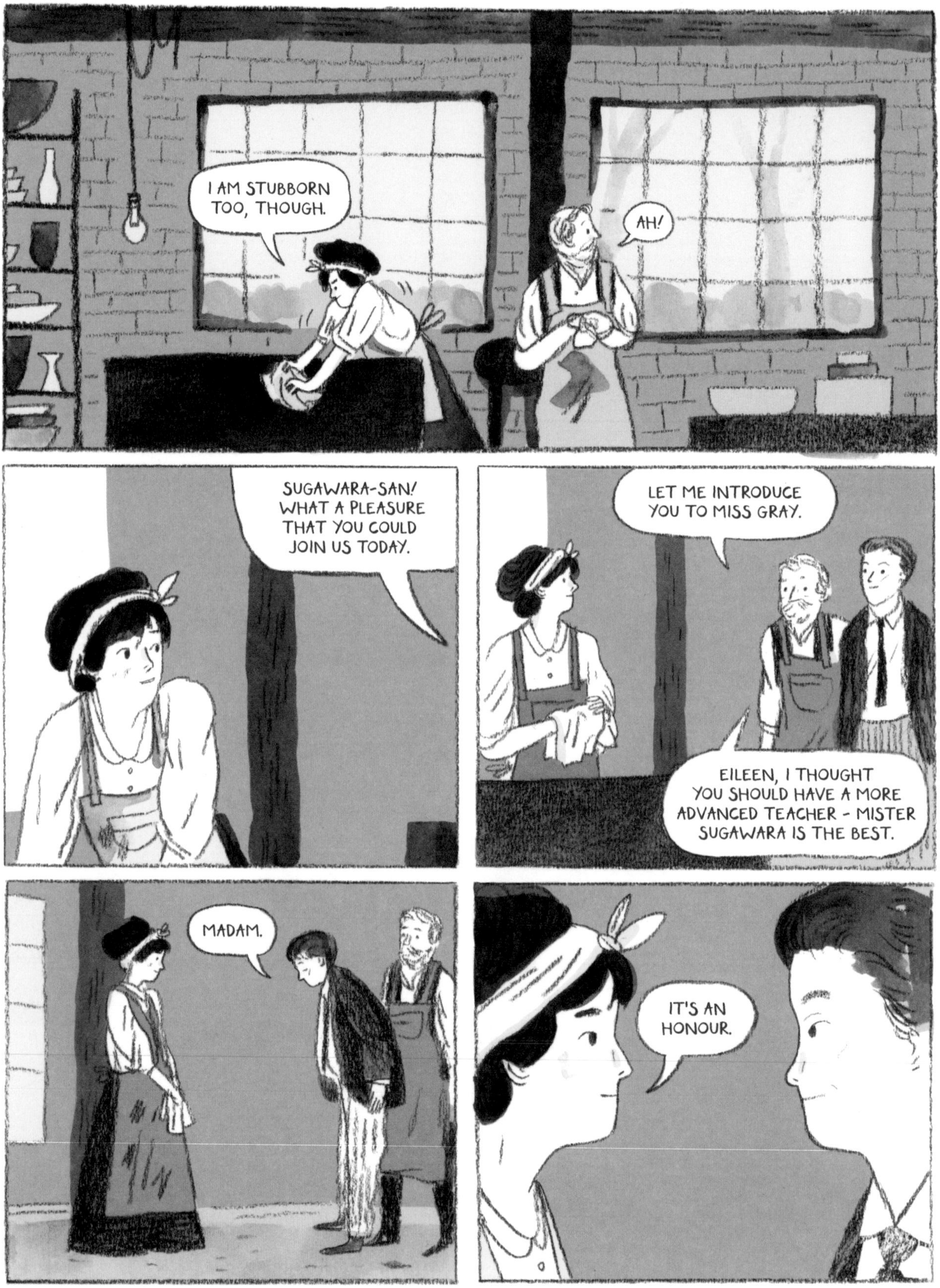
I AM STUBBORN TOO, THOUGH.
AH!
SUGAWARA-SAN! WHAT A PLEASURE THAT YOU COULD JOIN US TODAY.
LET ME INTRODUCE YOU TO MISS GRAY.
EILEEN, I THOUGHT YOU SHOULD HAVE A MORE ADVANCED TEACHER - MISTER SUGAWARA IS THE BEST.
MADAM.
IT'S AN HONOUR.

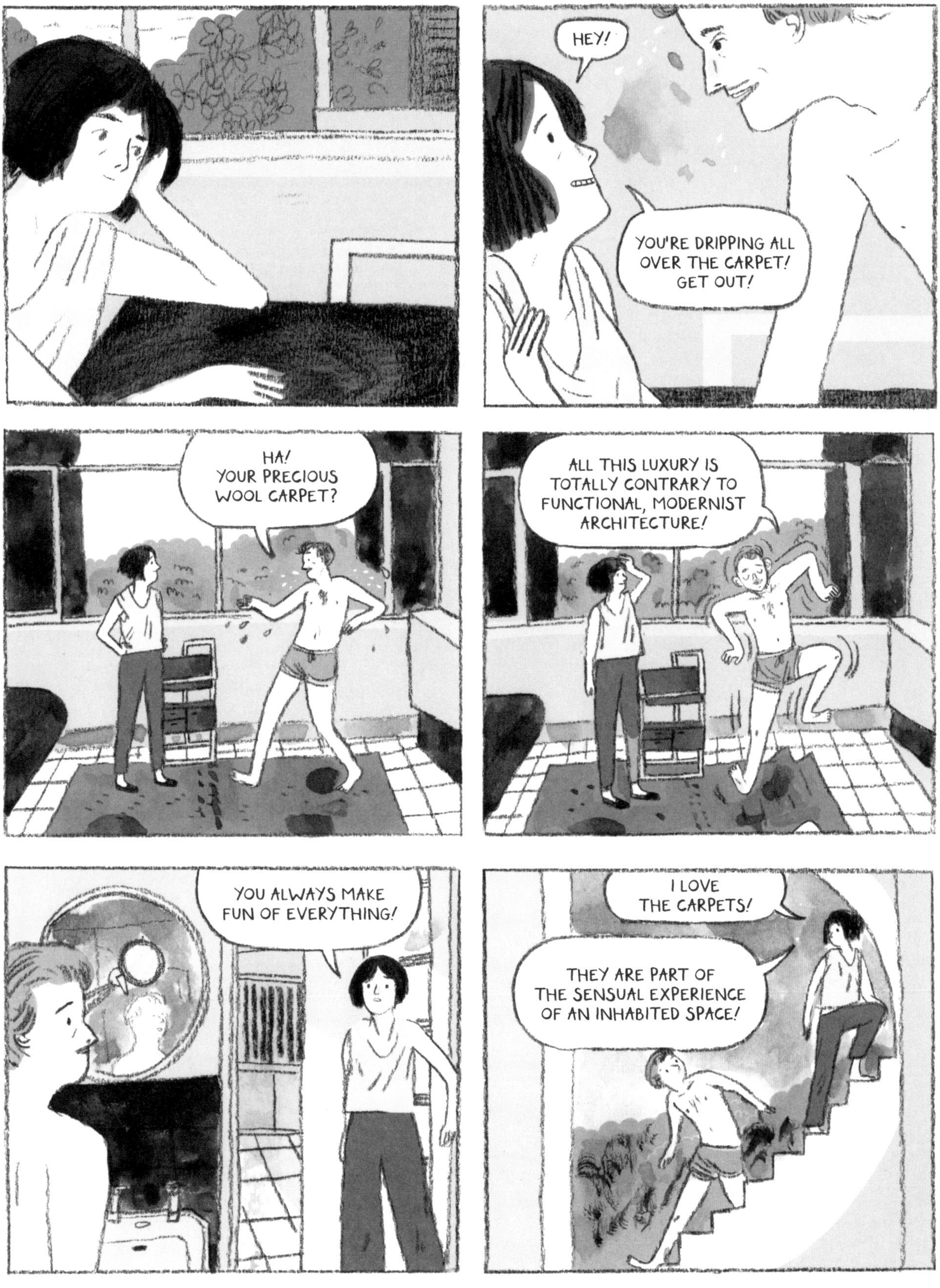
HEY!
YOU'RE DRIPPING ALL OVER THE CARPET! GET OUT!
HA! YOUR PRECIOUS WOOL CARPET?
ALL THIS LUXURY IS TOTALLY CONTRARY TO FUNCTIONAL, MODERNIST ARCHITECTURE!
YOU ALWAYS MAKE FUN OF EVERYTHING!
I LOVE THE CARPETS!
THEY ARE PART OF THE SENSUAL EXPERIENCE OF AN INHABITED SPACE!

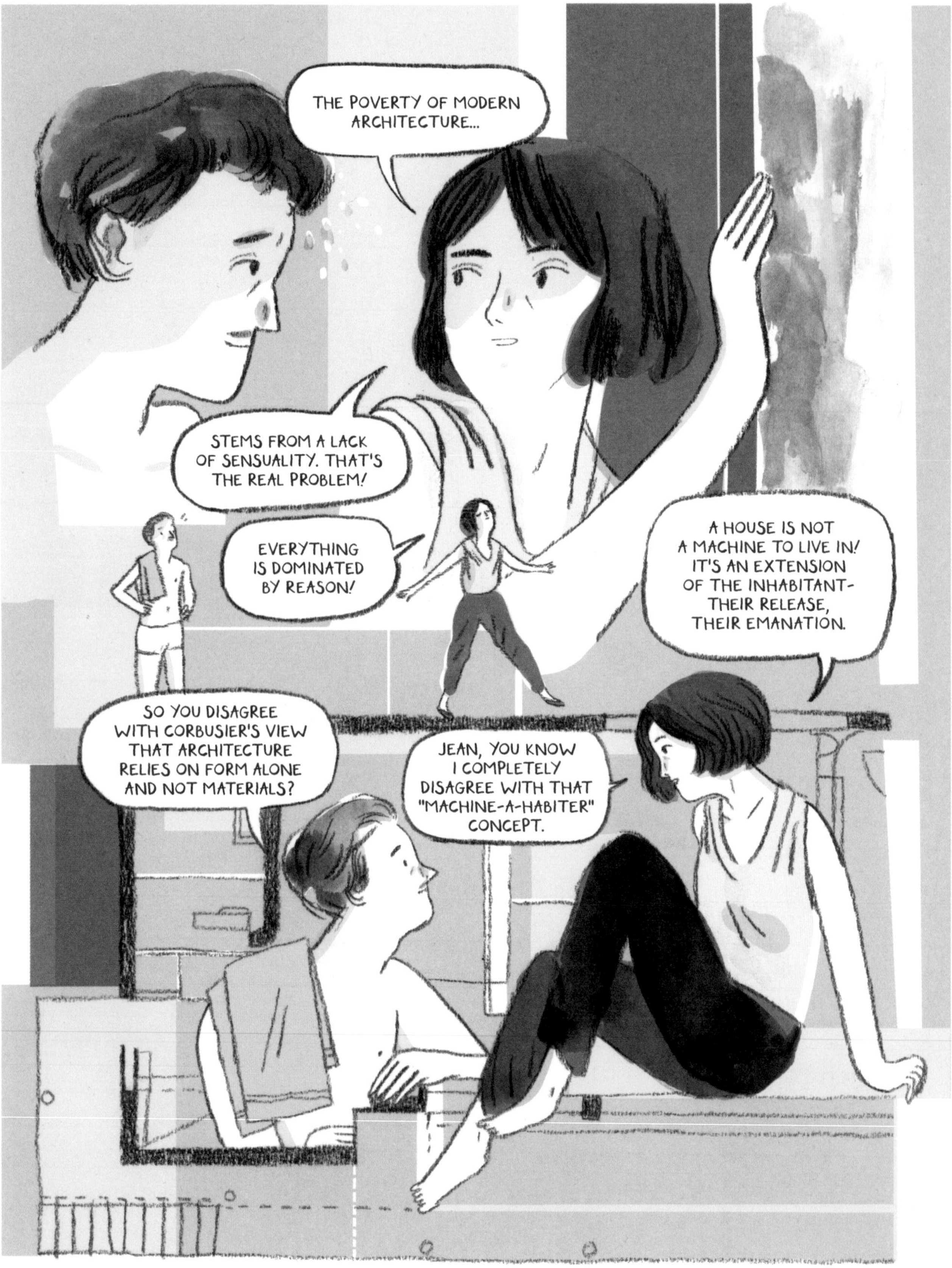
THE POVERTY OF MODERN ARCHITECTURE...
STEMS FROM A LACK OF SENSUALITY. THAT'S THE REAL PROBLEM!
EVERYTHING IS DOMINATED BY REASON!
A HOUSE IS NOT A MACHINE TO LIVE IN! IT'S AN EXTENSION OF THE INHABITANT- THEIR RELEASE, THEIR EMANATION.
SO YOU DISAGREE WITH CORBUSIER'S VIEW THAT ARCHITECTURE RELIES ON FORM ALONE AND NOT MATERIALS?
JEAN, YOU KNOW I COMPLETELY DISAGREE WITH THAT "MACHINE-A-HABITER" CONCEPT.

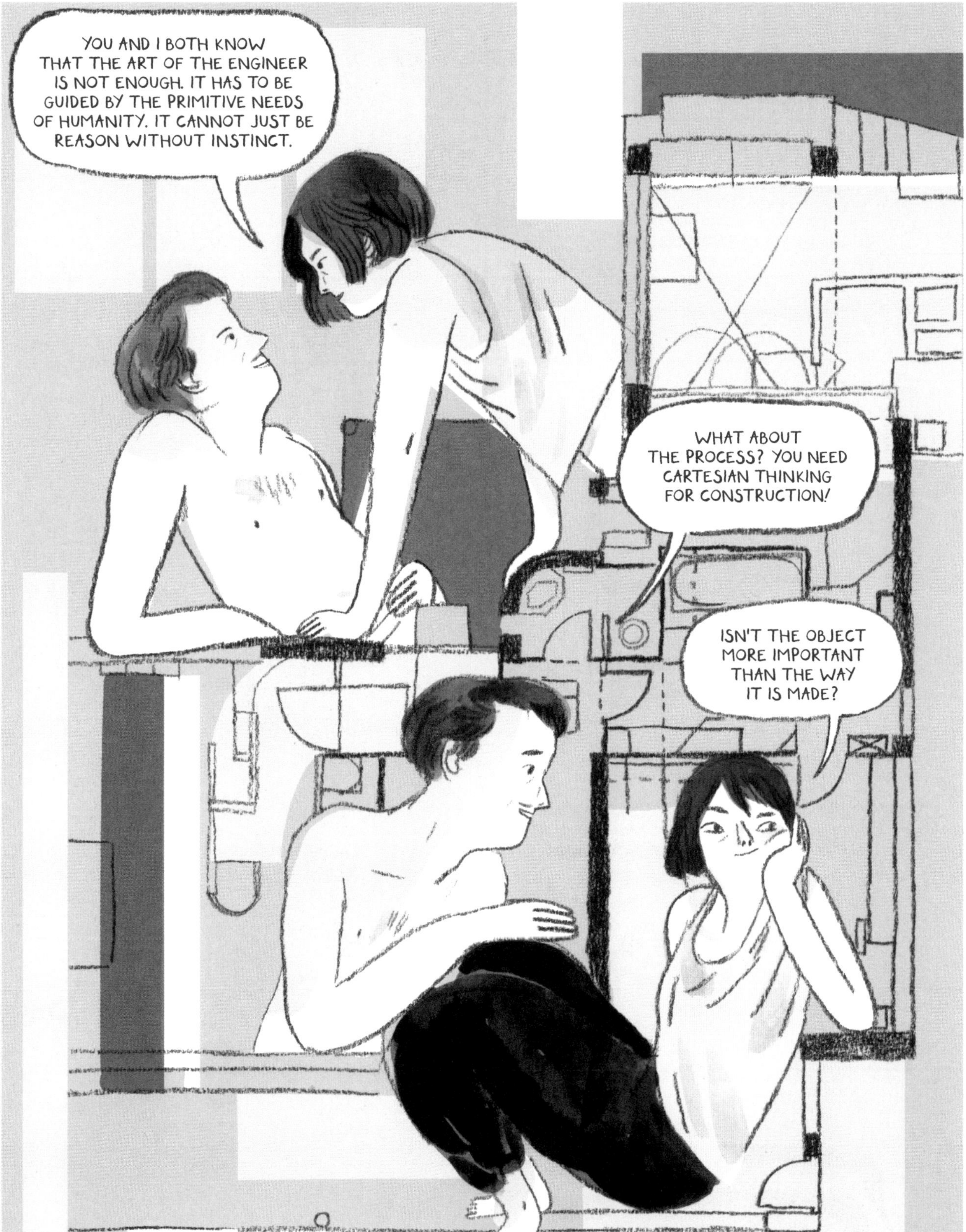
YOU AND I BOTH KNOW THAT THE ART OF THE ENGINEER IS NOT ENOUGH. IT HAS TO BE GUIDED BY THE PRIMITIVE NEEDS OF HUMANITY. IT CANNOT JUST BE REASON WITHOUT INSTINCT.
WHAT ABOUT THE PROCESS? YOU NEED CARTESIAN THINKING FOR CONSTRUCTION!
ISN'T THE OBJECT MORE IMPORTANT THAN THE WAY IT IS MADE?

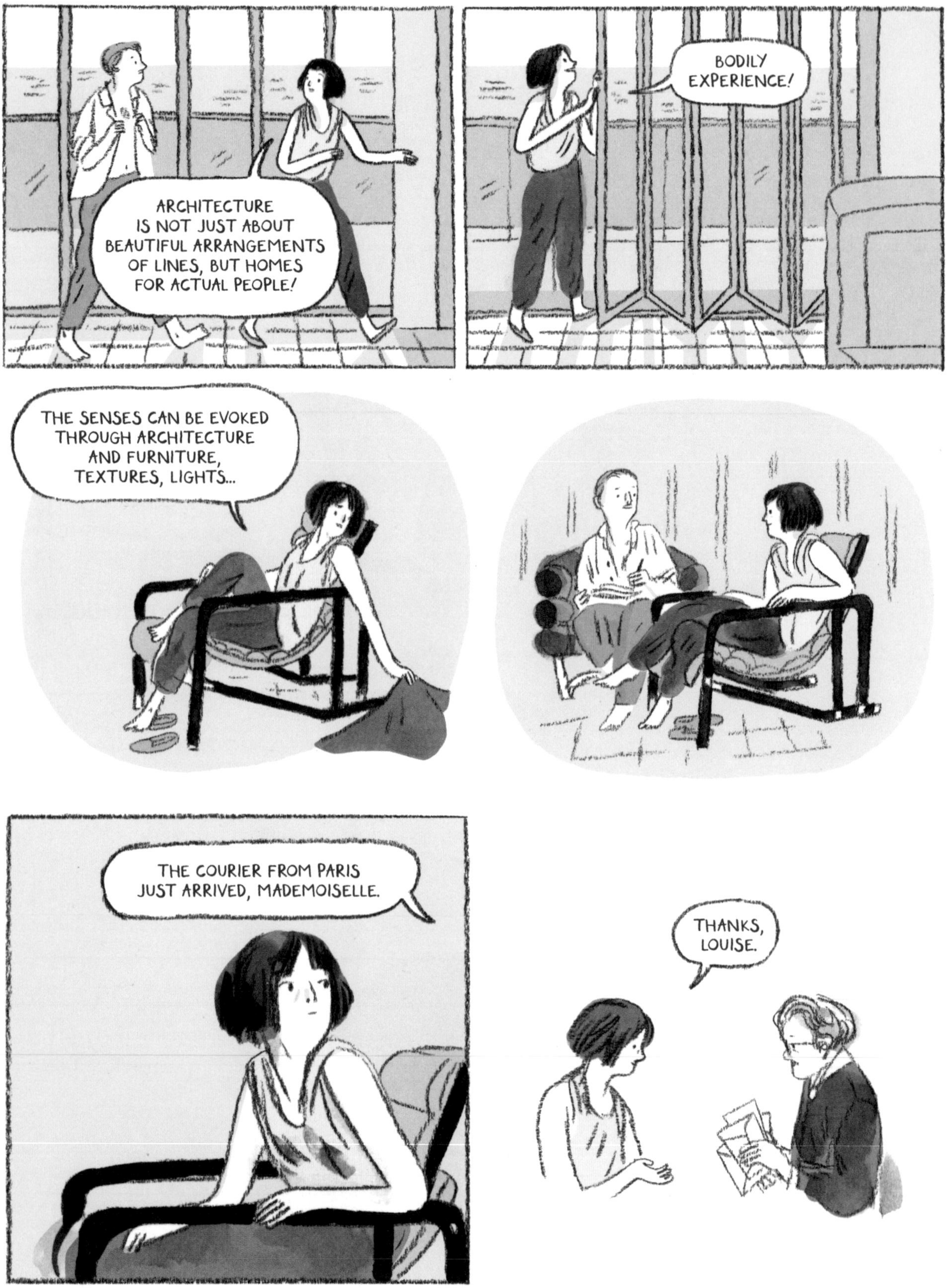
ARCHITECTURE IS NOT JUST ABOUT BEAUTIFUL ARRANGEMENTS OF LINES, BUT HOMES FOR ACTUAL PEOPLE!
BODILY EXPERIENCE!
THE SENSES CAN BE EVOKED THROUGH ARCHITECTURE AND FURNITURE, TEXTURES, LIGHTS...
THE COURIER FROM PARIS JUST ARRIVED, MADEMOISELLE.
THANKS, LOUISE.

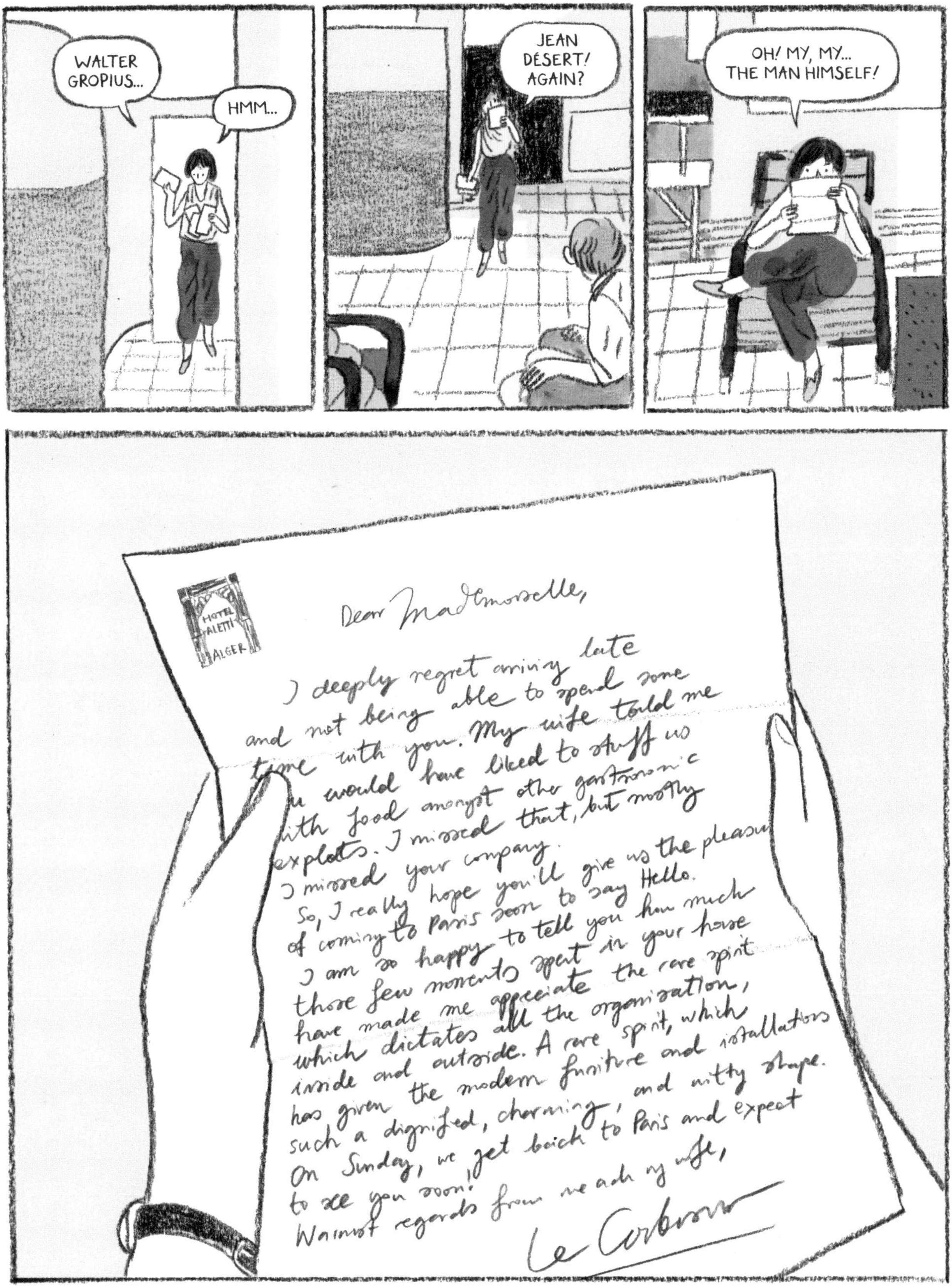
WALTER GROPIUS...
HMM...
JEAN DÉSERT! AGAIN?
OH! MY, MY... THE MAN HIMSELF!
HOTEL ALETTI ALGER
Dear Mademoiselle,
I deeply regret arriving late
and not being able to spend some
time with you. My wife told me
would have liked to stuff us
food amongst other gastronomic
exploits. I missed that, but mostly
I missed your company.
So, I really hope you'll give us the pleasu
of coming to Paris soon to say Hello.
I am so happy to tell you how much
those few moments spent in your house
have made me appreciate the rare spirit
which dictates all the organisation,
inside and outside. A rare spirit, which
has given the modern furniture and installations
such a dignified, charming, and witty shape.
On Sunday, we get back to Paris and expect
to see you soon!
Warmest regards from me and my wife,
Le Corbusier

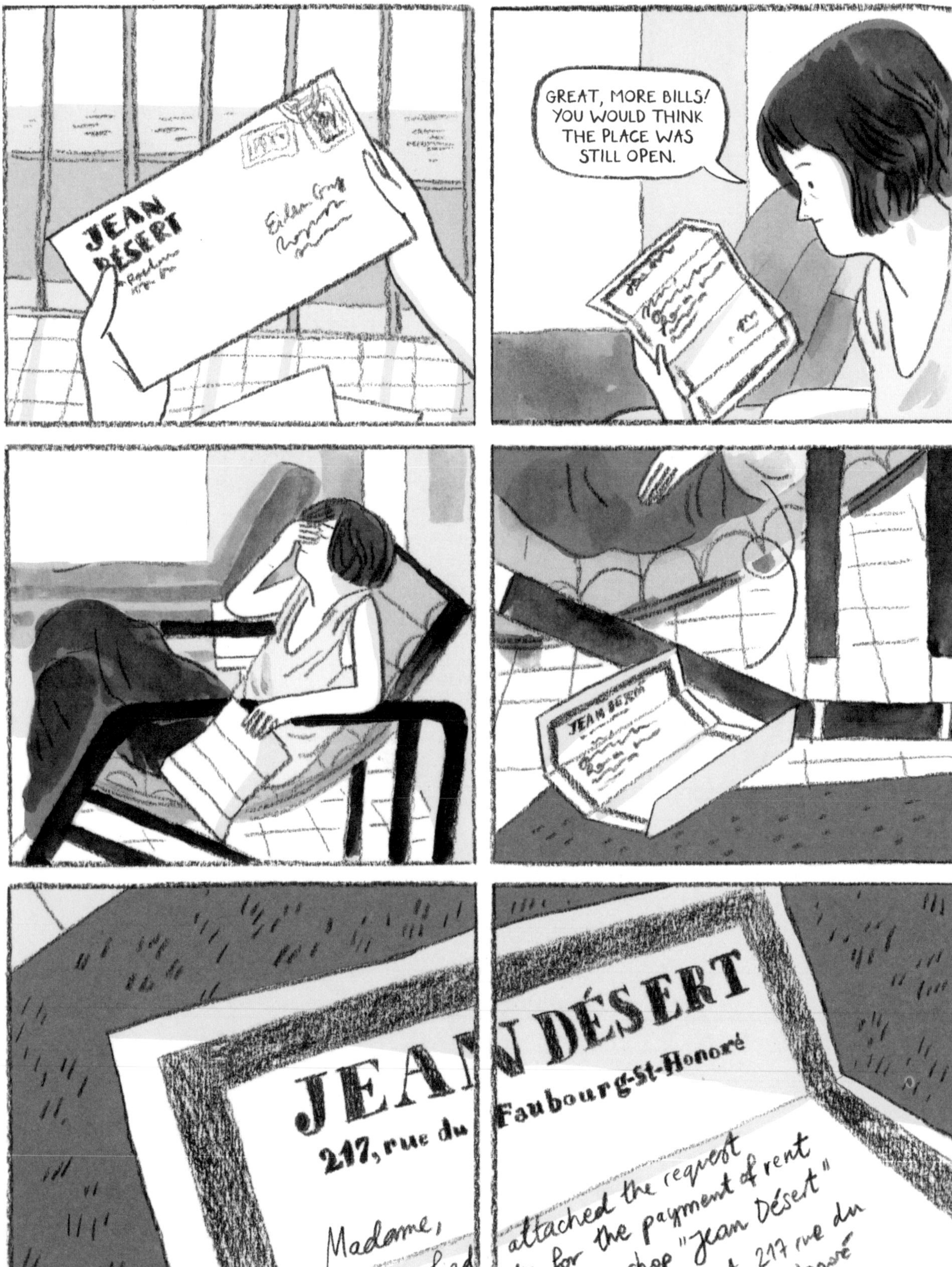

JEAN DÉSERT
GREAT, MORE BILLS! YOU WOULD THINK THE PLACE WAS STILL OPEN.
JEA
217, rue du
Madame,
N DÉSERT
Faubourg-St-Honoré
attached the request
ate for the payment of rent
the shop "Jean Désert"
at 217 rue du

JEAN DÉSERT

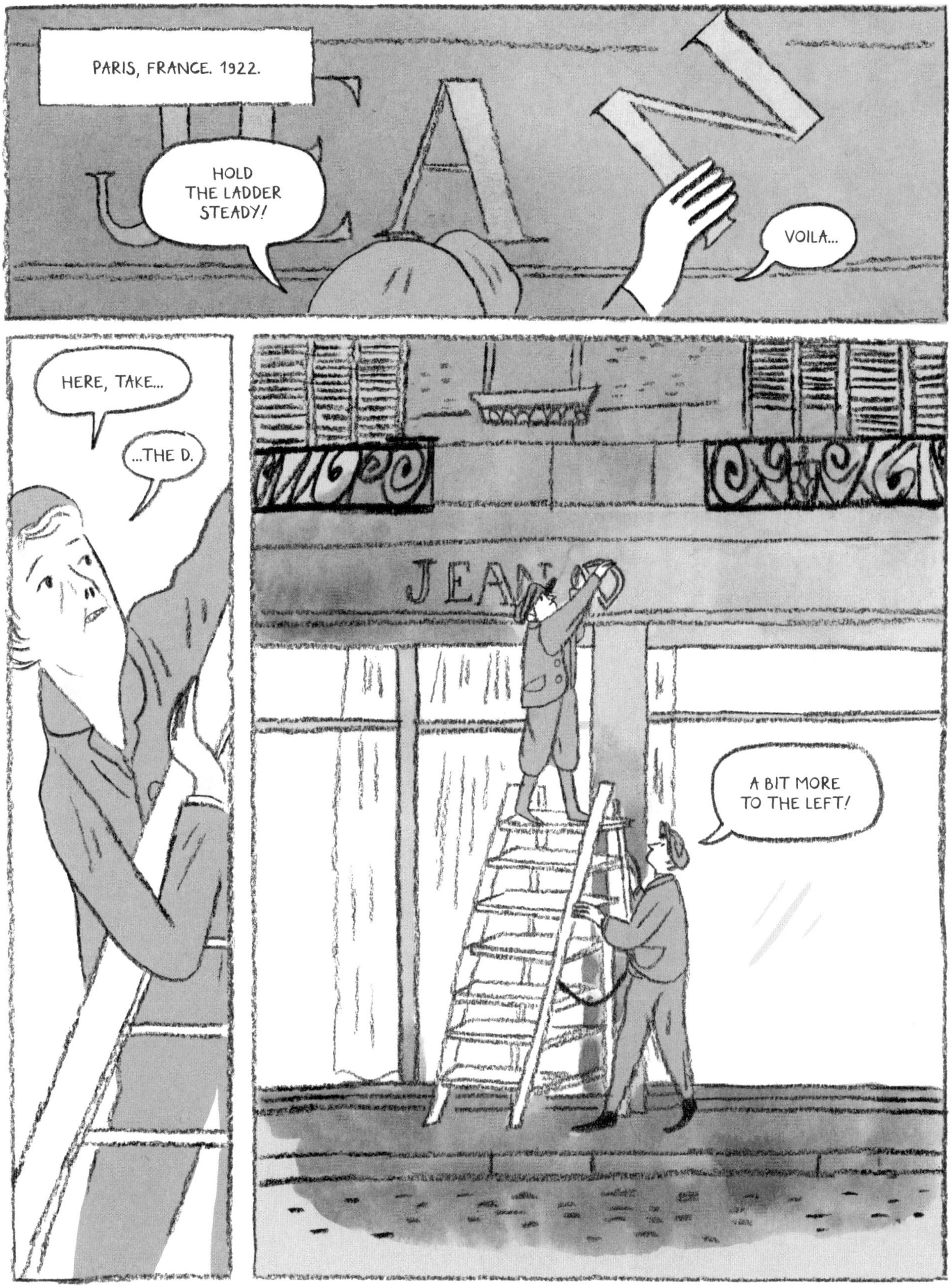
PARIS, FRANCE. 1922.
HOLD THE LADDER STEADY!
VOILA...
HERE, TAKE...
...THE D.
JEAN
A BIT MORE TO THE LEFT!

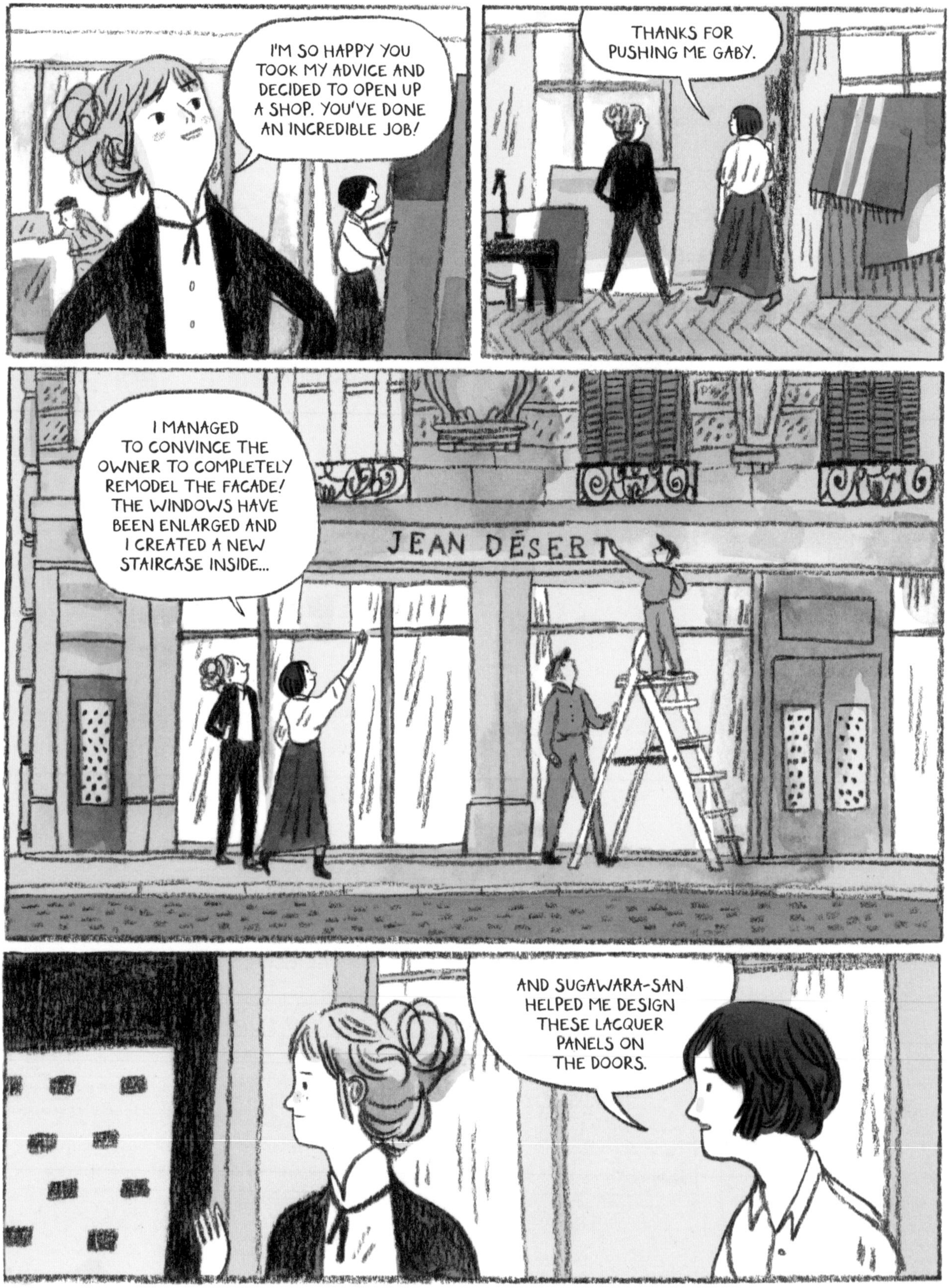
I'M SO HAPPY YOU TOOK MY ADVICE AND DECIDED TO OPEN UP A SHOP. YOU'VE DONE AN INCREDIBLE JOB!
THANKS FOR PUSHING ME GABY.
I MANAGED TO CONVINCE THE OWNER TO COMPLETELY REMODEL THE FACADE! THE WINDOWS HAVE BEEN ENLARGED AND I CREATED A NEW STAIRCASE INSIDE...
JEAN DÉSERT
AND SUGAWARA-SAN HELPED ME DESIGN THESE LACQUER PANELS ON THE DOORS.

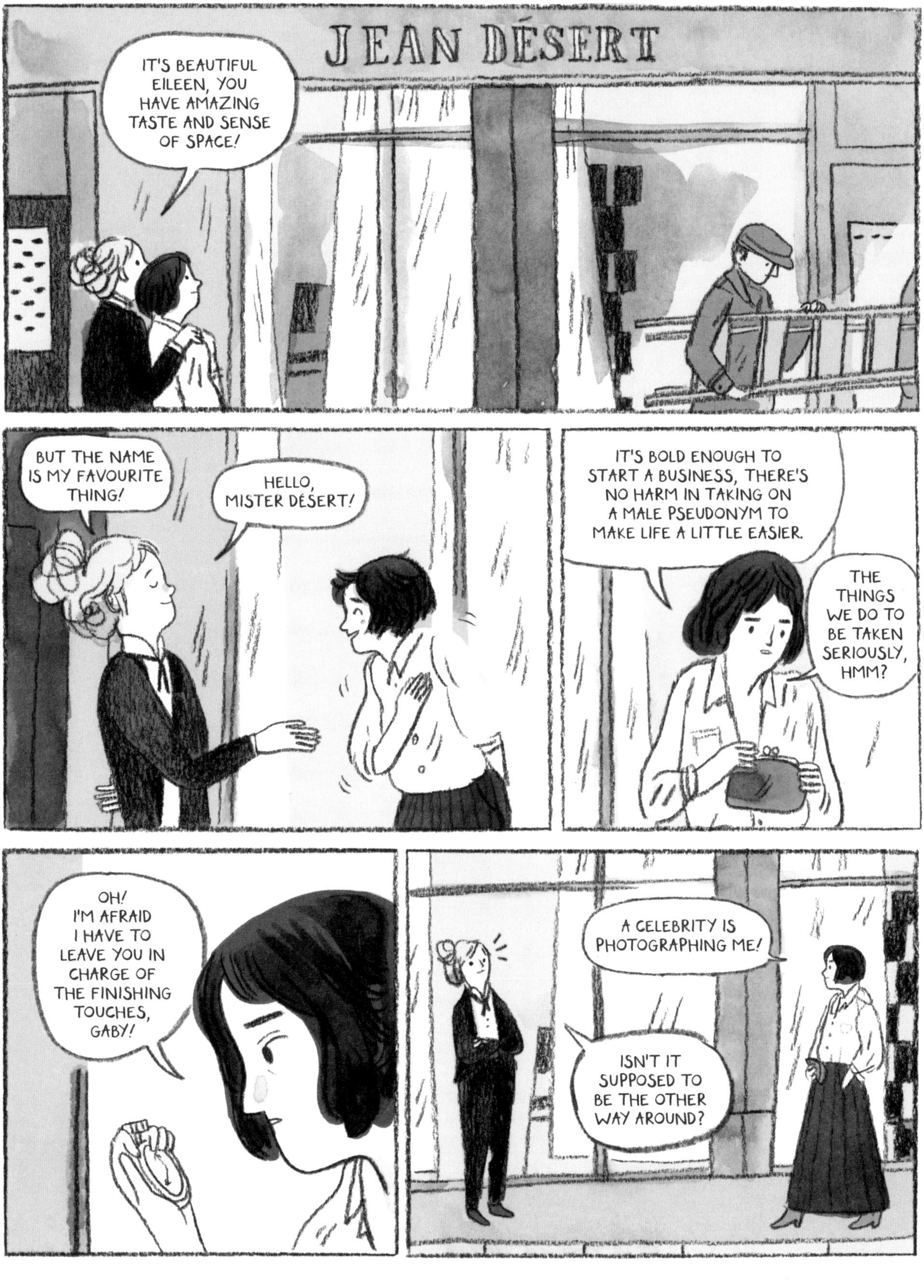
JEAN DÉSERT
IT'S BEAUTIFUL EILEEN, YOU HAVE AMAZING TASTE AND SENSE OF SPACE!
BUT THE NAME IS MY FAVOURITE THING!
HELLO, MISTER DÉSERT!
IT'S BOLD ENOUGH TO START A BUSINESS, THERE'S NO HARM IN TAKING ON A MALE PSEUDONYM TO MAKE LIFE A LITTLE EASIER.
THE THINGS WE DO TO BE TAKEN SERIOUSLY, HMM?
OH! I'M AFRAID I HAVE TO LEAVE YOU IN CHARGE OF THE FINISHING TOUCHES, GABY!
A CELEBRITY IS PHOTOGRAPHING ME!
ISN'T IT SUPPOSED TO BE THE OTHER WAY AROUND?

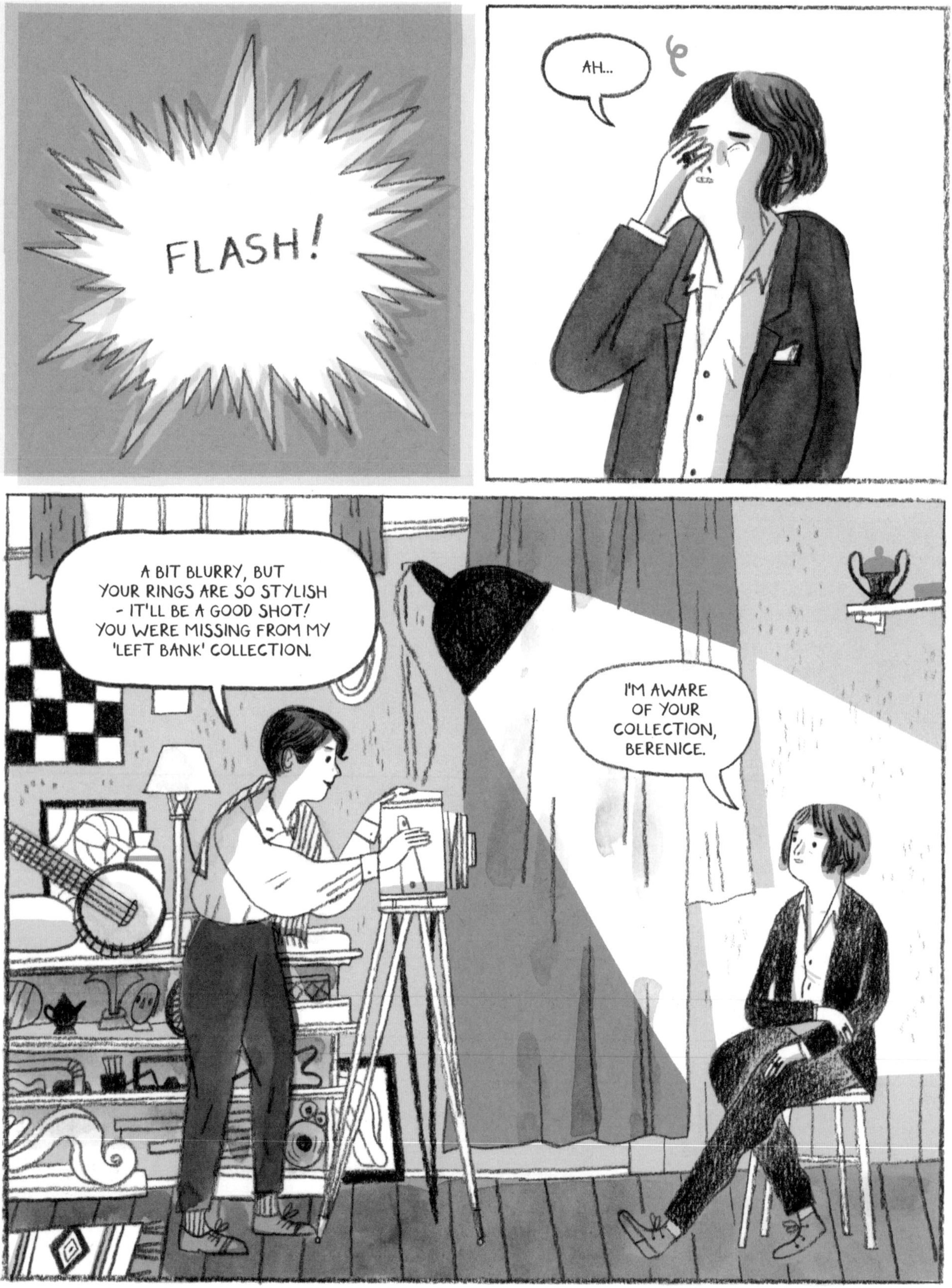
FLASH!
AH...
A BIT BLURRY, BUT YOUR RINGS ARE SO STYLISH - IT'LL BE A GOOD SHOT! YOU WERE MISSING FROM MY 'LEFT BANK' COLLECTION.
I'M AWARE OF YOUR COLLECTION, BERENICE.

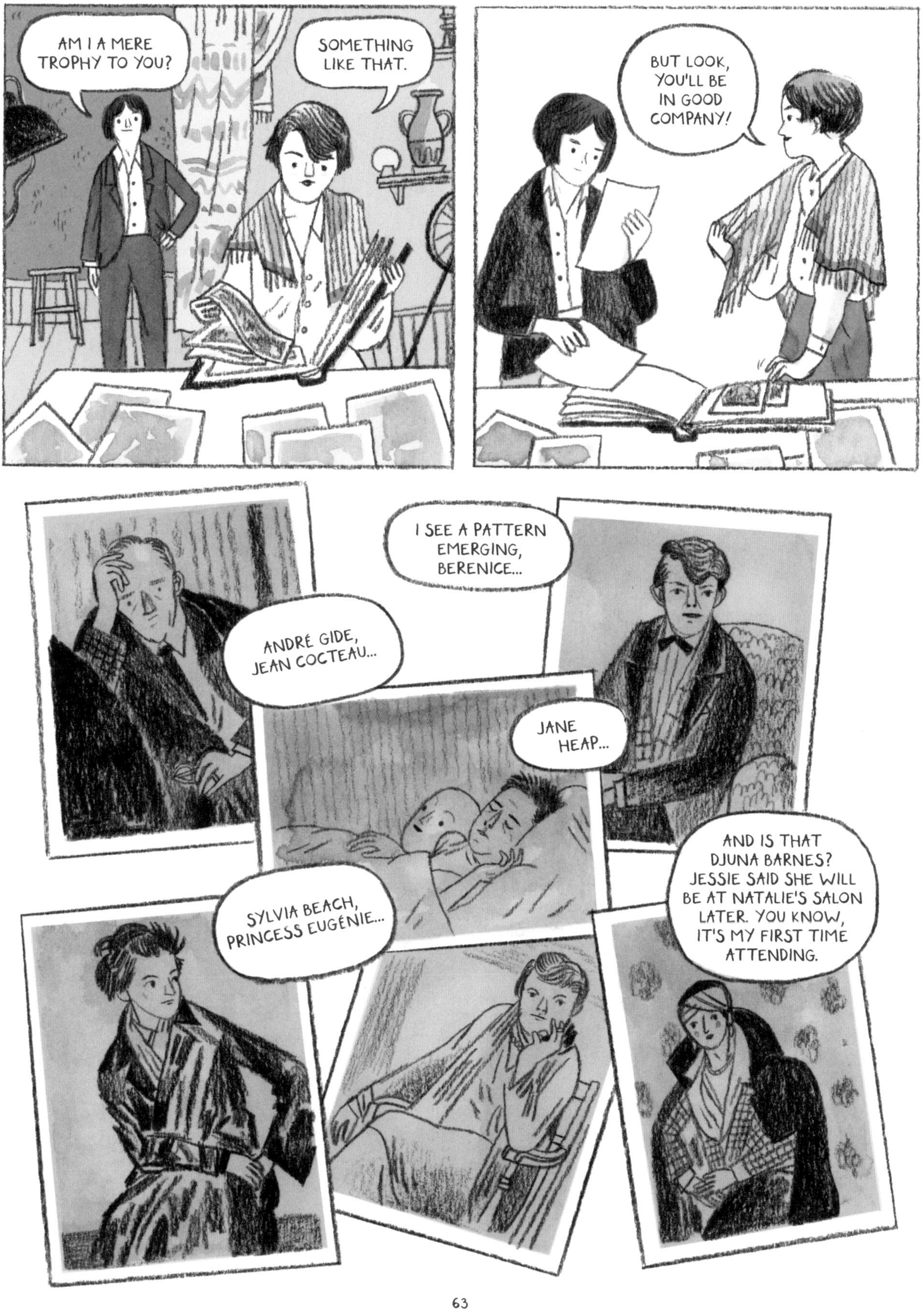
AM I A MERE TROPHY TO YOU?
SOMETHING LIKE THAT.
BUT LOOK, YOU'LL BE IN GOOD COMPANY!
I SEE A PATTERN EMERGING, BERENICE...
ANDRÉ GIDE, JEAN COCTEAU...
JANE HEAP...
SYLVIA BEACH, PRINCESS EUGÉNIE...
AND IS THAT DJUNA BARNES? JESSIE SAID SHE WILL BE AT NATALIE'S SALON LATER. YOU KNOW, IT'S MY FIRST TIME ATTENDING.

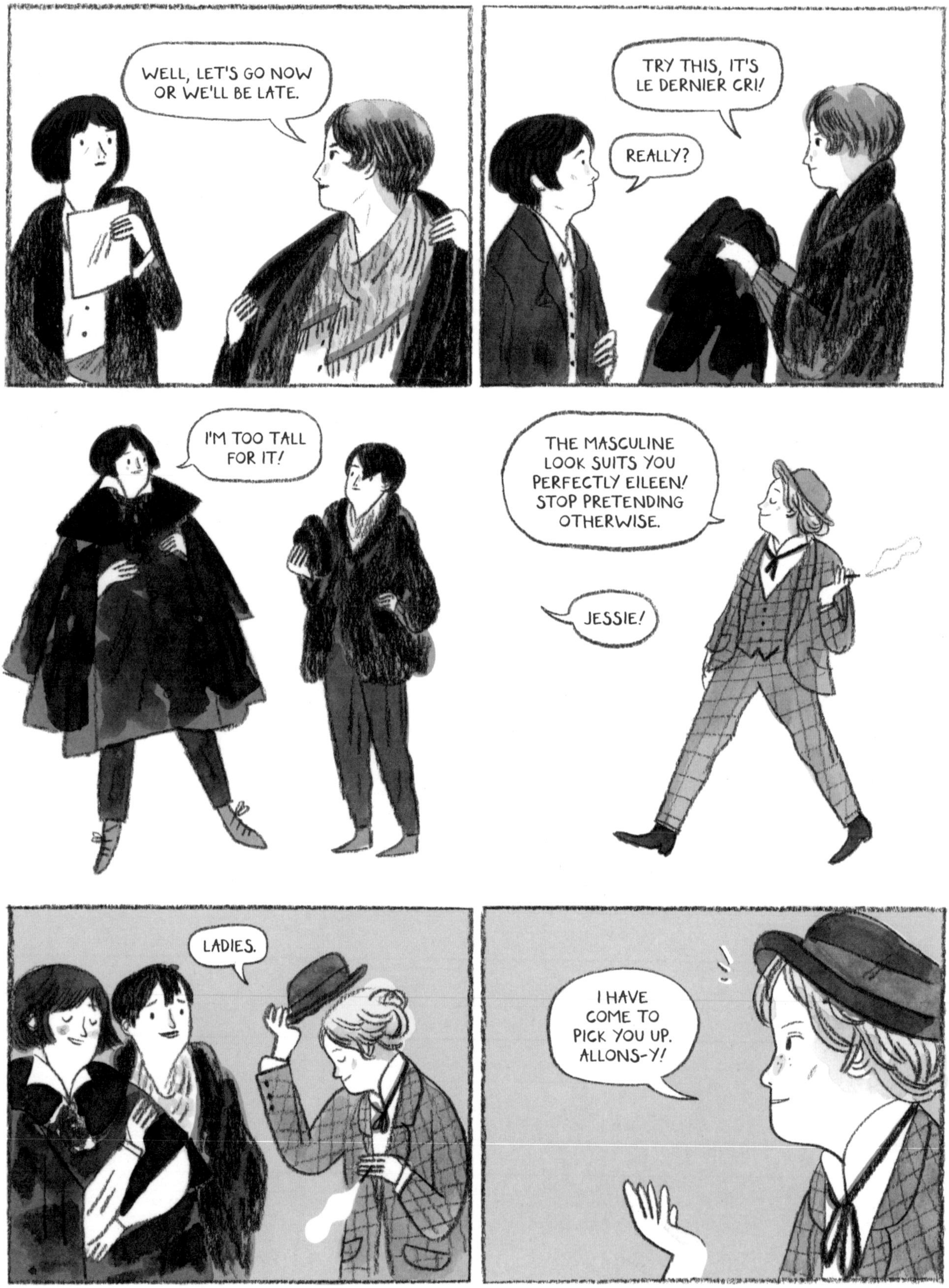
WELL, LET'S GO NOW OR WE'LL BE LATE.
TRY THIS, IT'S LE DERNIER CRI!
REALLY?
I'M TOO TALL FOR IT!
THE MASCULINE LOOK SUITS YOU PERFECTLY EILEEN! STOP PRETENDING OTHERWISE.
JESSIE!
LADIES.
!
I HAVE COME TO PICK YOU UP. ALLONS-Y!

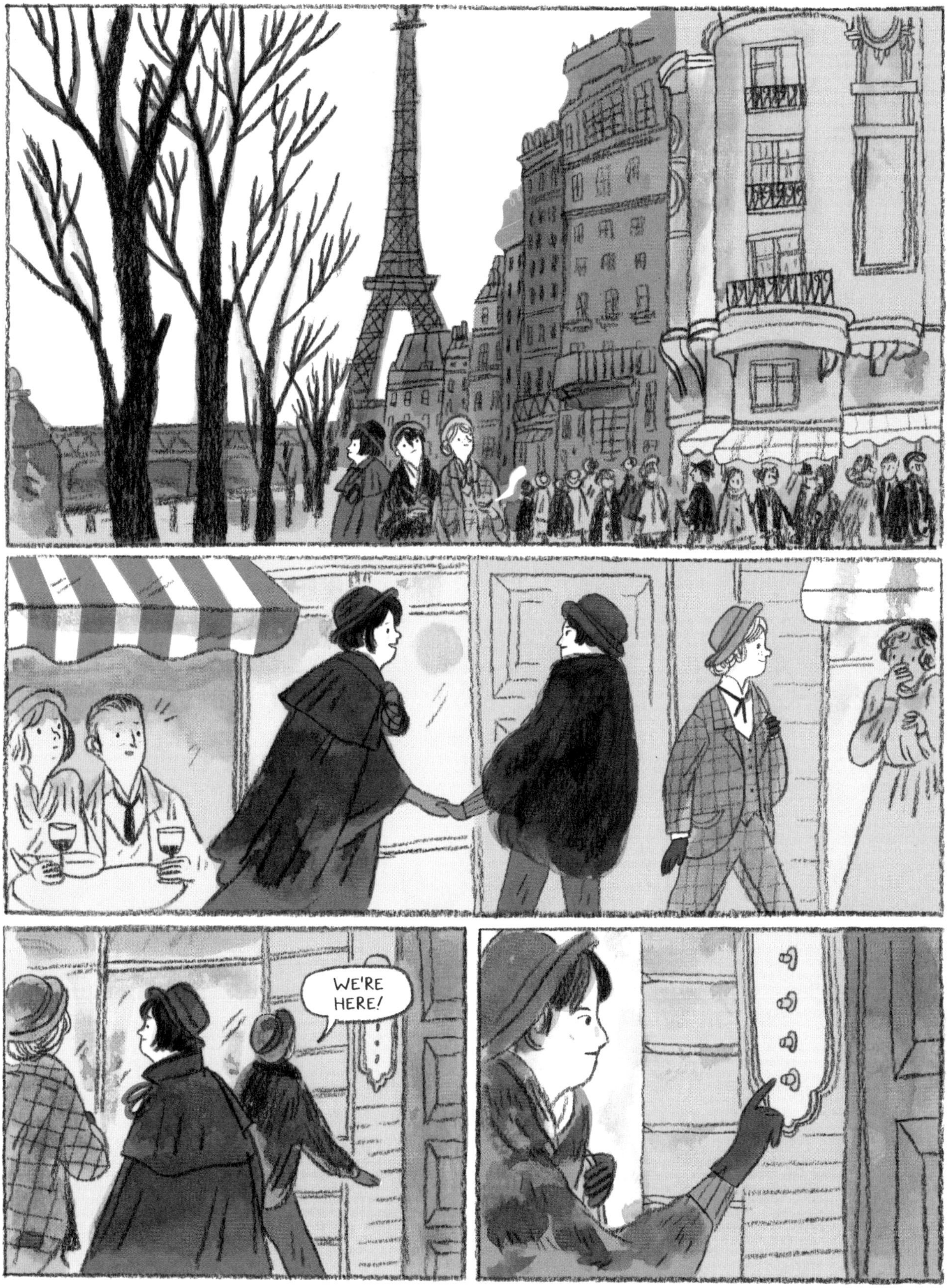
WE'RE HERE!

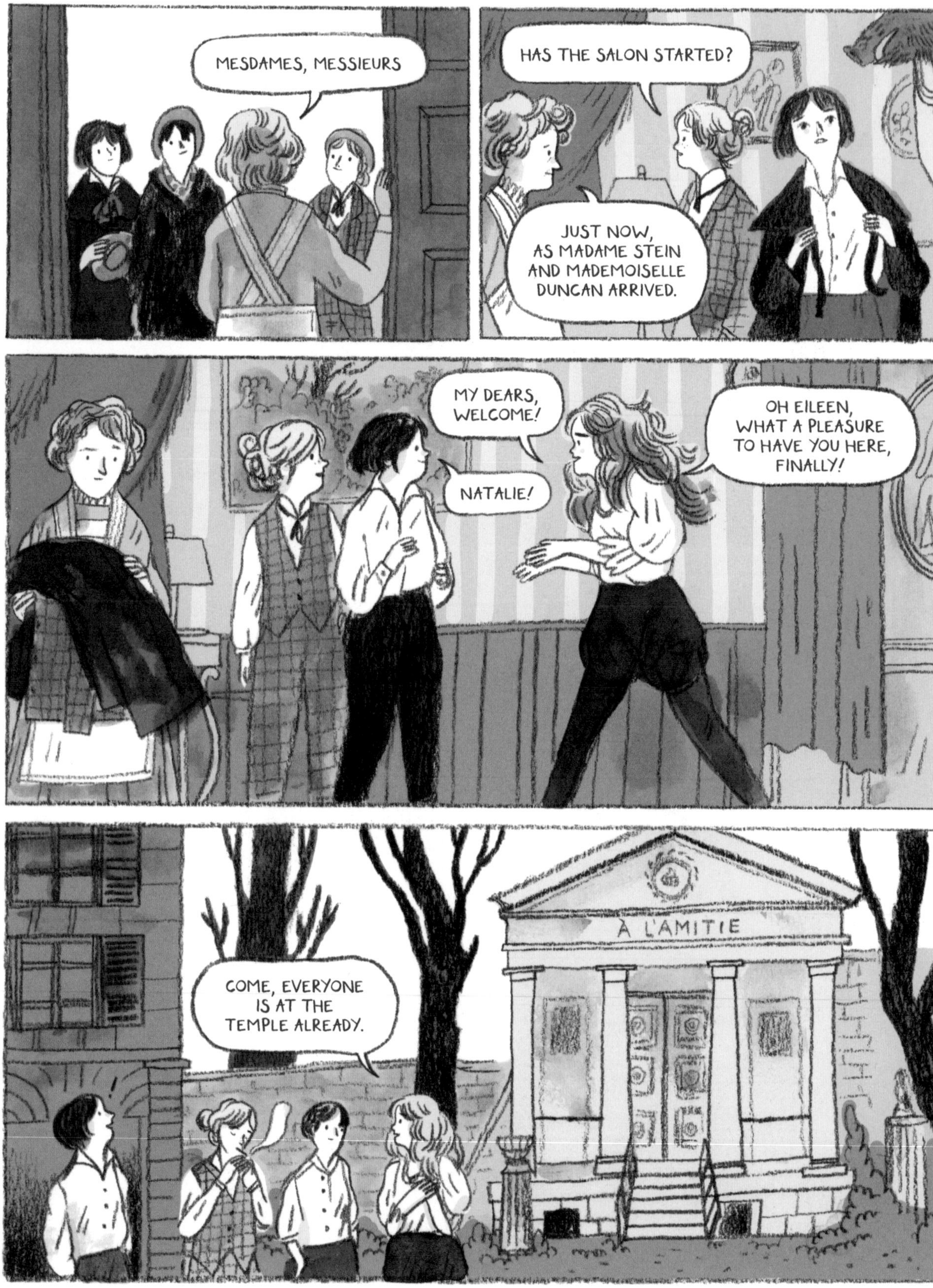
MESDAMES, MESSIEURS
HAS THE SALON STARTED?
JUST NOW, AS MADAME STEIN AND MADEMOISELLE DUNCAN ARRIVED.
MY DEARS, WELCOME!
NATALIE!
OH EILEEN, WHAT A PLEASURE TO HAVE YOU HERE, FINALLY!
À L'AMITIE
COME, EVERYONE IS AT THE TEMPLE ALREADY.

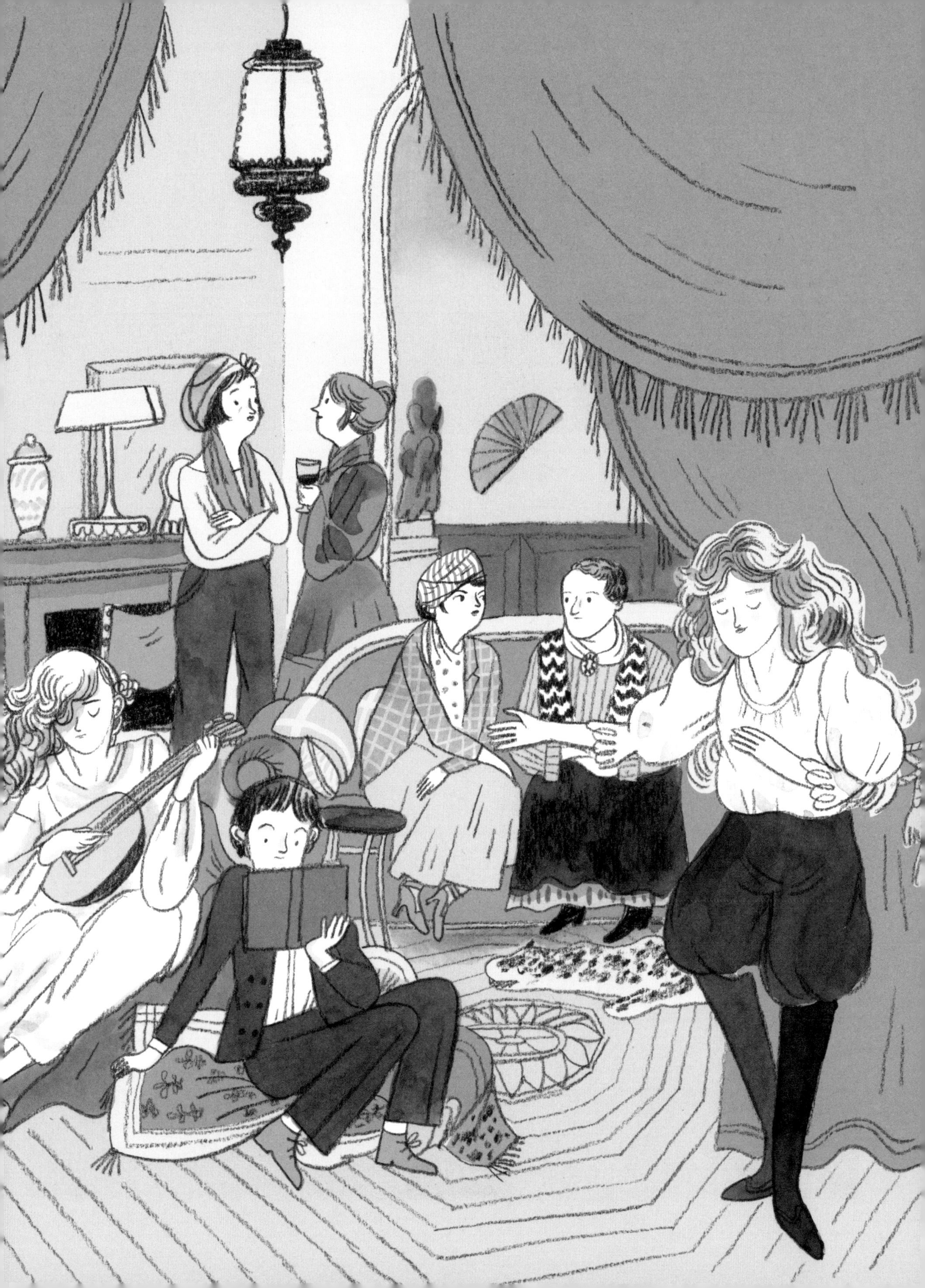

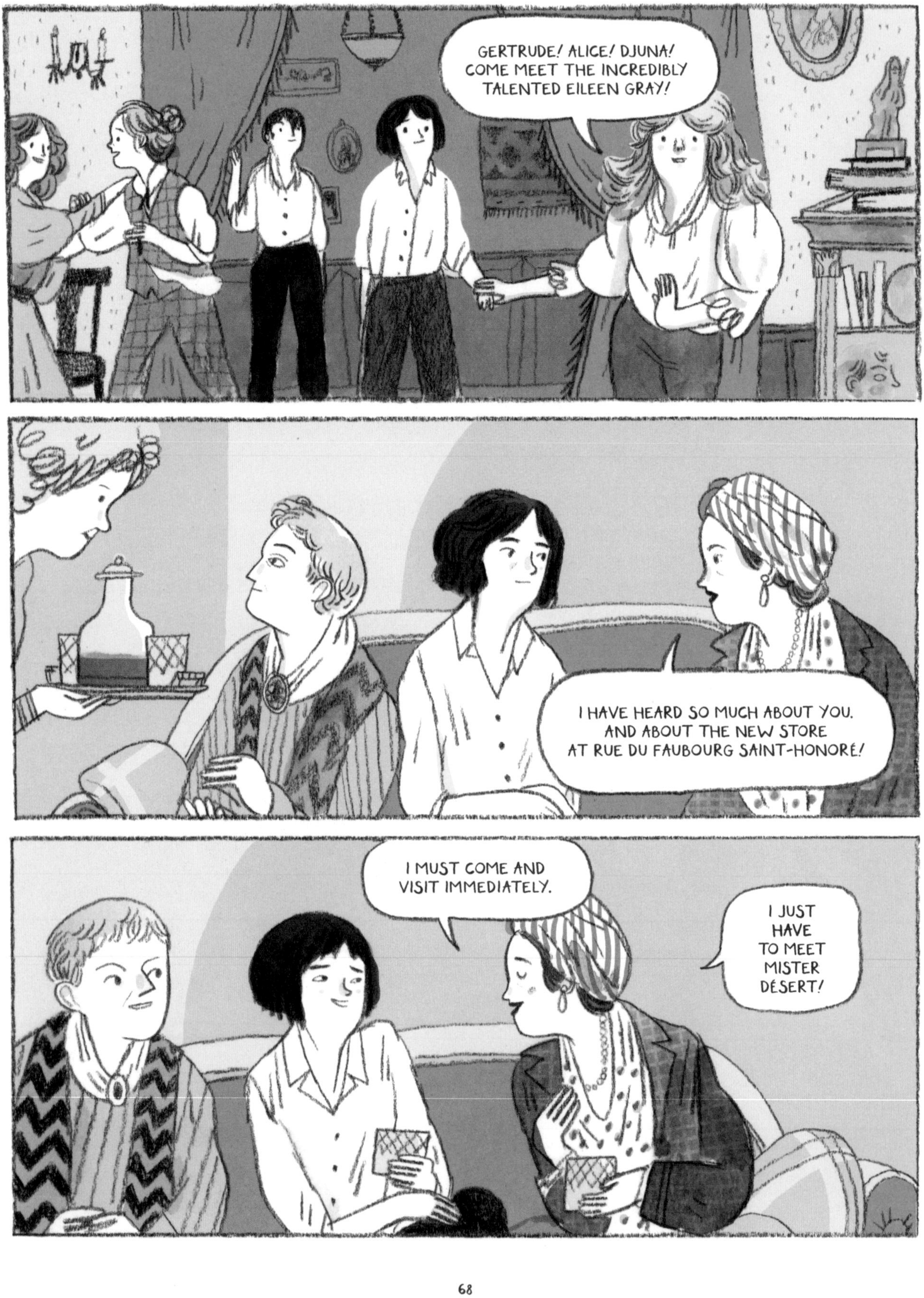
GERTRUDE! ALICE! DJUNA! COME MEET THE INCREDIBLY TALENTED EILEEN GRAY!
I HAVE HEARD SO MUCH ABOUT YOU. AND ABOUT THE NEW STORE AT RUE DU FAUBOURG SAINT-HONORÉ!
I MUST COME AND VISIT IMMEDIATELY.
I JUST HAVE TO MEET MISTER DÉSERT!

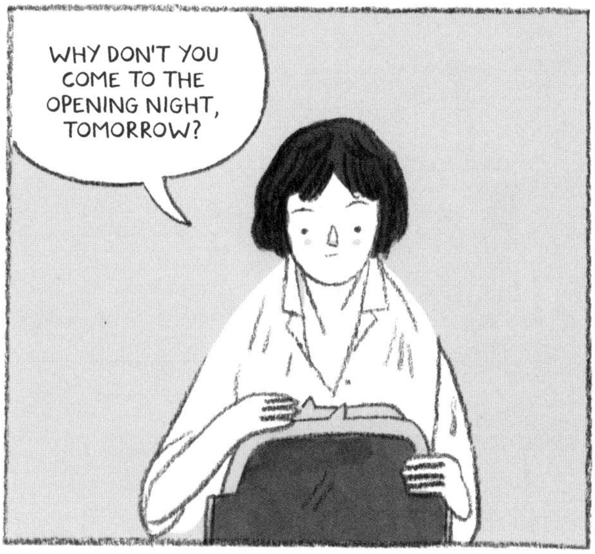
WHY DON'T YOU COME TO THE OPENING NIGHT, TOMORROW?

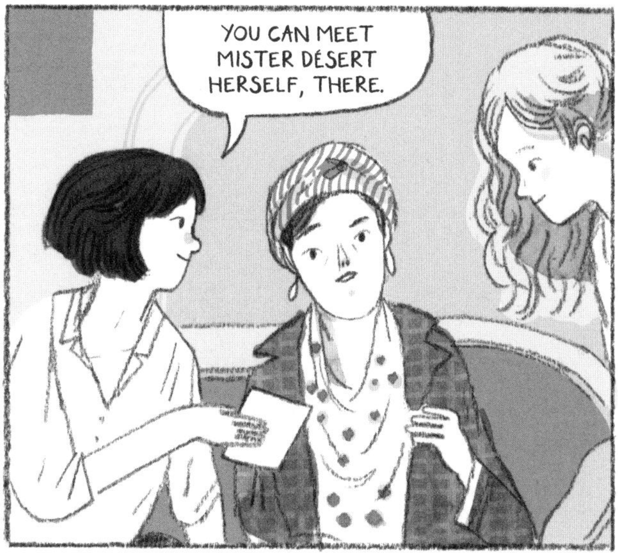
YOU CAN MEET MISTER DÉSERT HERSELF, THERE.

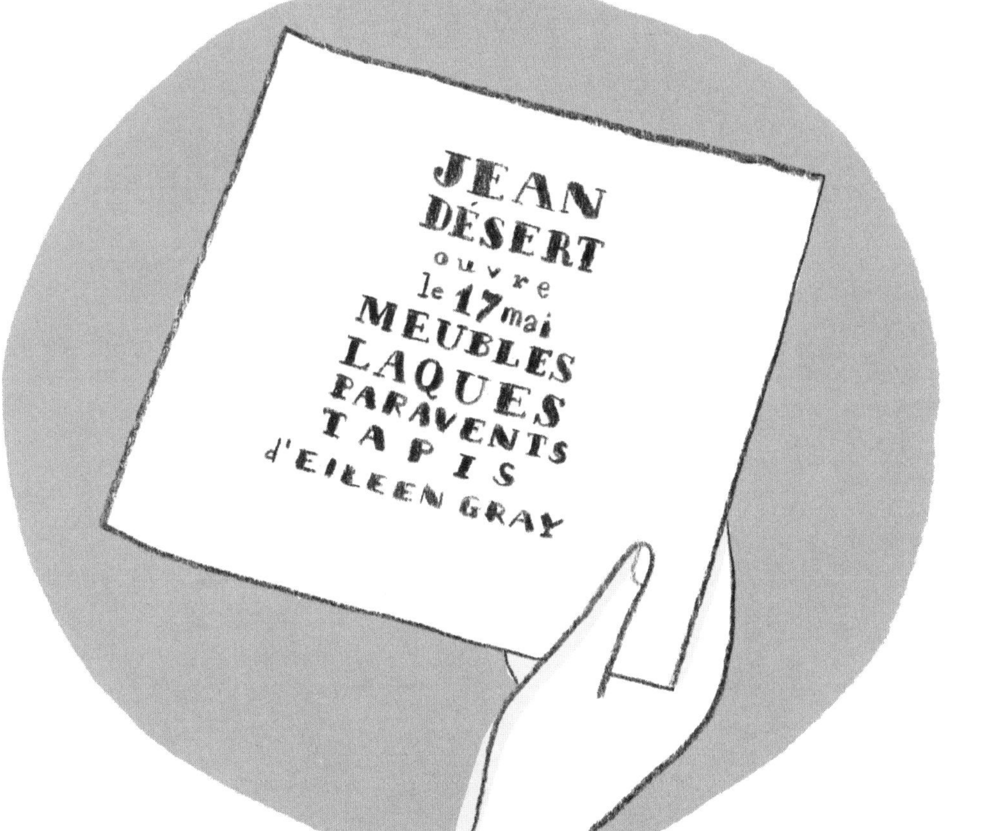
JEAN
DÉSERT
ouvre
le 17 mai
MEUBLES
LAQUES
PARAVENTS
TAPIS
d'EILEEN GRAY

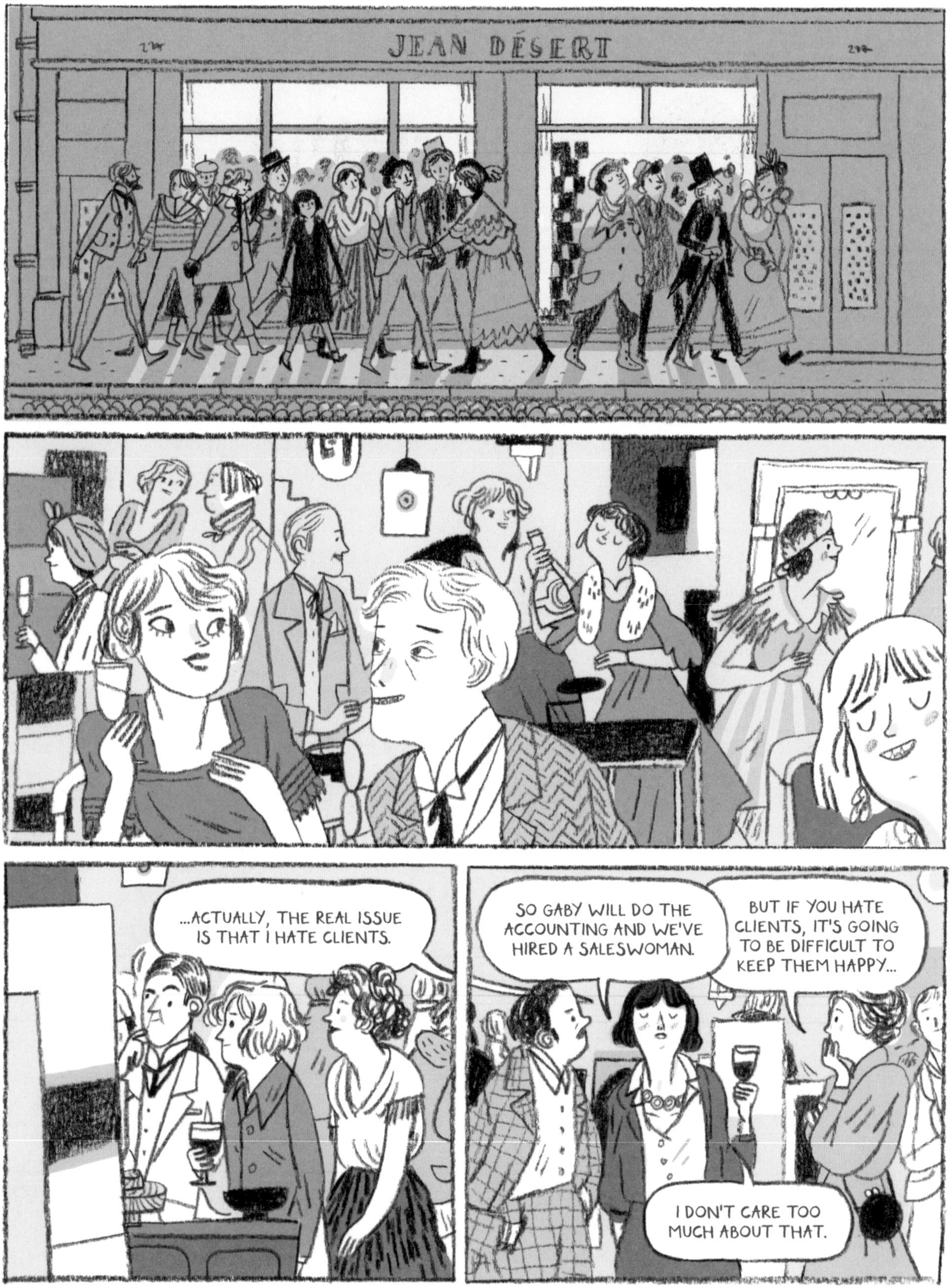

JEAN DÉSERT
...ACTUALLY, THE REAL ISSUE IS THAT I HATE CLIENTS.
SO GABY WILL DO THE ACCOUNTING AND WE'VE HIRED A SALESWOMAN.
BUT IF YOU HATE CLIENTS, IT'S GOING TO BE DIFFICULT TO KEEP THEM HAPPY...
I DON'T CARE TOO MUCH ABOUT THAT.

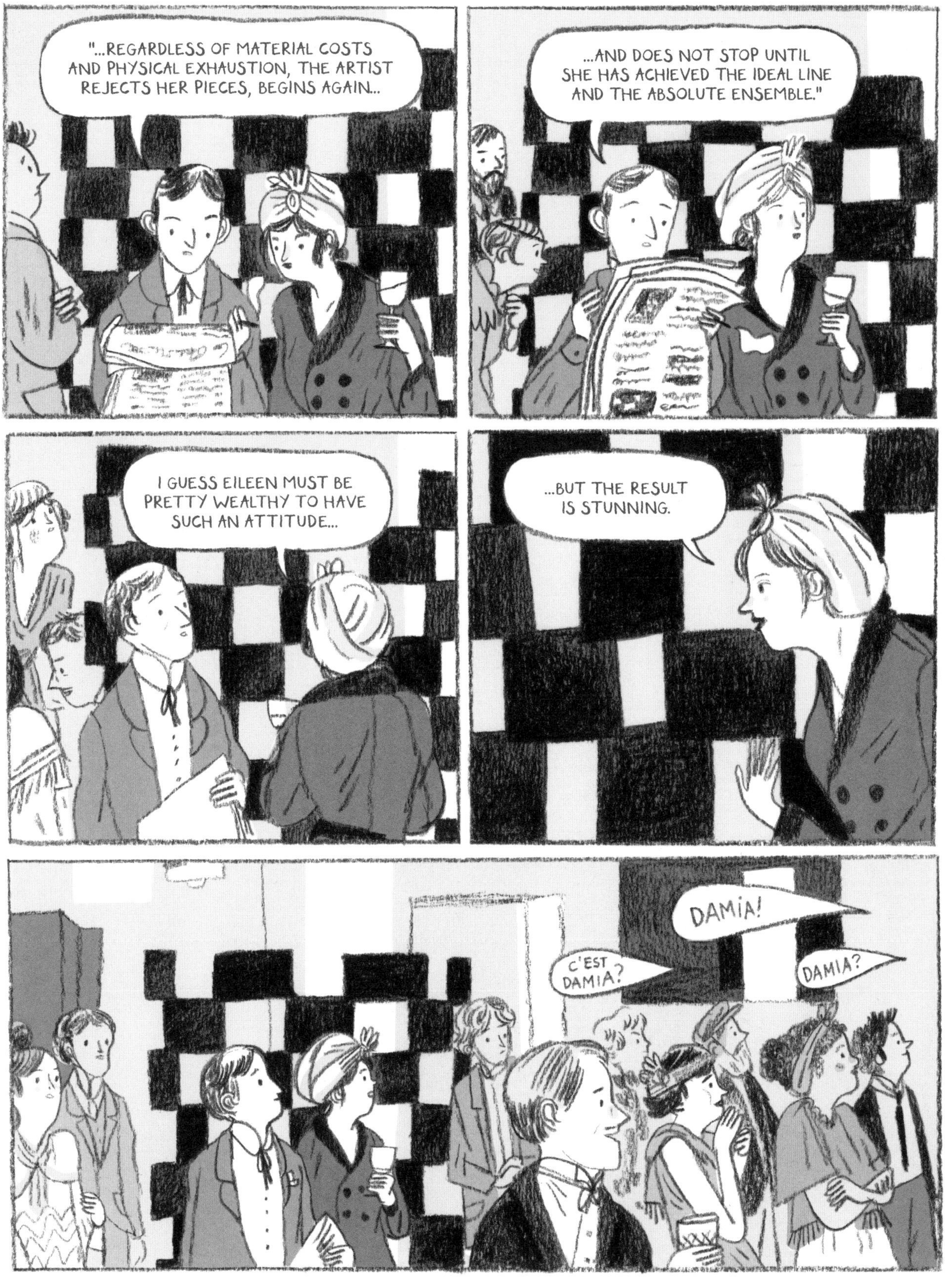
"...REGARDLESS OF MATERIAL COSTS AND PHYSICAL EXHAUSTION, THE ARTIST REJECTS HER PIECES, BEGINS AGAIN...
...AND DOES NOT STOP UNTIL SHE HAS ACHIEVED THE IDEAL LINE AND THE ABSOLUTE ENSEMBLE."
I GUESS EILEEN MUST BE PRETTY WEALTHY TO HAVE SUCH AN ATTITUDE...
...BUT THE RESULT IS STUNNING.
DAMIA!
C'EST DAMIA?
DAMIA?

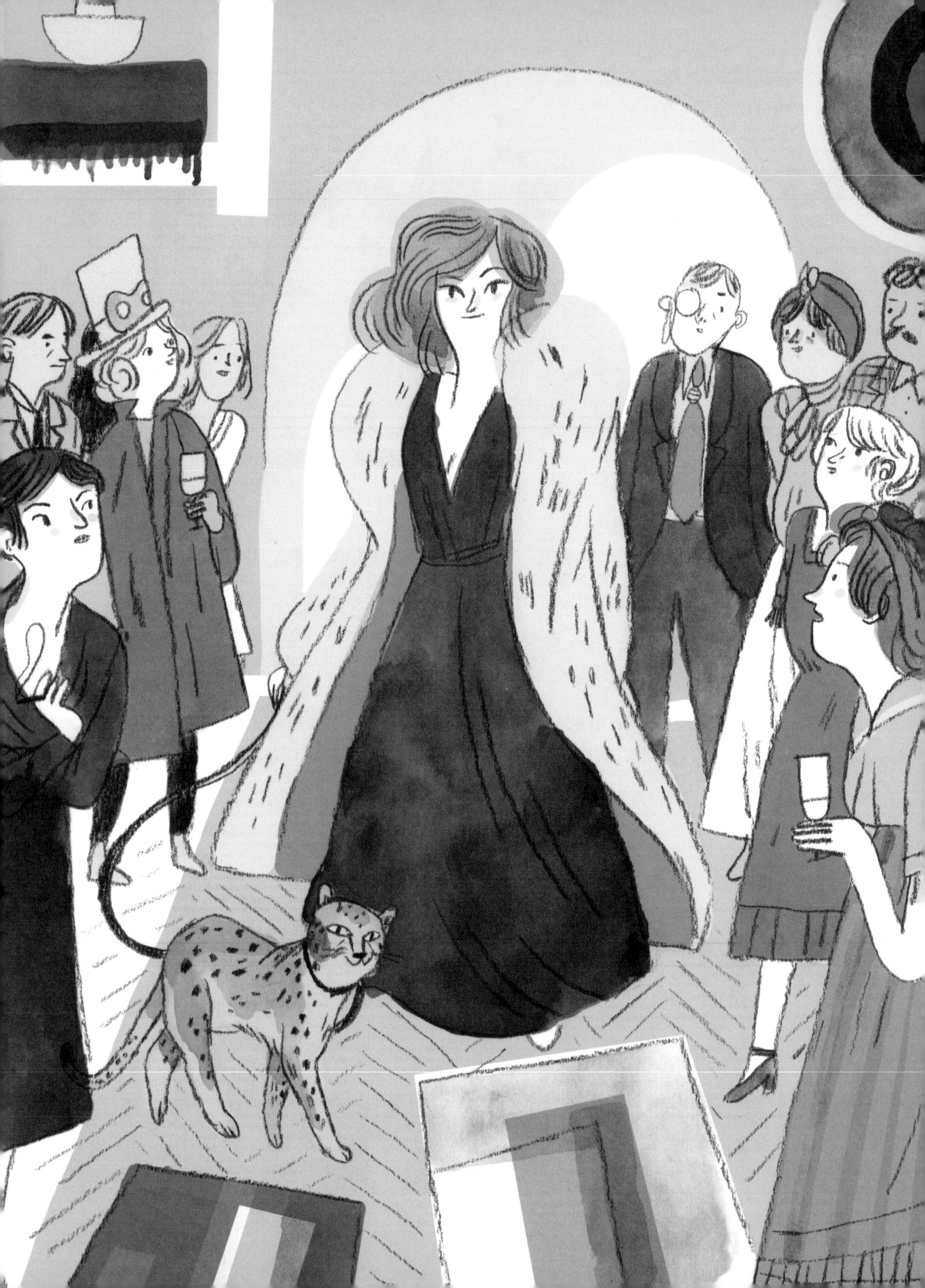

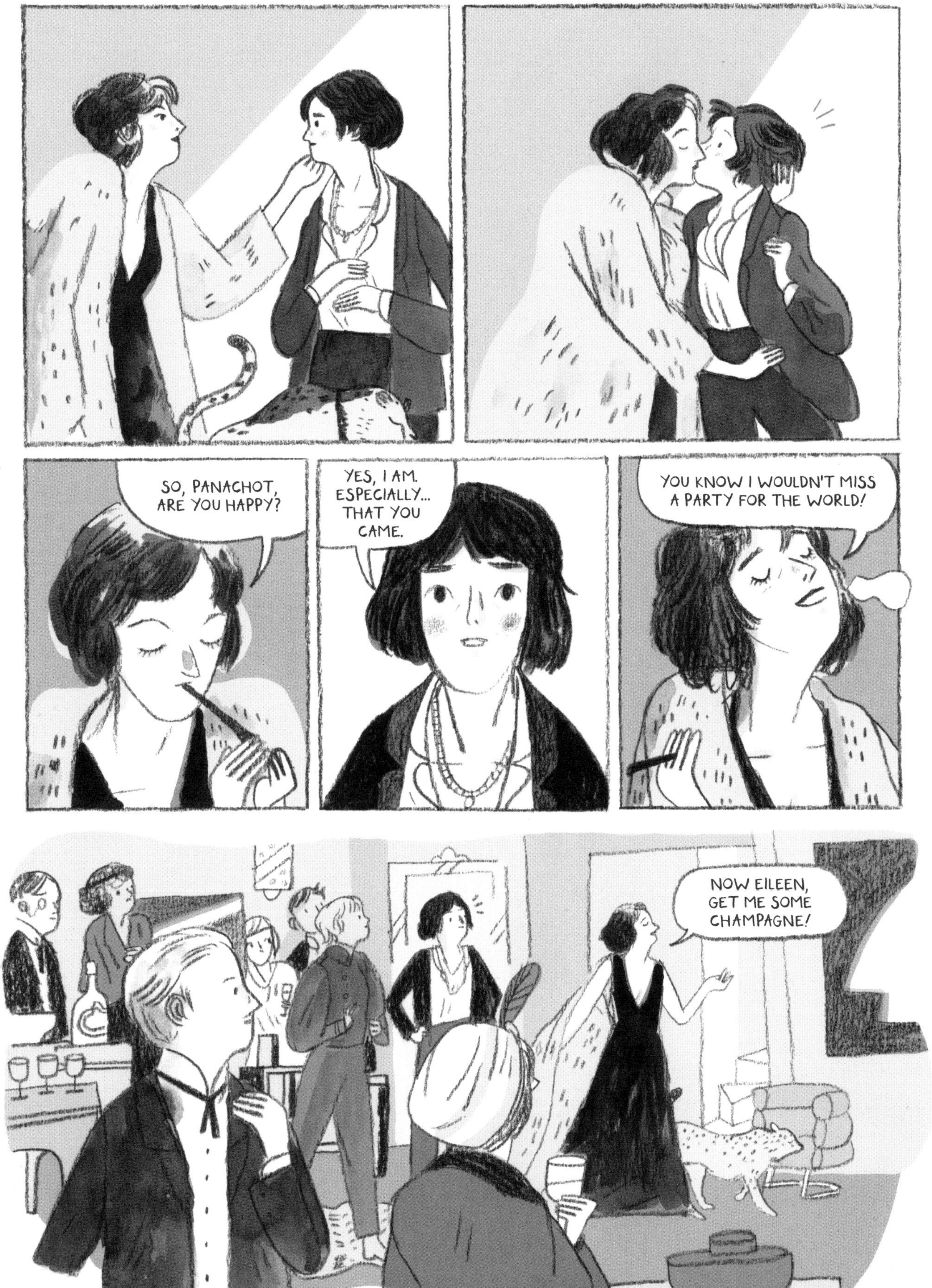
SO, PANACHOT, ARE YOU HAPPY?
YES, I AM. ESPECIALLY... THAT YOU CAME.
YOU KNOW I WOULDN'T MISS A PARTY FOR THE WORLD!
NOW EILEEN, GET ME SOME CHAMPAGNE!

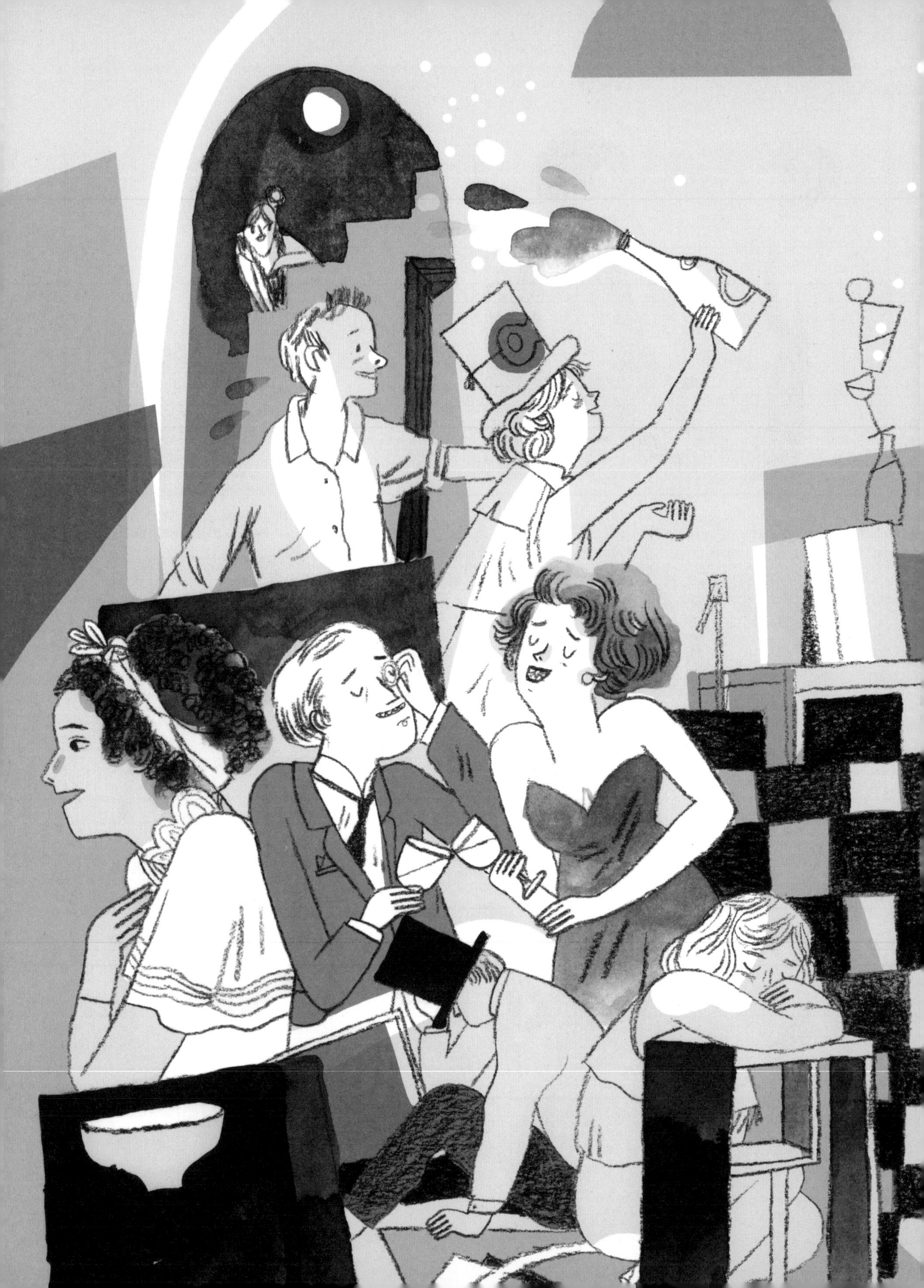

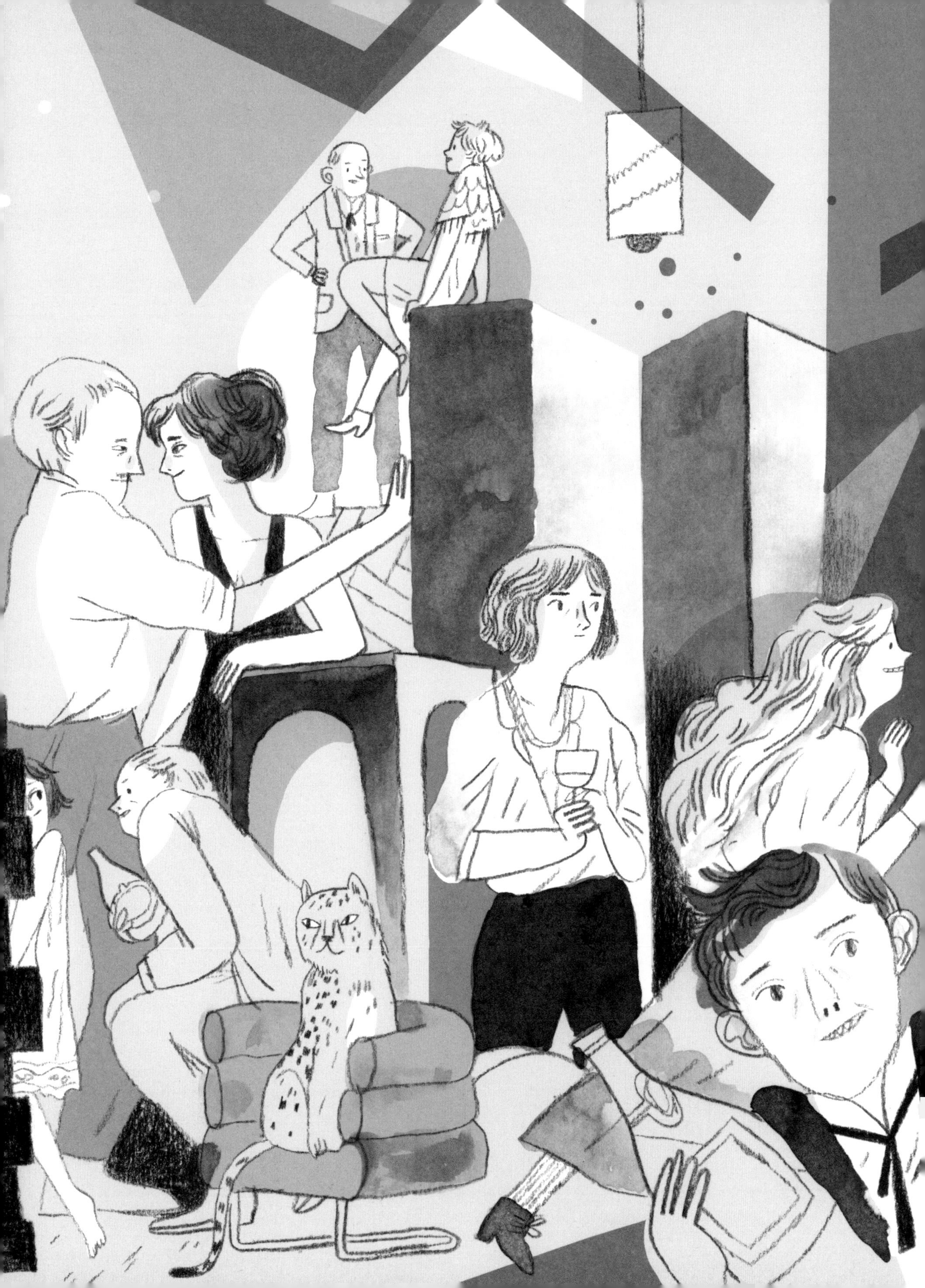

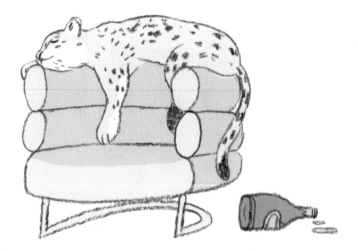

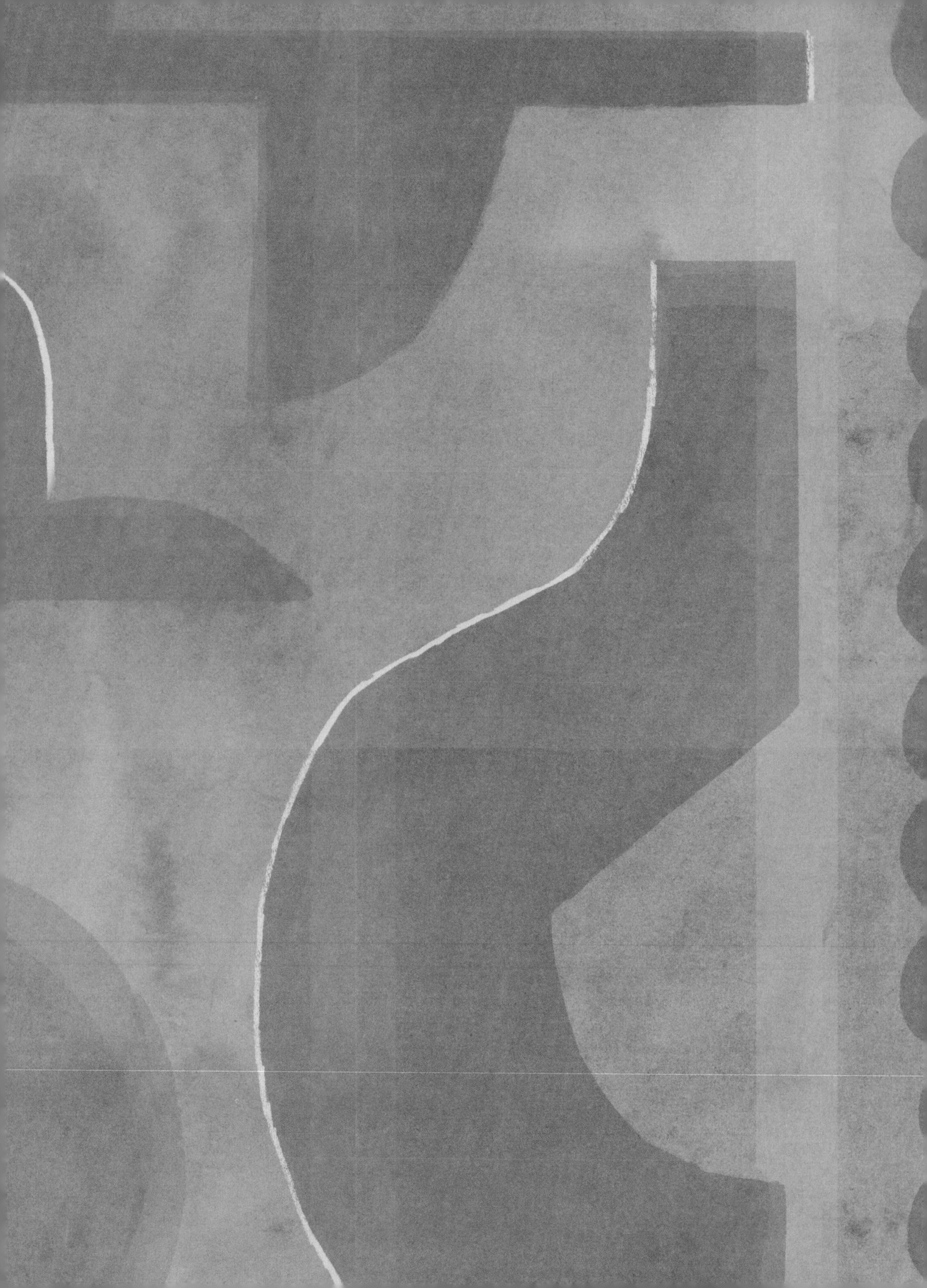

EILEEN & JEAN

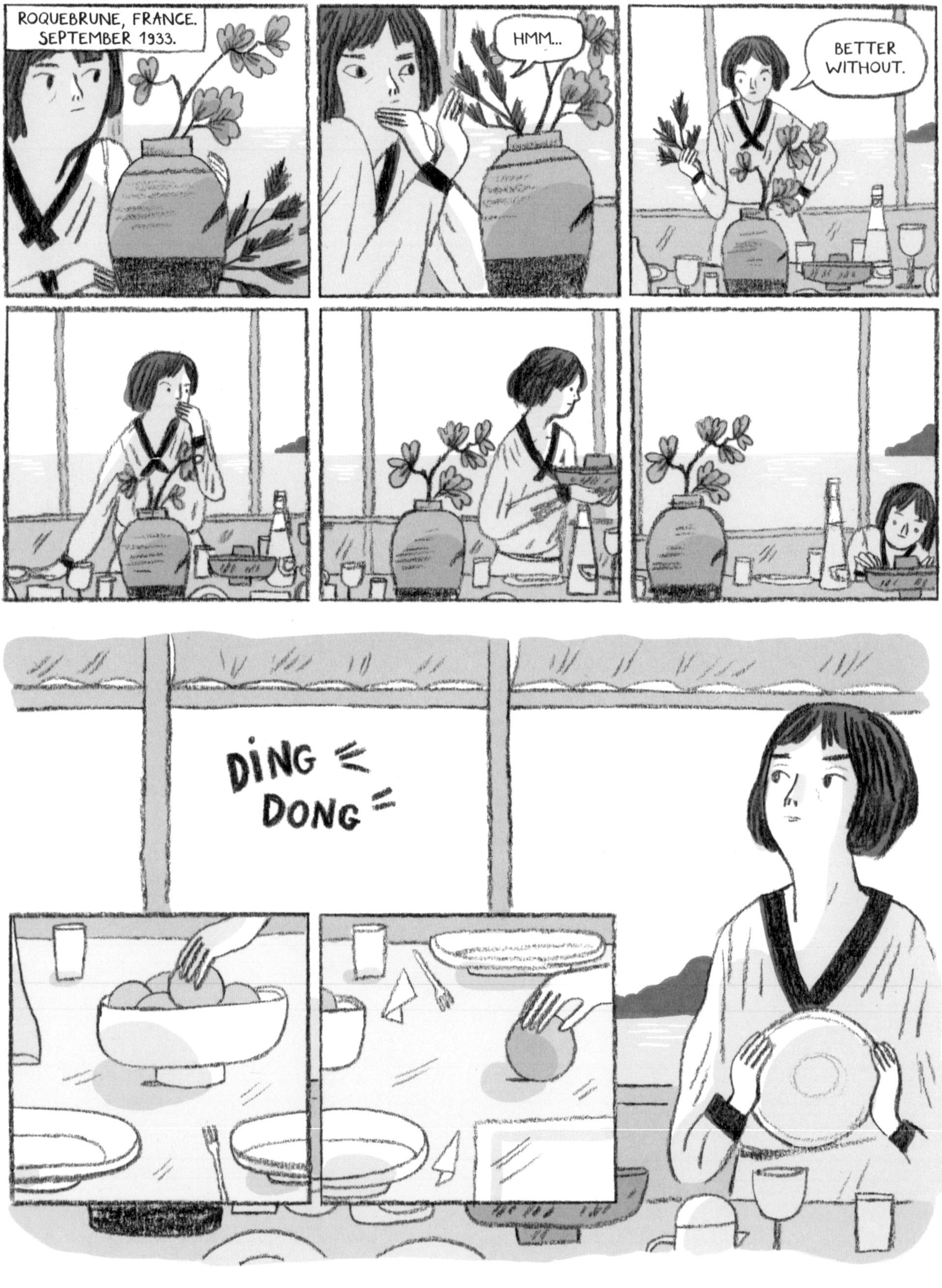
ROQUEBRUNE, FRANCE. SEPTEMBER 1933.
HMM...
BETTER WITHOUT.
DING
DONG

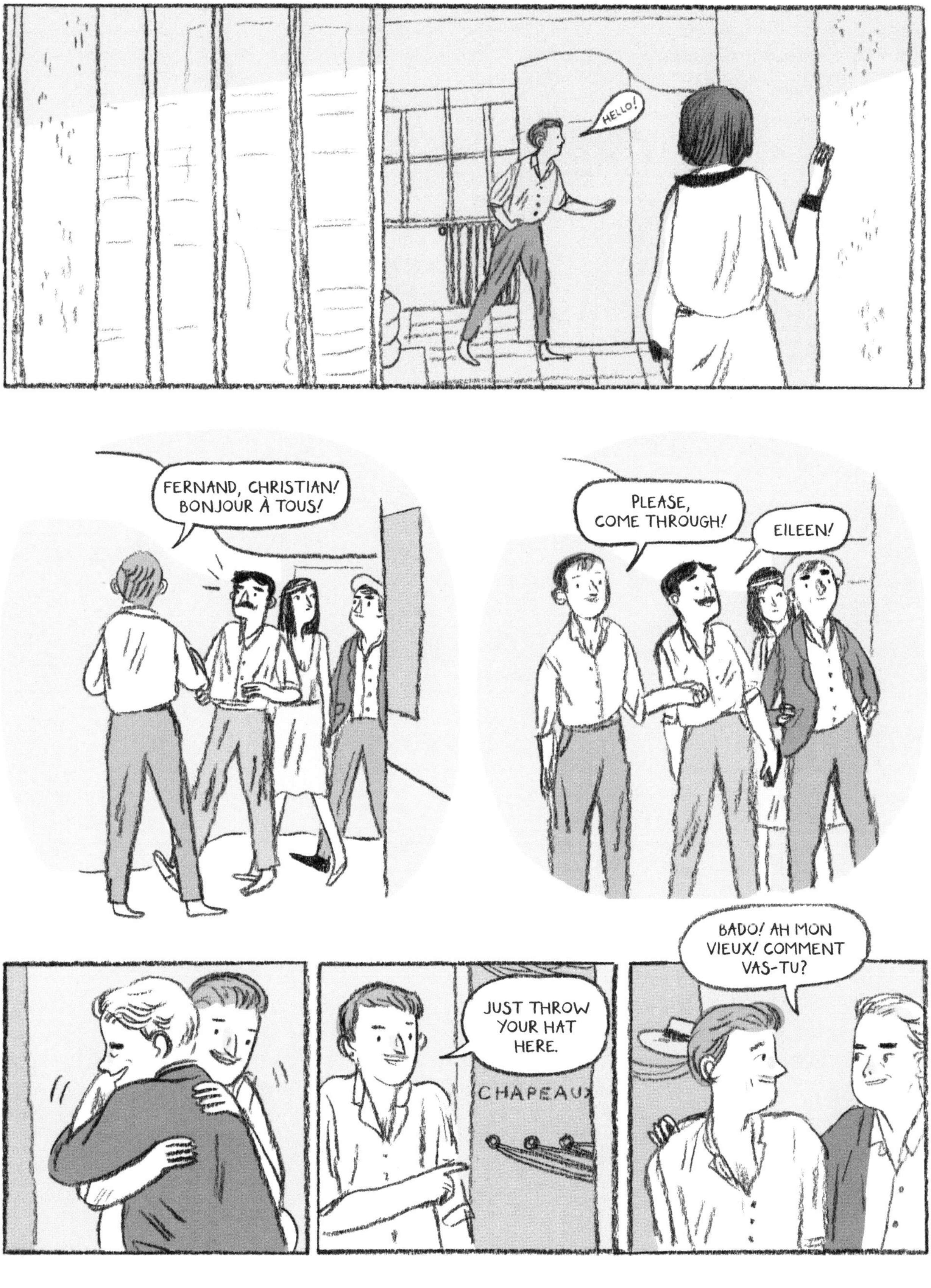
HELLO!
FERNAND, CHRISTIAN! BONJOUR À TOUS!
PLEASE, COME THROUGH!
EILEEN!
JUST THROW YOUR HAT HERE.
CHAPEAUX
BADO! AH MON VIEUX! COMMENT VAS-TU?

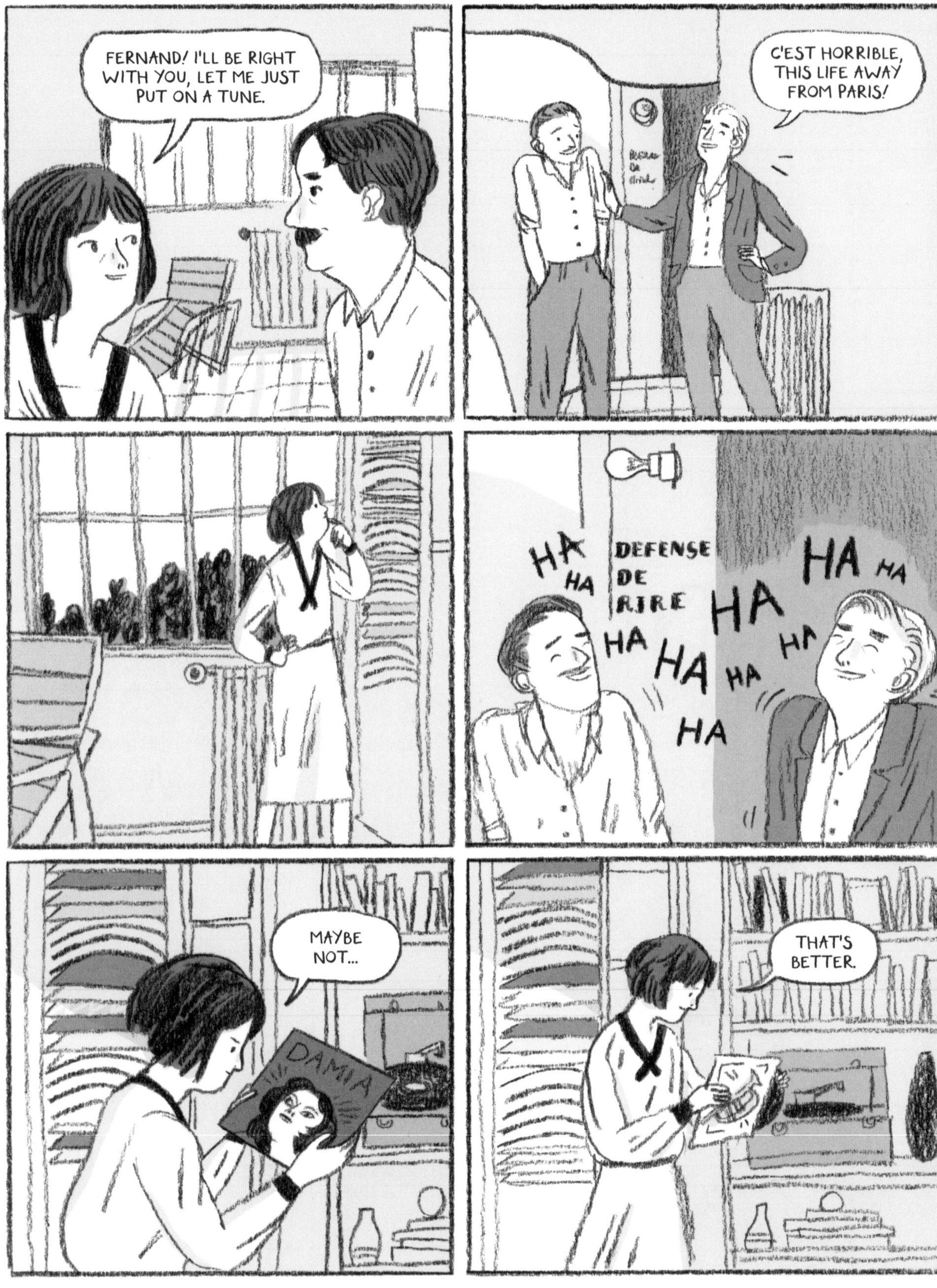

FERNAND! I'LL BE RIGHT WITH YOU, LET ME JUST PUT ON A TUNE.
C'EST HORRIBLE, THIS LIFE AWAY FROM PARIS!
HA
HA
DEFENSE DE RIRE
HA HA
HA
HA
HA
HA
HA
HA
HA
MAYBE NOT...
DAMIA
THAT'S BETTER.

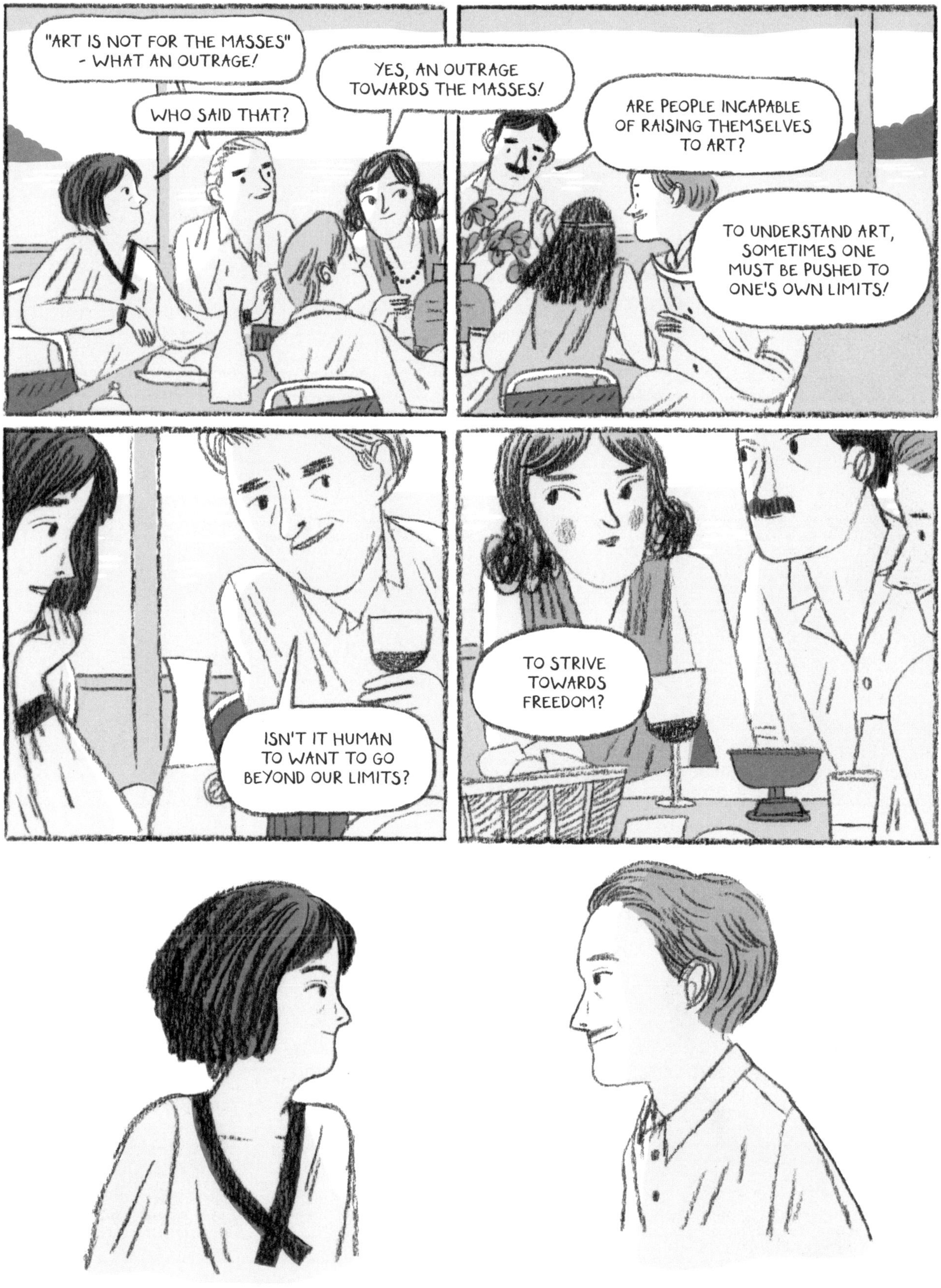
"ART IS NOT FOR THE MASSES" - WHAT AN OUTRAGE!
WHO SAID THAT?
YES, AN OUTRAGE TOWARDS THE MASSES!
ARE PEOPLE INCAPABLE OF RAISING THEMSELVES TO ART?
TO UNDERSTAND ART, SOMETIMES ONE MUST BE PUSHED TO ONE'S OWN LIMITS!
ISN'T IT HUMAN TO WANT TO GO BEYOND OUR LIMITS?
TO STRIVE TOWARDS FREEDOM?

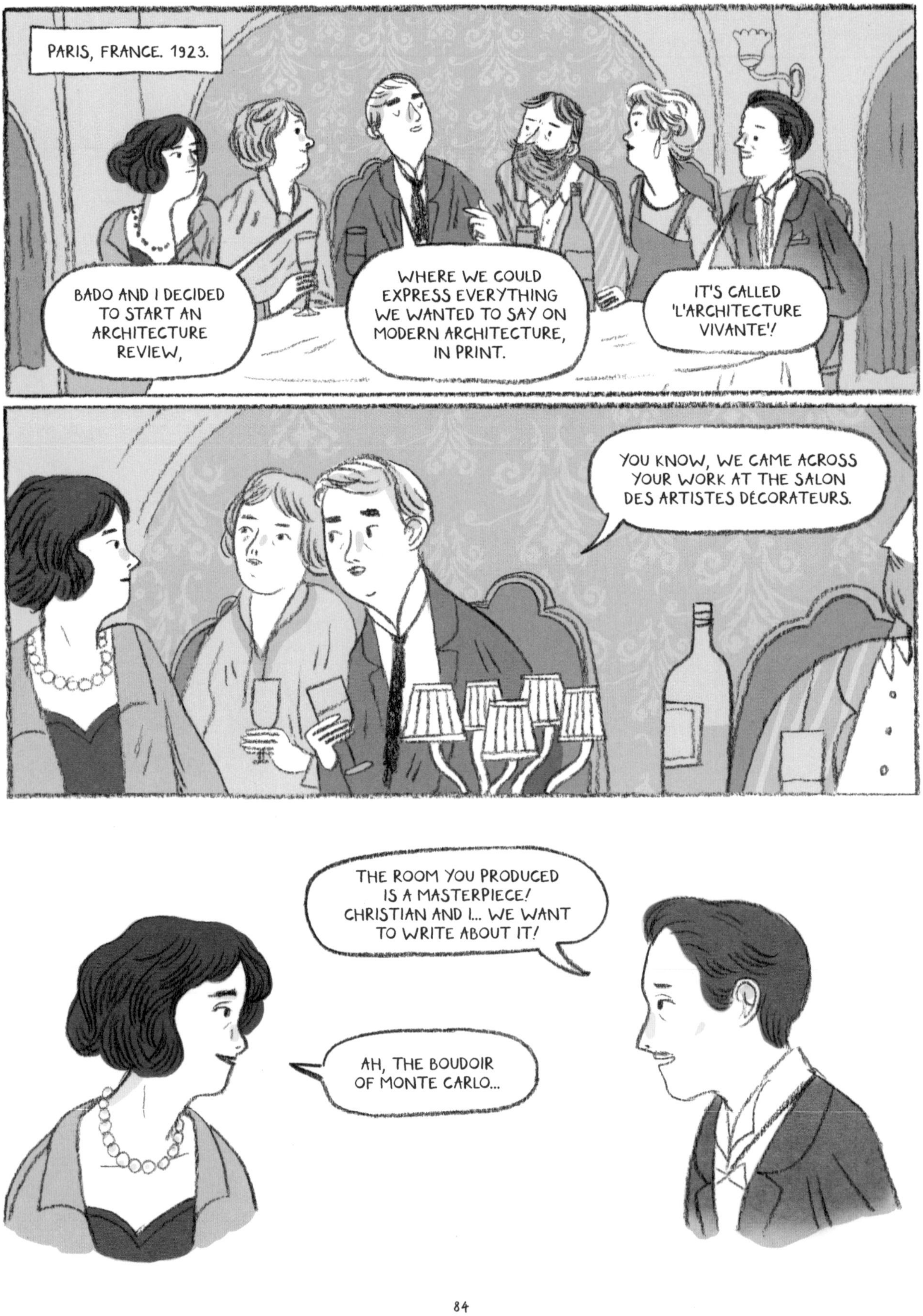
PARIS, FRANCE. 1923.
BADO AND I DECIDED TO START AN ARCHITECTURE REVIEW,
WHERE WE COULD EXPRESS EVERYTHING WE WANTED TO SAY ON MODERN ARCHITECTURE, IN PRINT.
IT'S CALLED 'L'ARCHITECTURE VIVANTE'!
YOU KNOW, WE CAME ACROSS YOUR WORK AT THE SALON DES ARTISTES DÉCORATEURS.
THE ROOM YOU PRODUCED IS A MASTERPIECE! CHRISTIAN AND I... WE WANT TO WRITE ABOUT IT!
AH, THE BOUDOIR OF MONTE CARLO...

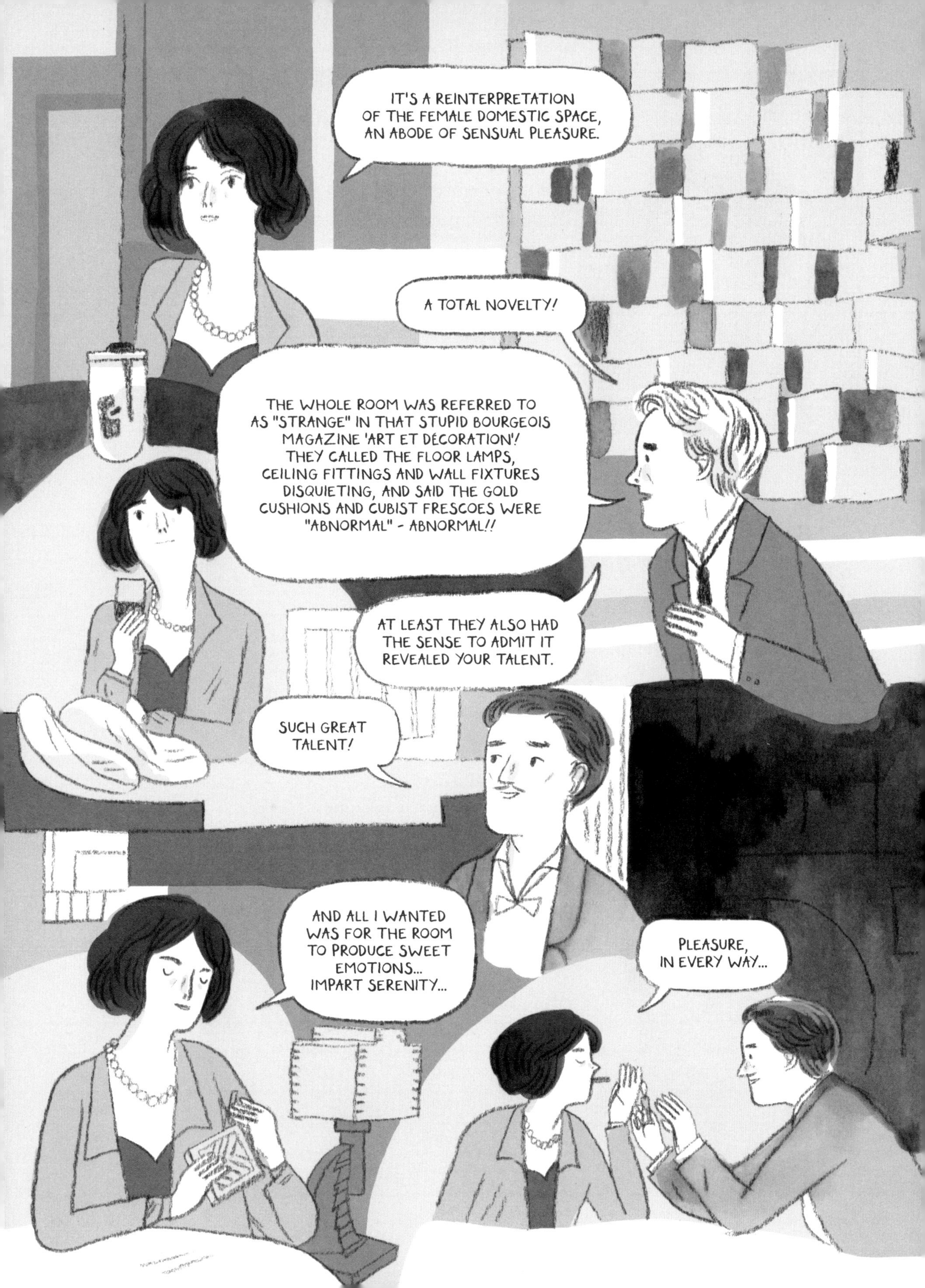

IT'S A REINTERPRETATION OF THE FEMALE DOMESTIC SPACE, AN ABODE OF SENSUAL PLEASURE.
A TOTAL NOVELTY!
THE WHOLE ROOM WAS REFERRED TO AS "STRANGE" IN THAT STUPID BOURGEOIS MAGAZINE 'ART ET DÉCORATION'! THEY CALLED THE FLOOR LAMPS, CEILING FITTINGS AND WALL FIXTURES DISQUIETING, AND SAID THE GOLD CUSHIONS AND CUBIST FRESCOES WERE "ABNORMAL" - ABNORMAL!!
AT LEAST THEY ALSO HAD THE SENSE TO ADMIT IT REVEALED YOUR TALENT.
SUCH GREAT TALENT!
AND ALL I WANTED WAS FOR THE ROOM TO PRODUCE SWEET EMOTIONS... IMPART SERENITY...
PLEASURE, IN EVERY WAY...

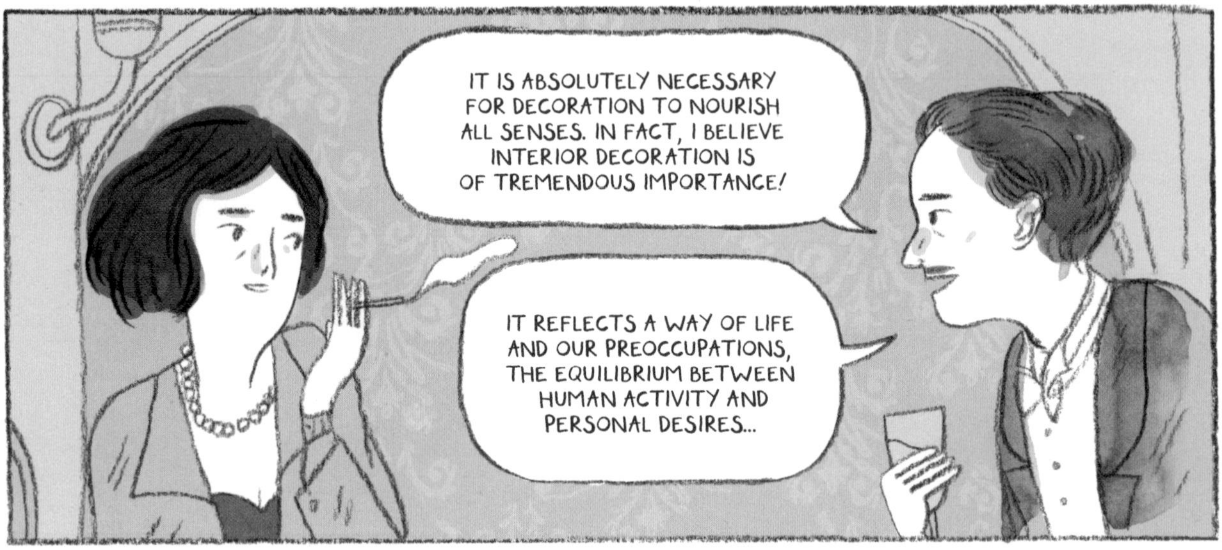
IT IS ABSOLUTELY NECESSARY FOR DECORATION TO NOURISH ALL SENSES. IN FACT, I BELIEVE INTERIOR DECORATION IS OF TREMENDOUS IMPORTANCE!
IT REFLECTS A WAY OF LIFE AND OUR PREOCCUPATIONS, THE EQUILIBRIUM BETWEEN HUMAN ACTIVITY AND PERSONAL DESIRES...

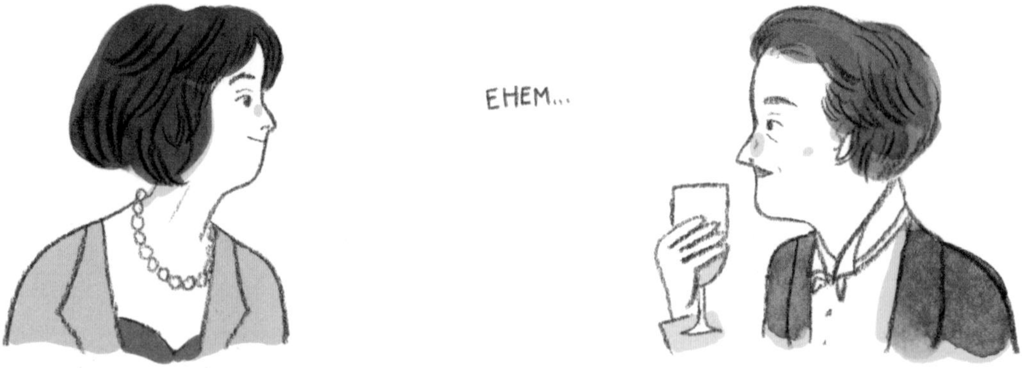
EHEM...

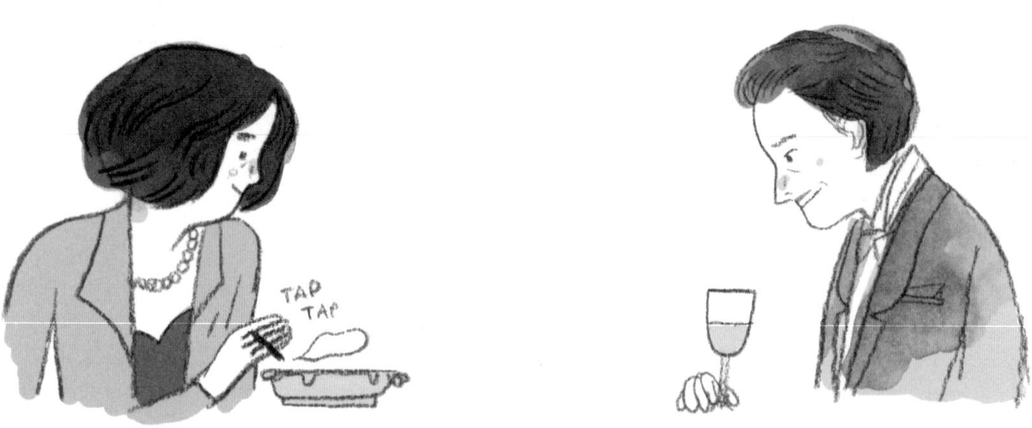
TAP
TAP

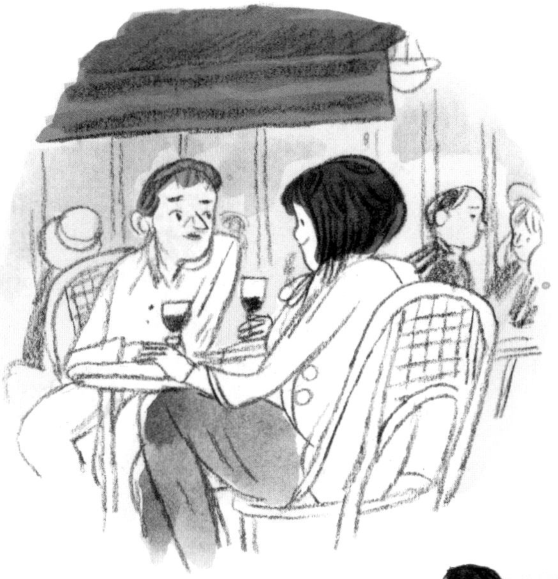
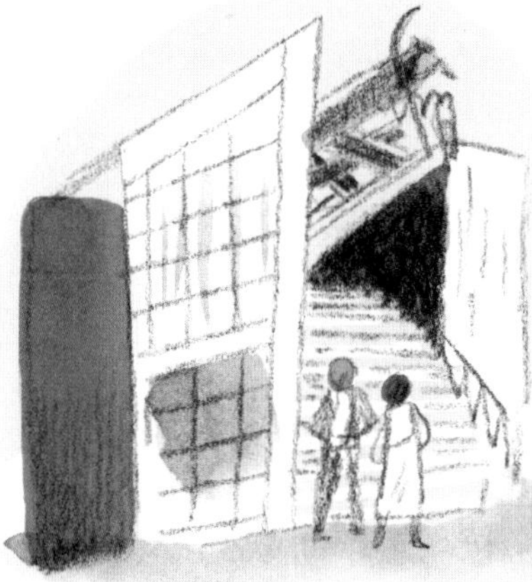
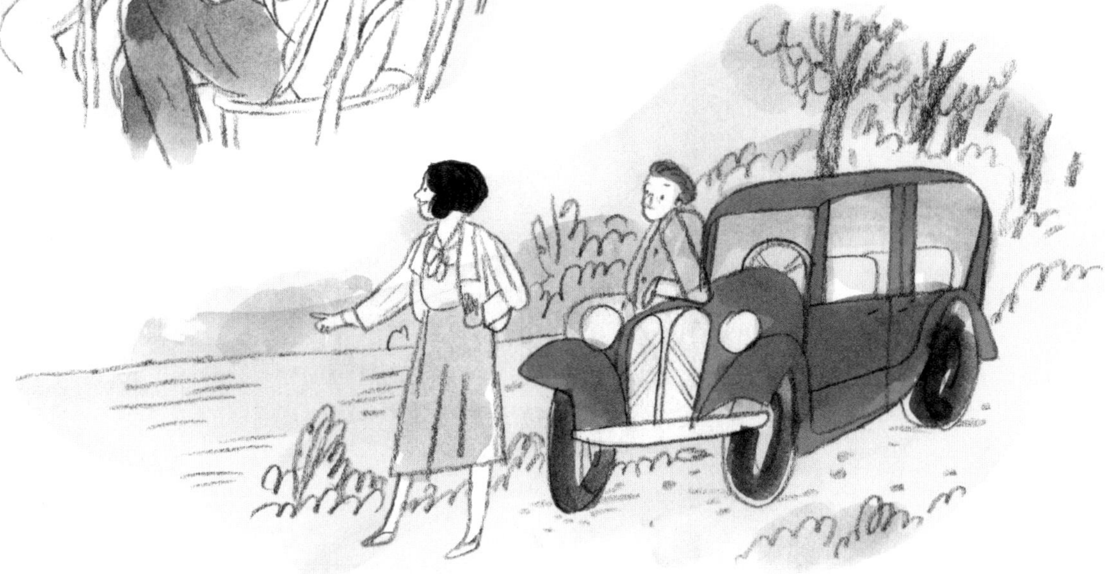
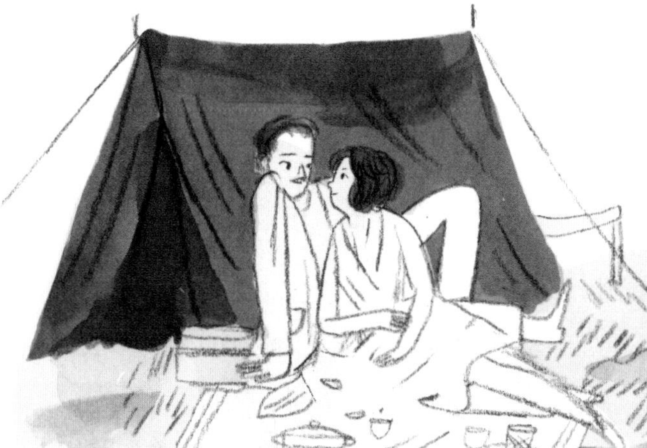
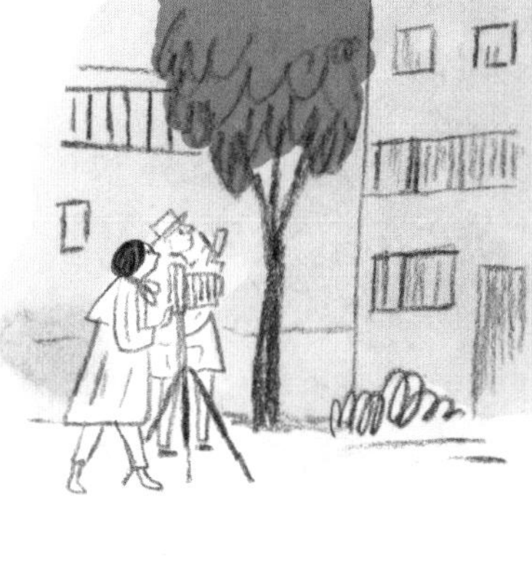

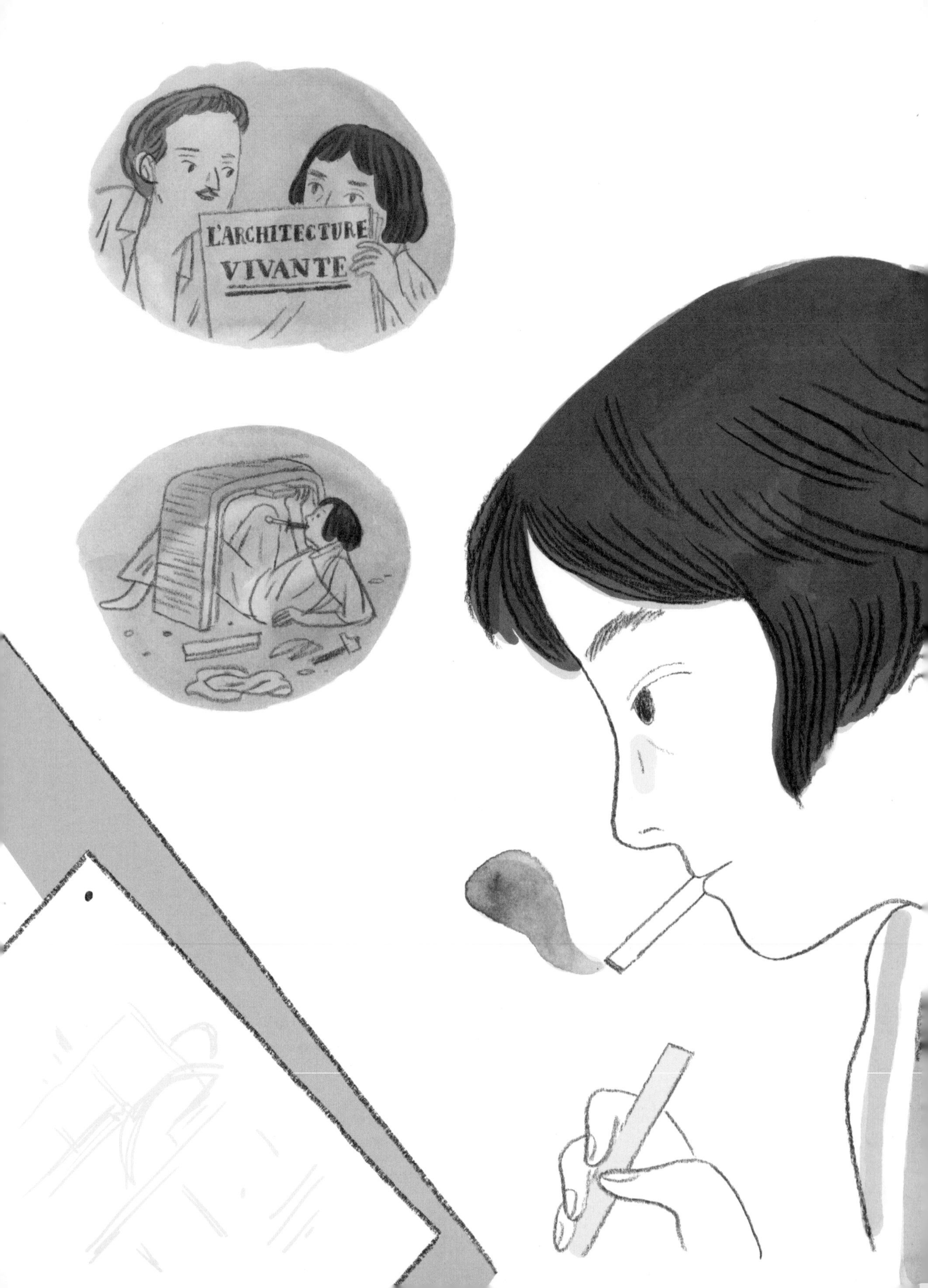
L'ARCHITECTURE
VIVANTE

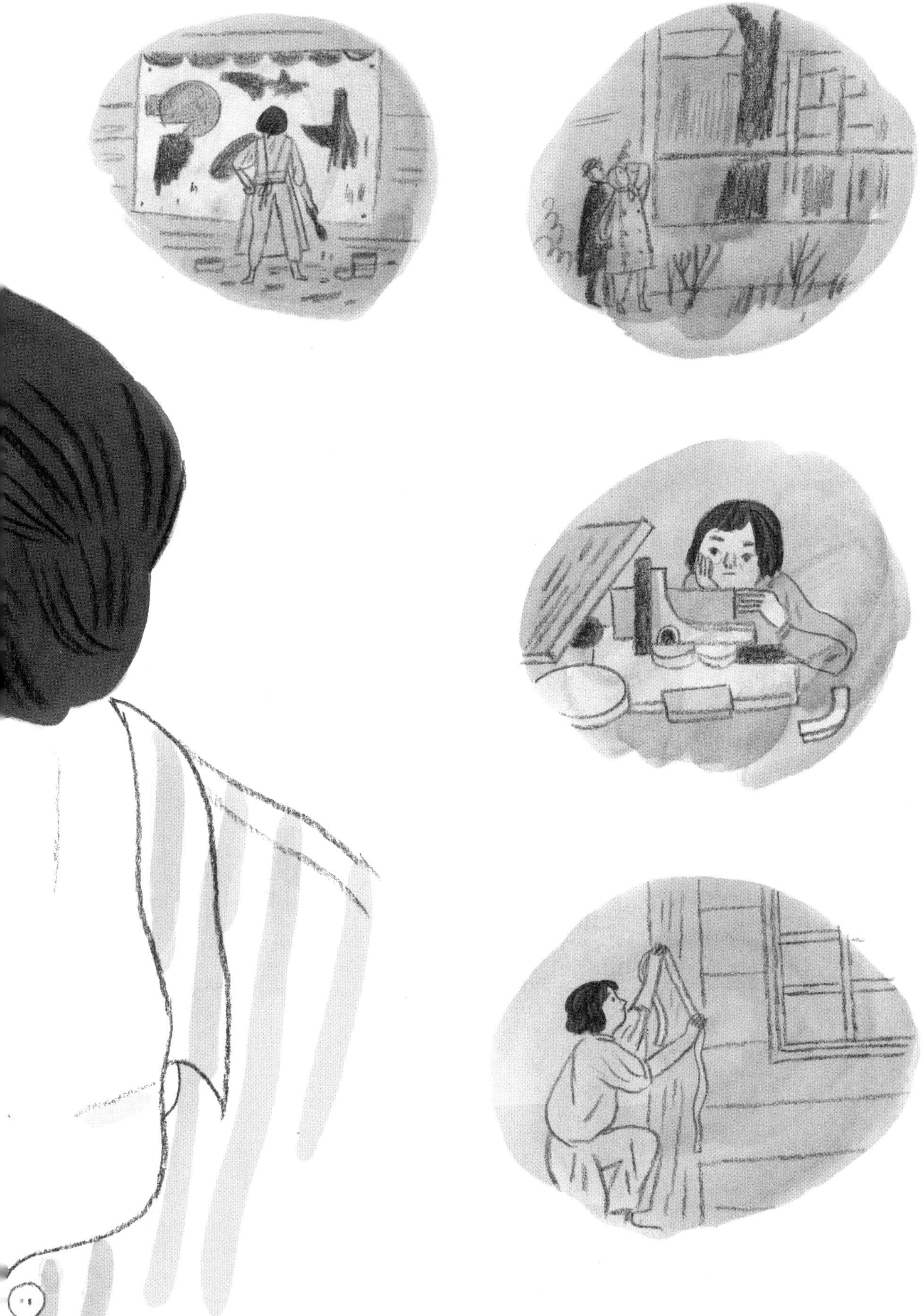

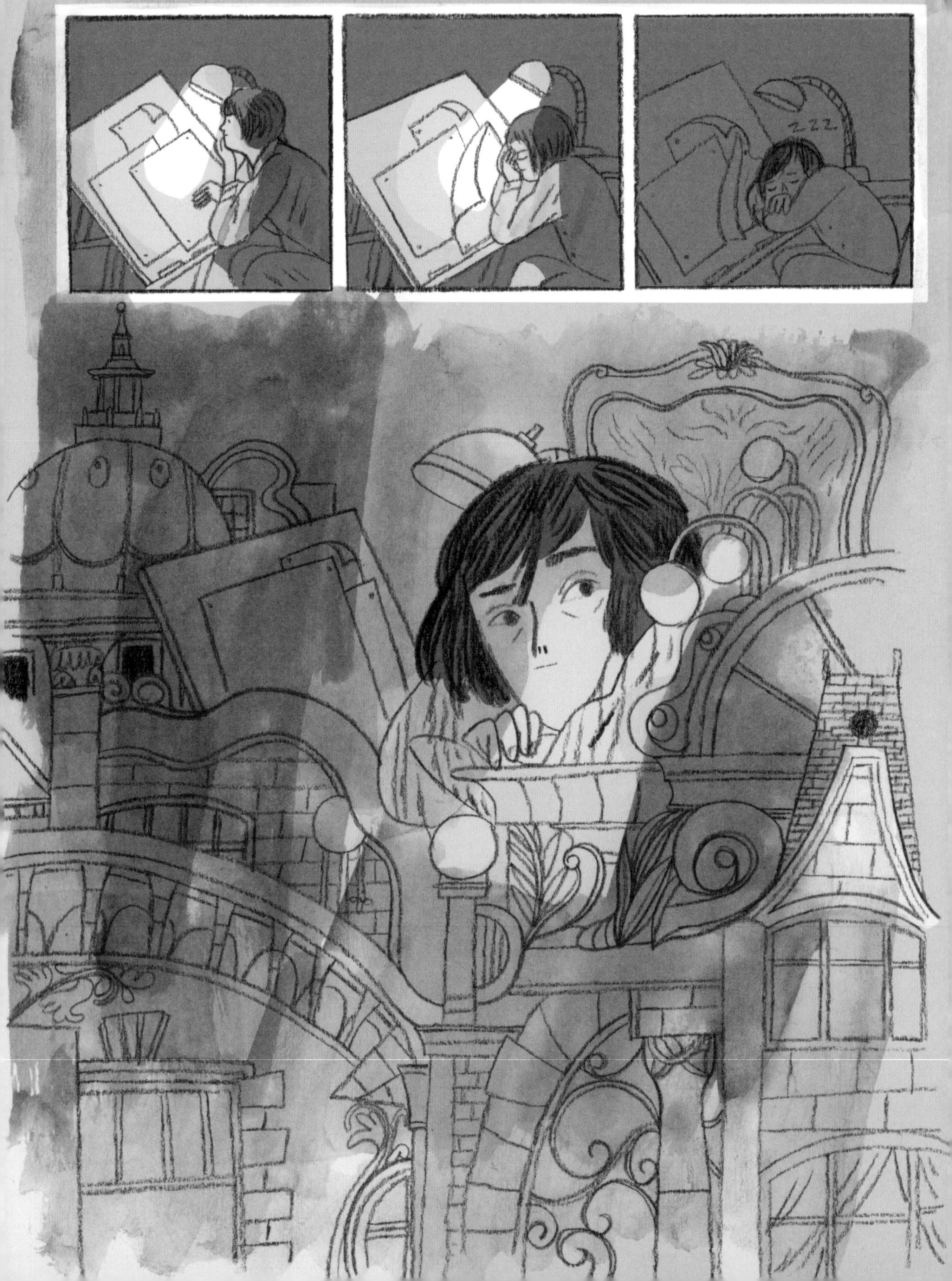
ZZZ

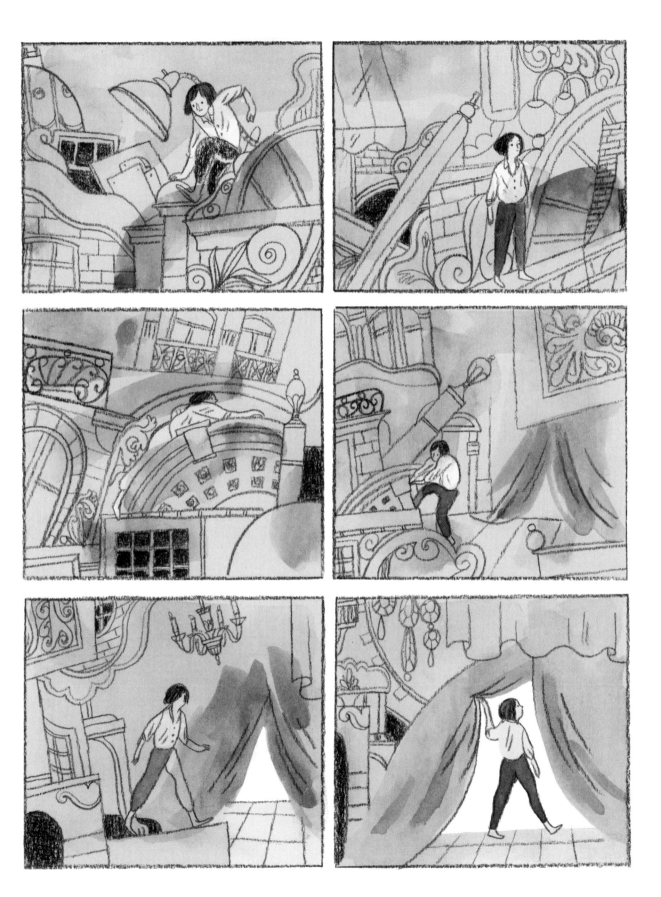

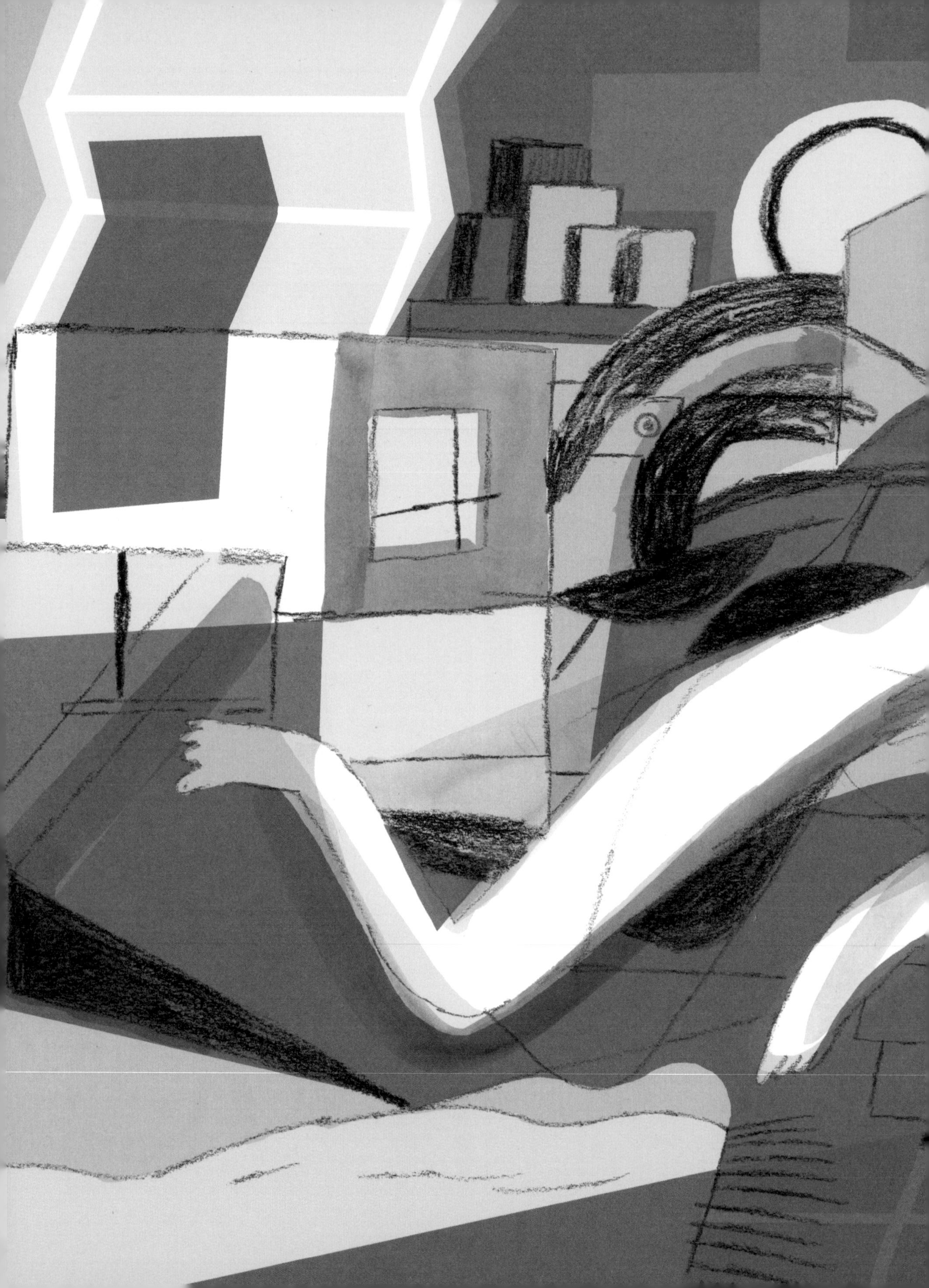

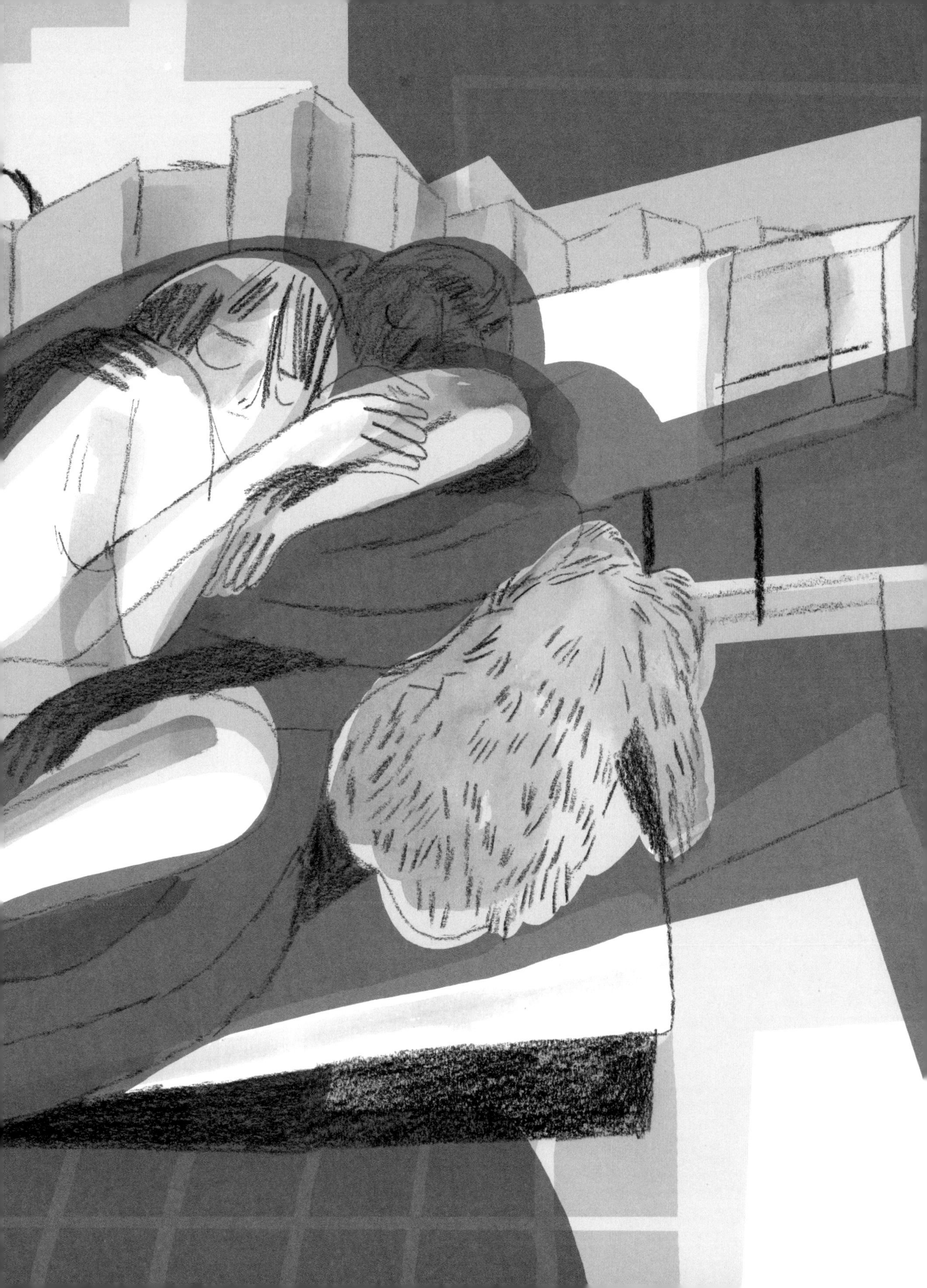

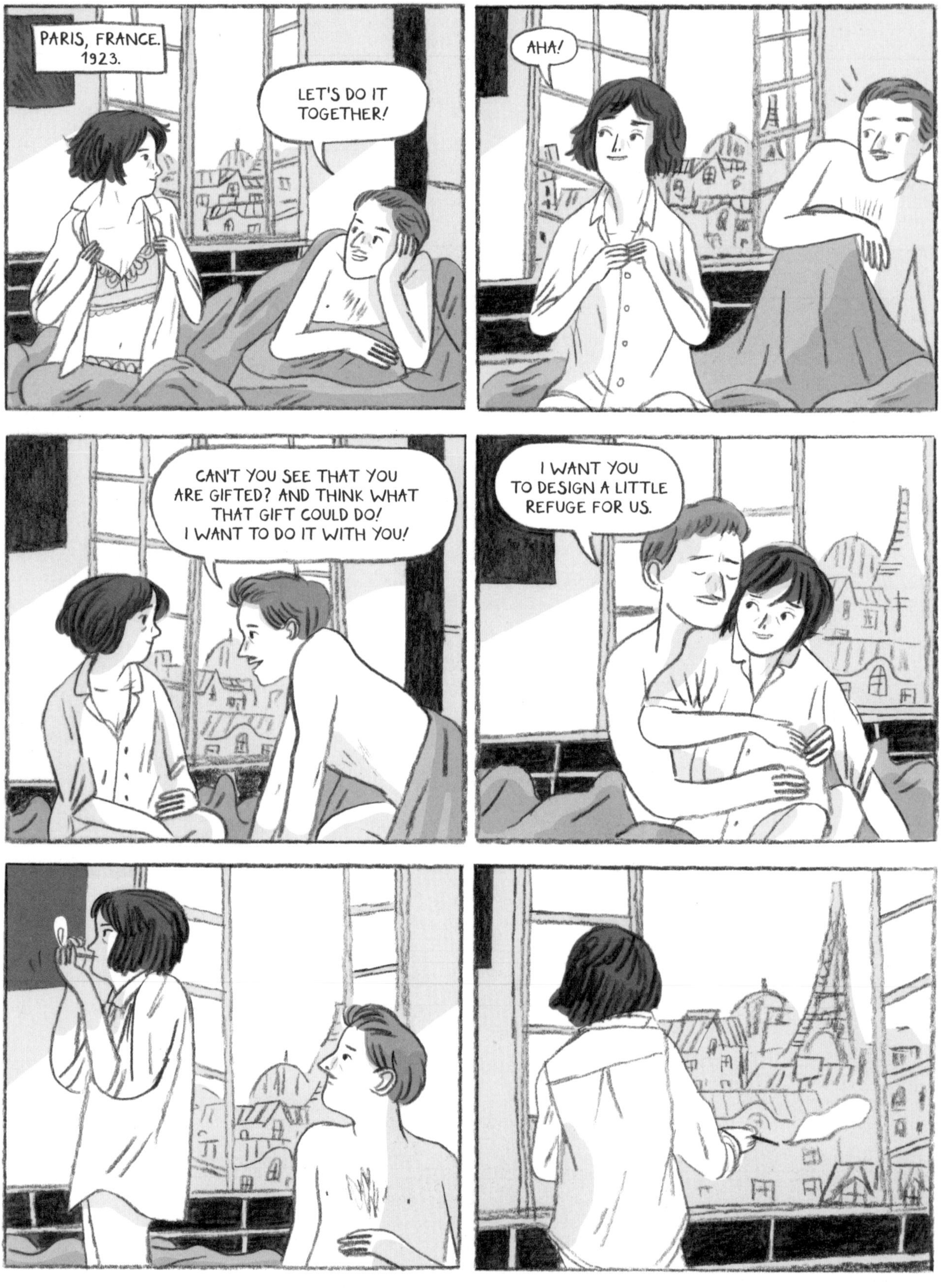
PARIS, FRANCE. 1923.
LET'S DO IT TOGETHER!
AHA!
CAN'T YOU SEE THAT YOU ARE GIFTED? AND THINK WHAT THAT GIFT COULD DO! I WANT TO DO IT WITH YOU!
I WANT YOU TO DESIGN A LITTLE REFUGE FOR US.

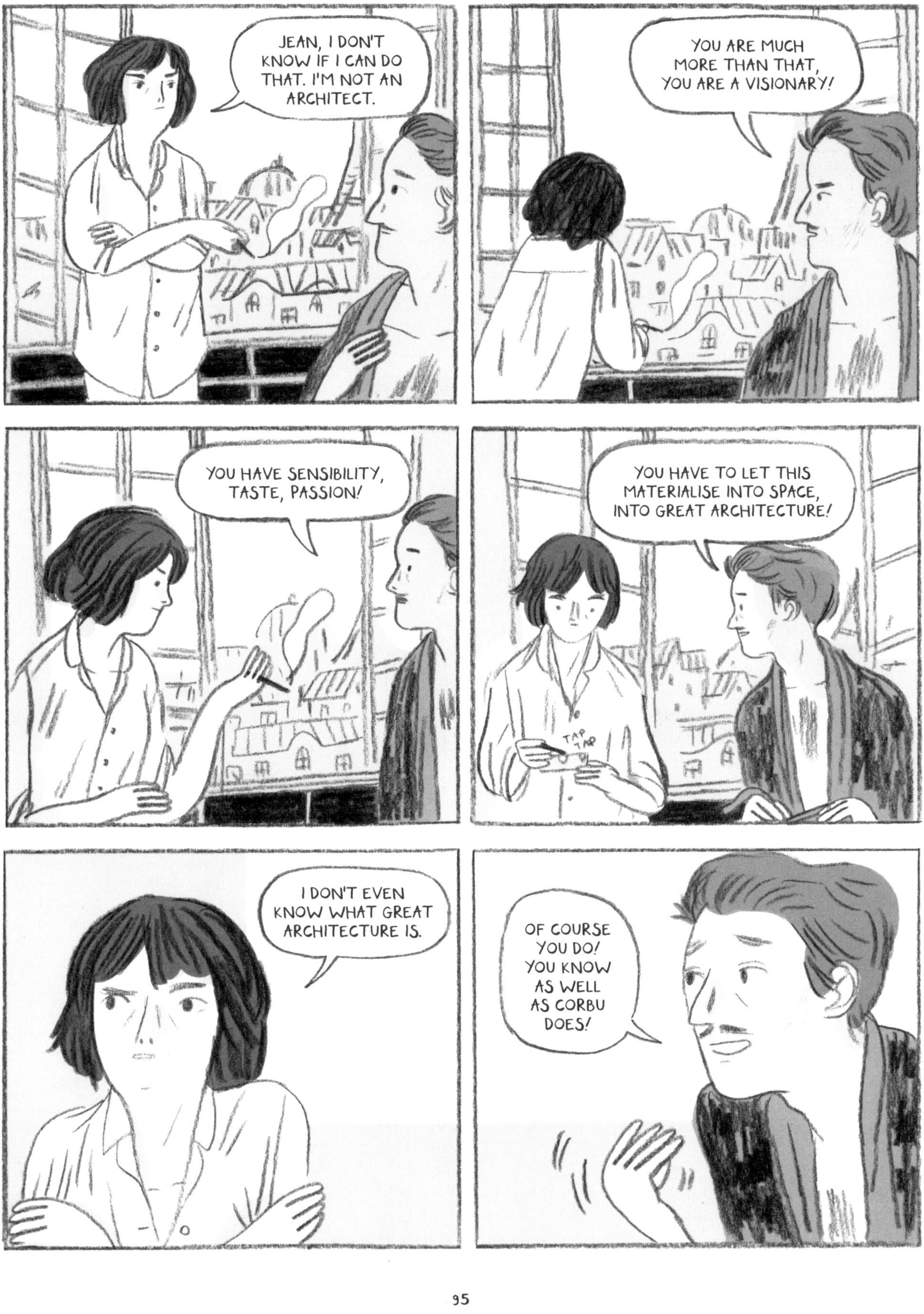
JEAN, I DON'T KNOW IF I CAN DO THAT. I'M NOT AN ARCHITECT.
YOU ARE MUCH MORE THAN THAT, YOU ARE A VISIONARY!
YOU HAVE SENSIBILITY, TASTE, PASSION!
YOU HAVE TO LET THIS MATERIALISE INTO SPACE, INTO GREAT ARCHITECTURE!
TAP TAP
I DON'T EVEN KNOW WHAT GREAT ARCHITECTURE IS.
OF COURSE YOU DO! YOU KNOW AS WELL AS CORBU DOES!

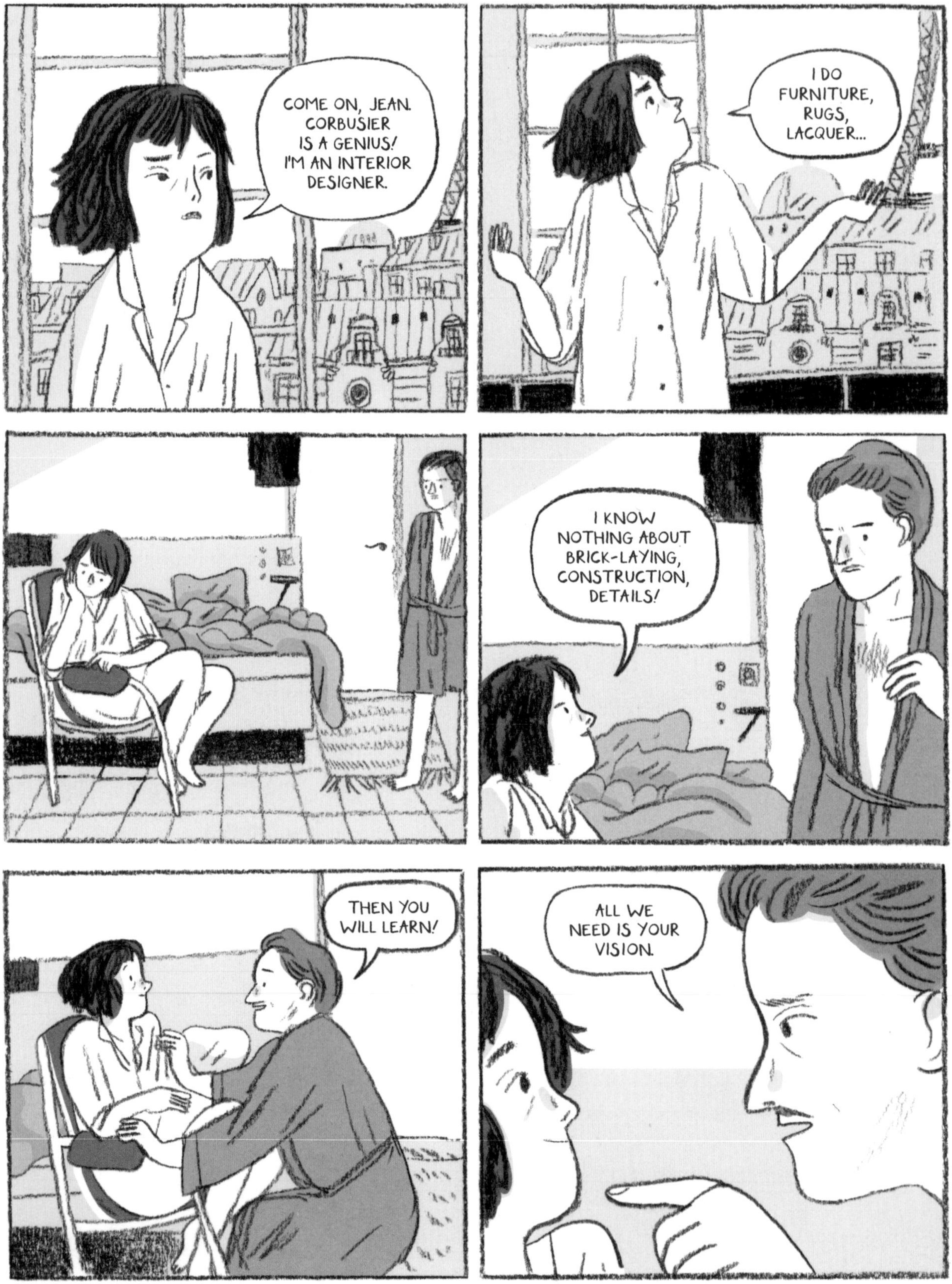
COME ON, JEAN. CORBUSIER IS A GENIUS! I'M AN INTERIOR DESIGNER.
I DO FURNITURE, RUGS, LACQUER...
I KNOW NOTHING ABOUT BRICK-LAYING, CONSTRUCTION, DETAILS!
THEN YOU WILL LEARN!
ALL WE NEED IS YOUR VISION.

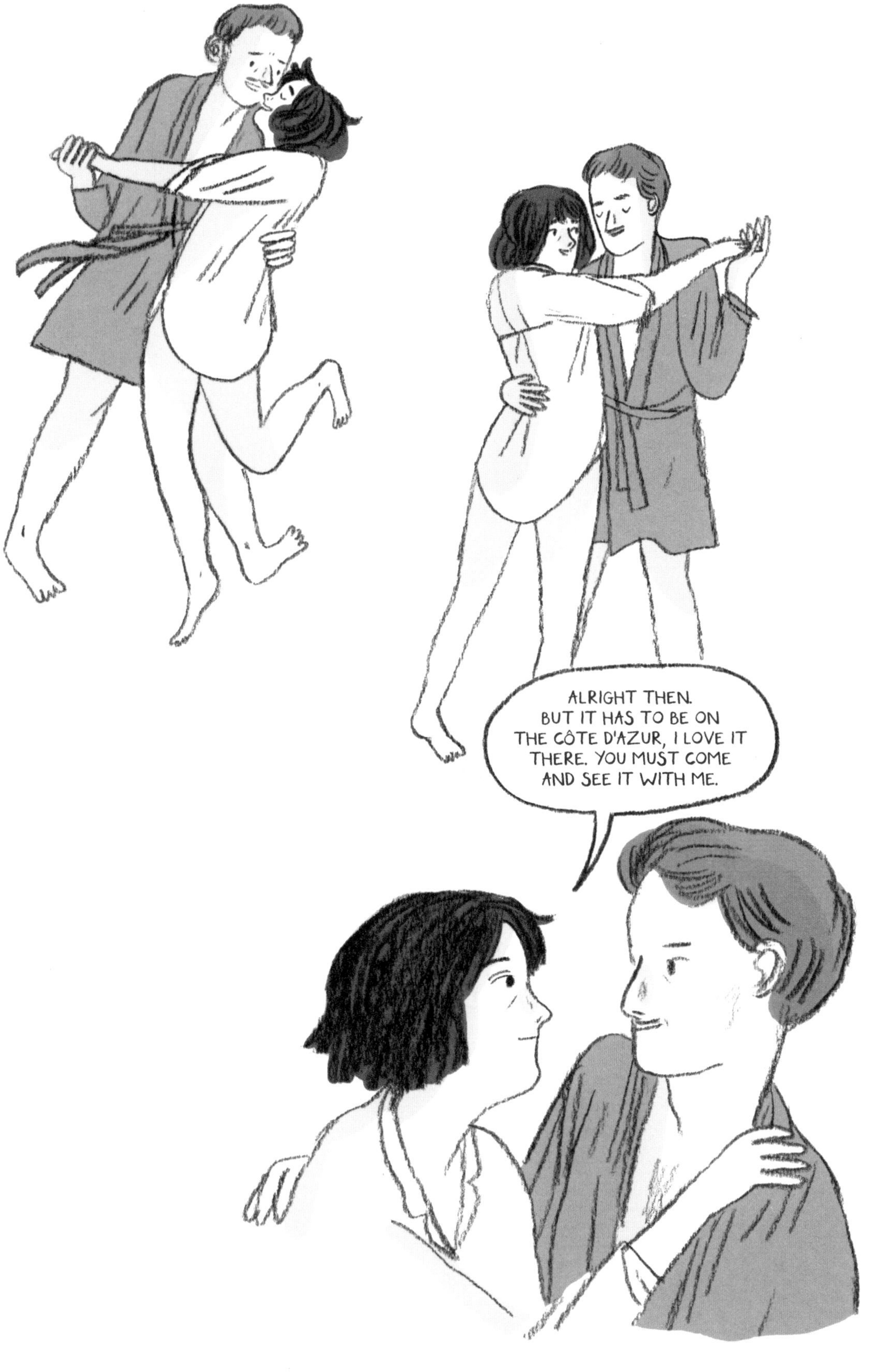
ALRIGHT THEN. BUT IT HAS TO BE ON THE CÔTE D'AZUR, I LOVE IT THERE. YOU MUST COME AND SEE IT WITH ME.

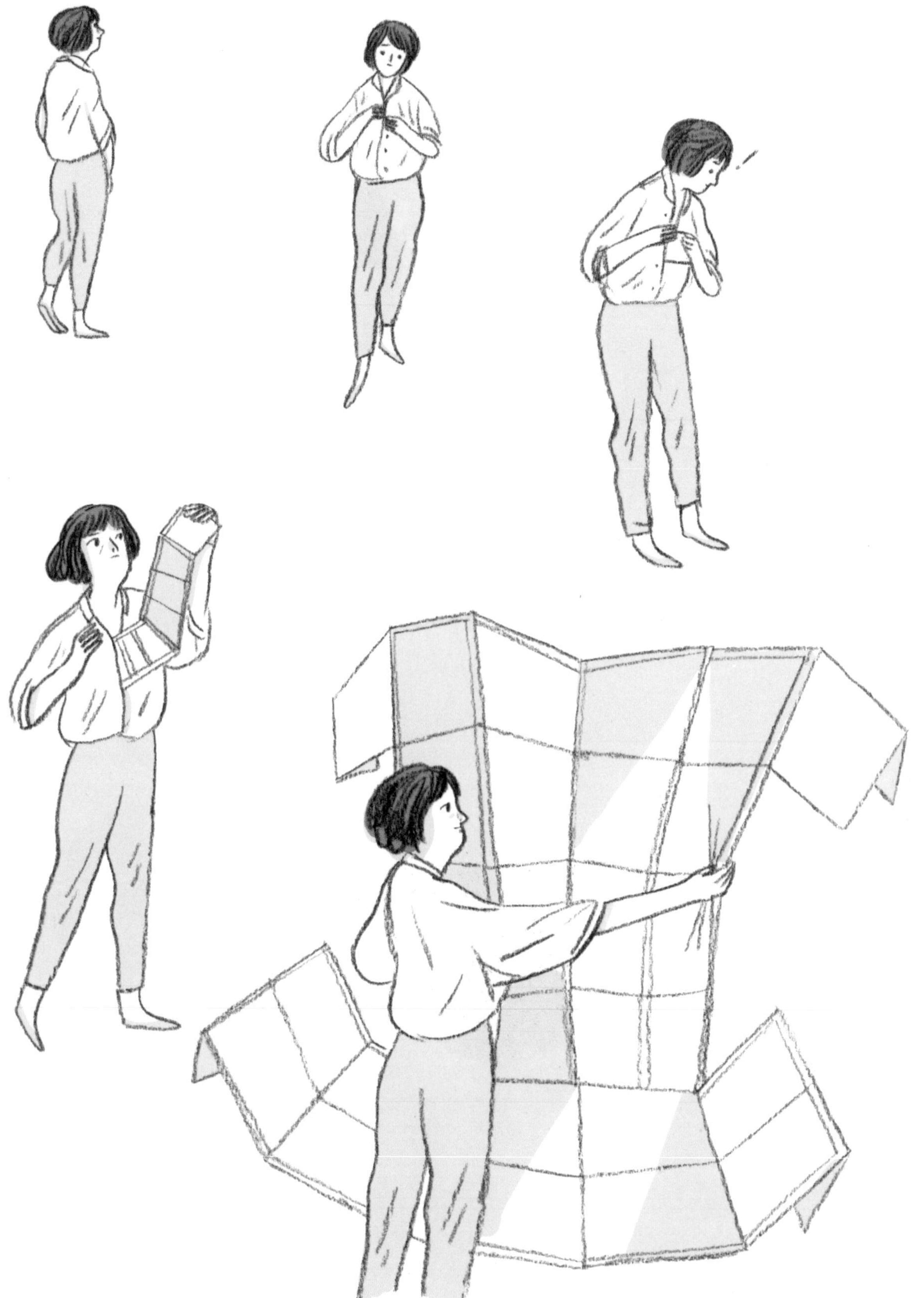

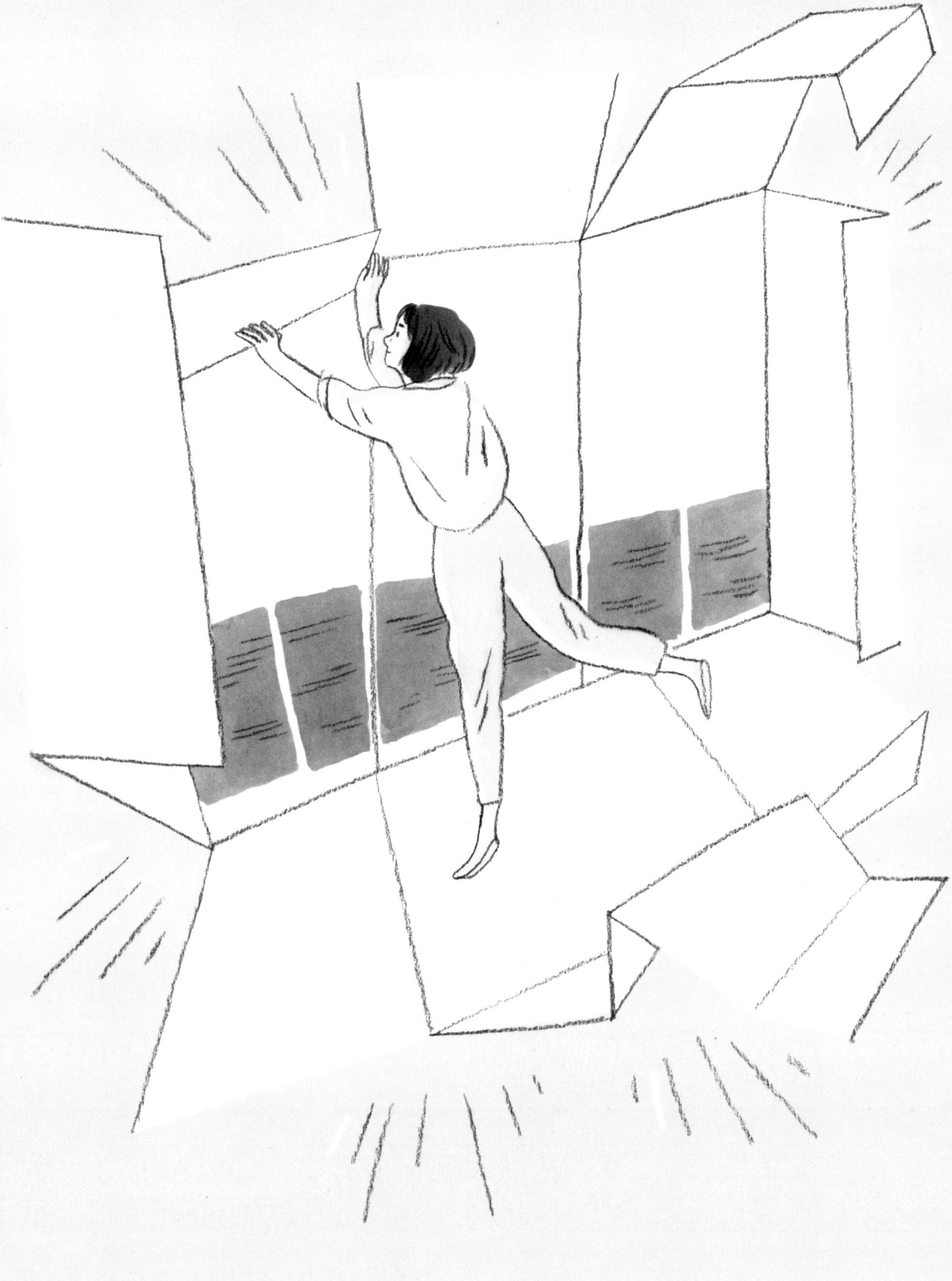

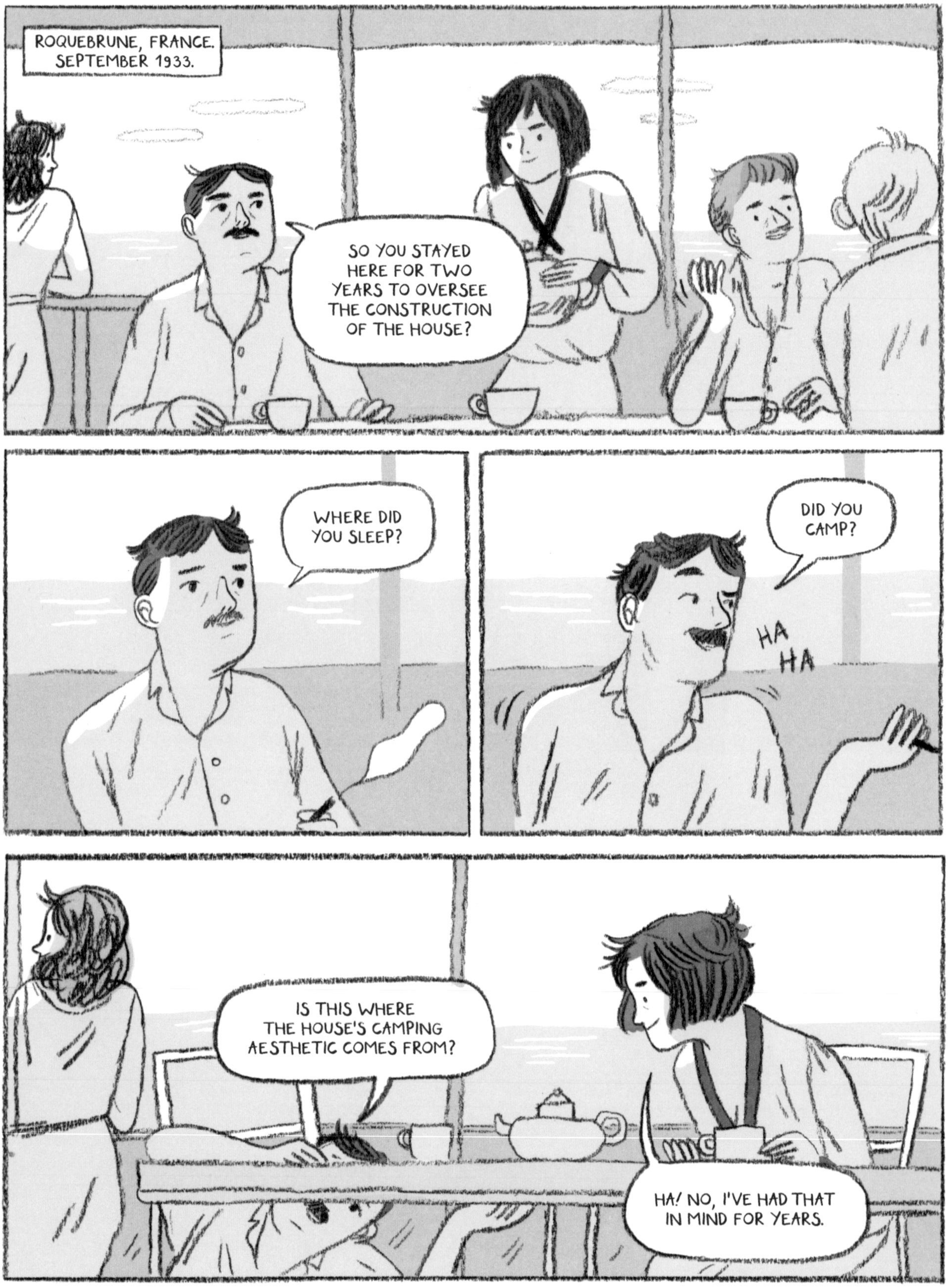
ROQUEBRUNE, FRANCE. SEPTEMBER 1933.
SO YOU STAYED HERE FOR TWO YEARS TO OVERSEE THE CONSTRUCTION OF THE HOUSE?
WHERE DID YOU SLEEP?
DID YOU CAMP?
HA HA
IS THIS WHERE THE HOUSE'S CAMPING AESTHETIC COMES FROM?
HA! NO, I'VE HAD THAT IN MIND FOR YEARS.

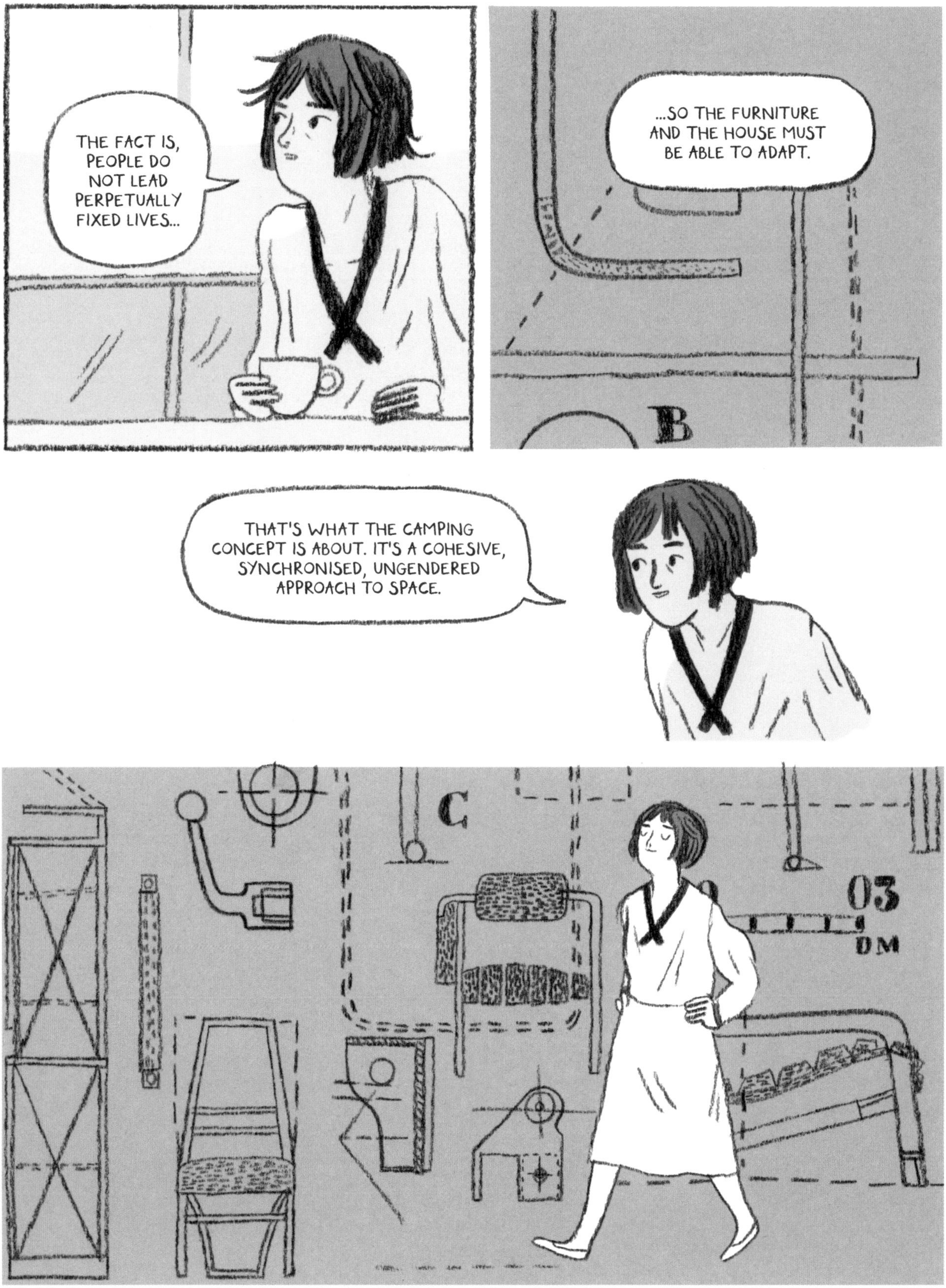
THE FACT IS, PEOPLE DO NOT LEAD PERPETUALLY FIXED LIVES...
...SO THE FURNITURE AND THE HOUSE MUST BE ABLE TO ADAPT.
B
THAT'S WHAT THE CAMPING CONCEPT IS ABOUT. IT'S A COHESIVE, SYNCHRONISED, UNGENDERED APPROACH TO SPACE.
C
03
DM

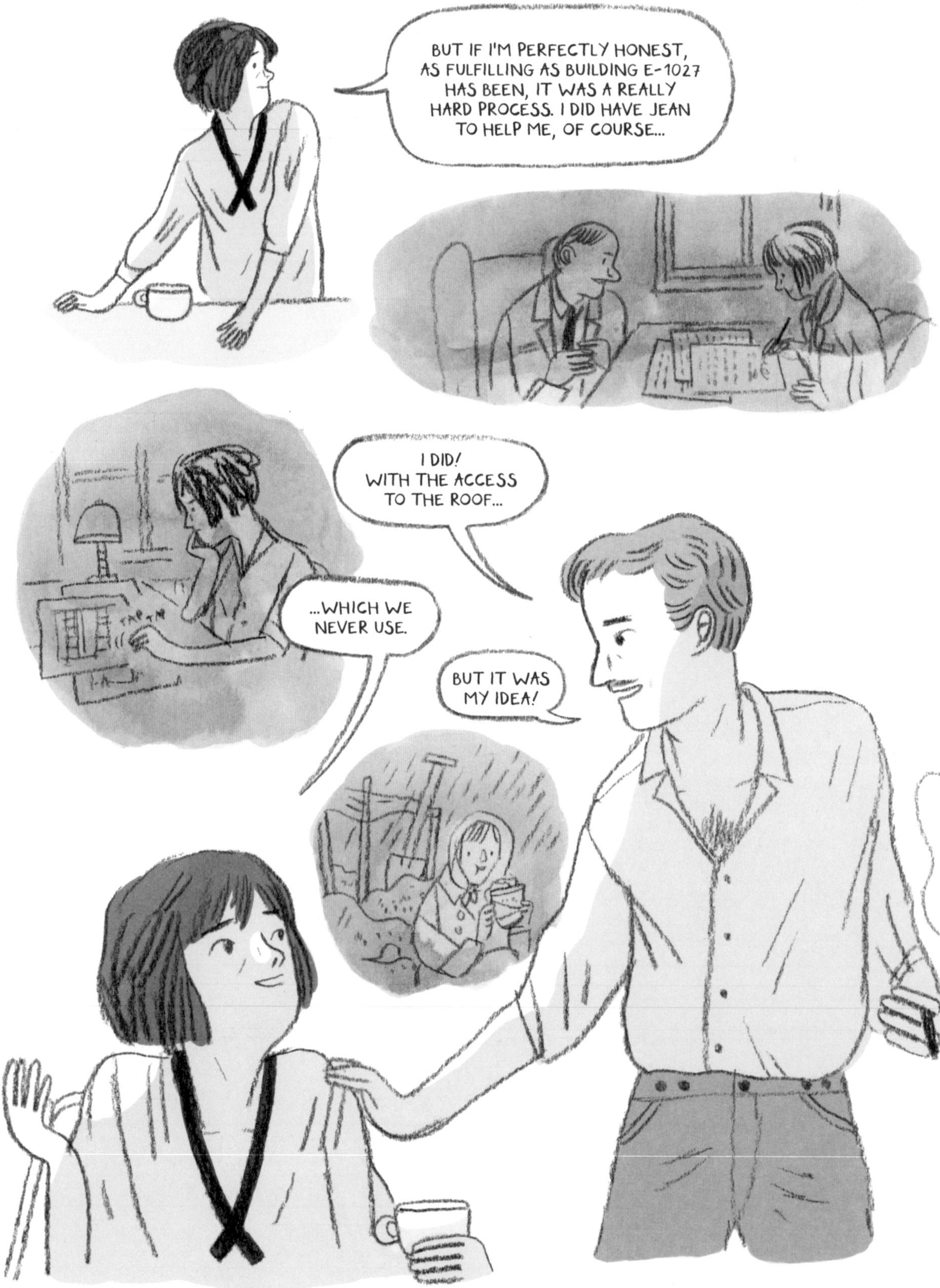
BUT IF I'M PERFECTLY HONEST, AS FULFILLING AS BUILDING E-1027 HAS BEEN, IT WAS A REALLY HARD PROCESS. I DID HAVE JEAN TO HELP ME, OF COURSE...
I DID! WITH THE ACCESS TO THE ROOF...
...WHICH WE NEVER USE.
BUT IT WAS MY IDEA!
TAP TAP

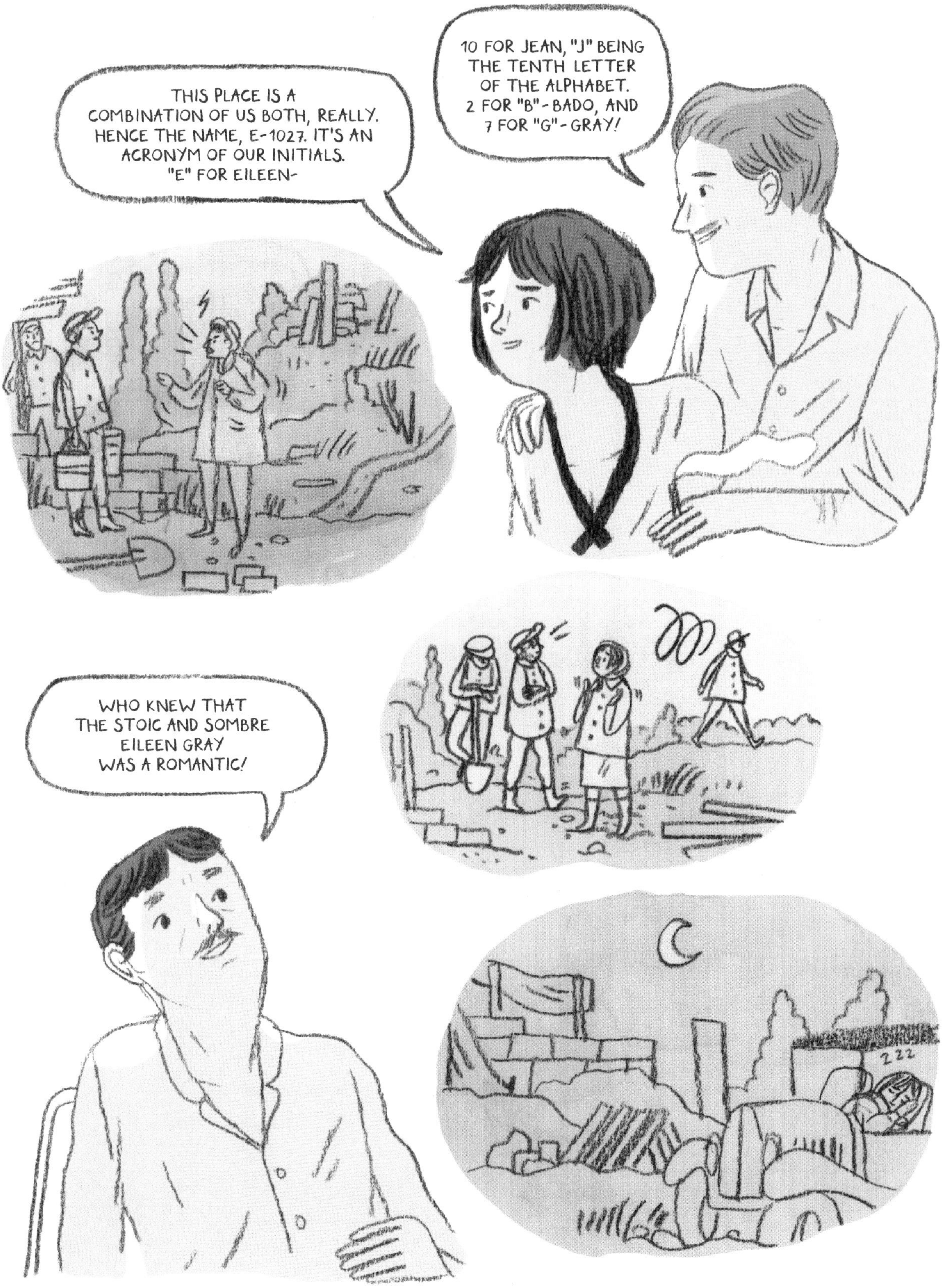
THIS PLACE IS A COMBINATION OF US BOTH, REALLY. HENCE THE NAME, E-1027. IT'S AN ACRONYM OF OUR INITIALS. "E" FOR EILEEN-
10 FOR JEAN, "J" BEING THE TENTH LETTER OF THE ALPHABET. 2 FOR "B"-BADO, AND 7 FOR "G"-GRAY!
WHO KNEW THAT THE STOIC AND SOMBRE EILEEN GRAY WAS A ROMANTIC!
ZZZ

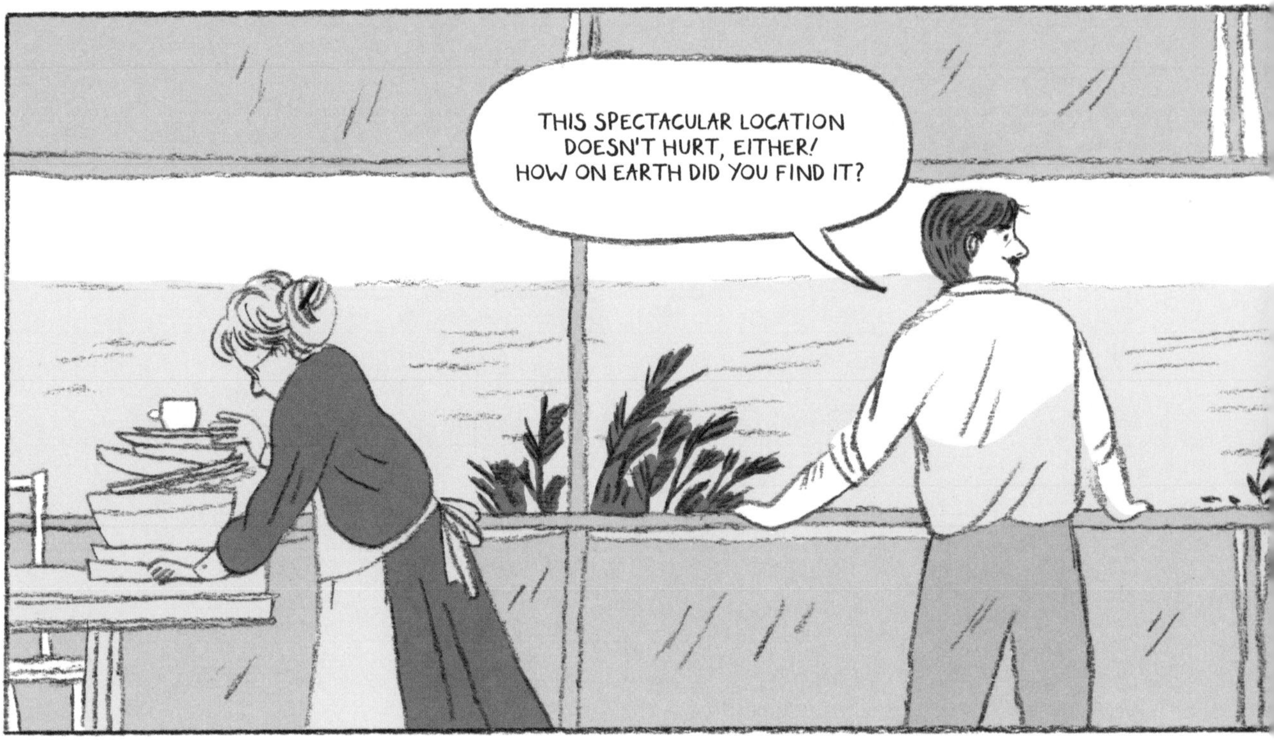
THIS SPECTACULAR LOCATION DOESN'T HURT, EITHER! HOW ON EARTH DID YOU FIND IT?

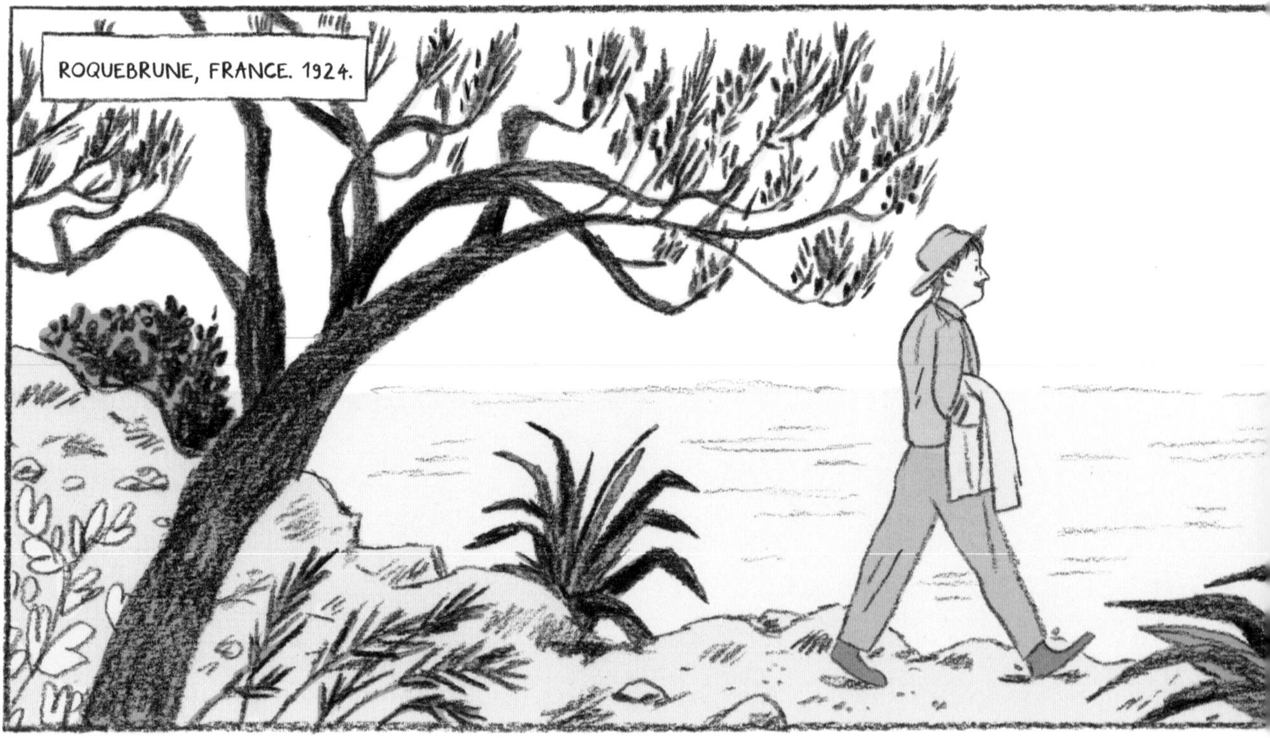
ROQUEBRUNE, FRANCE. 1924.

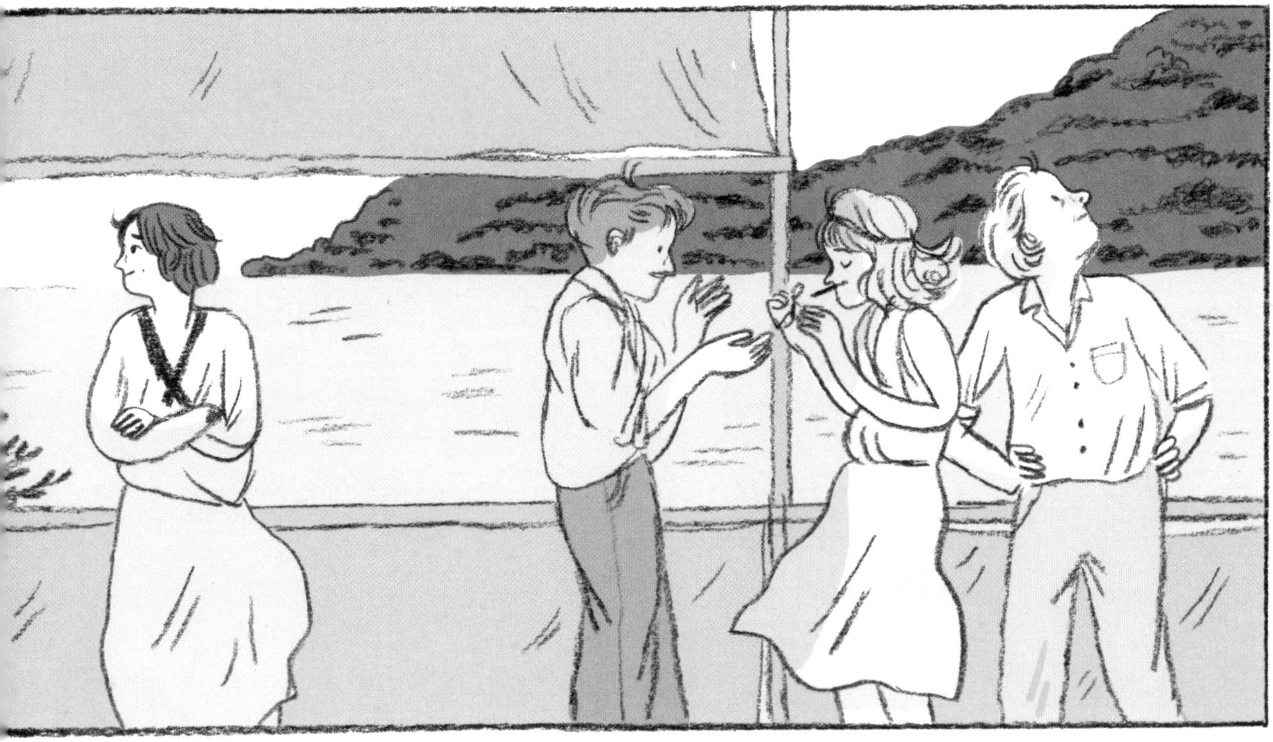

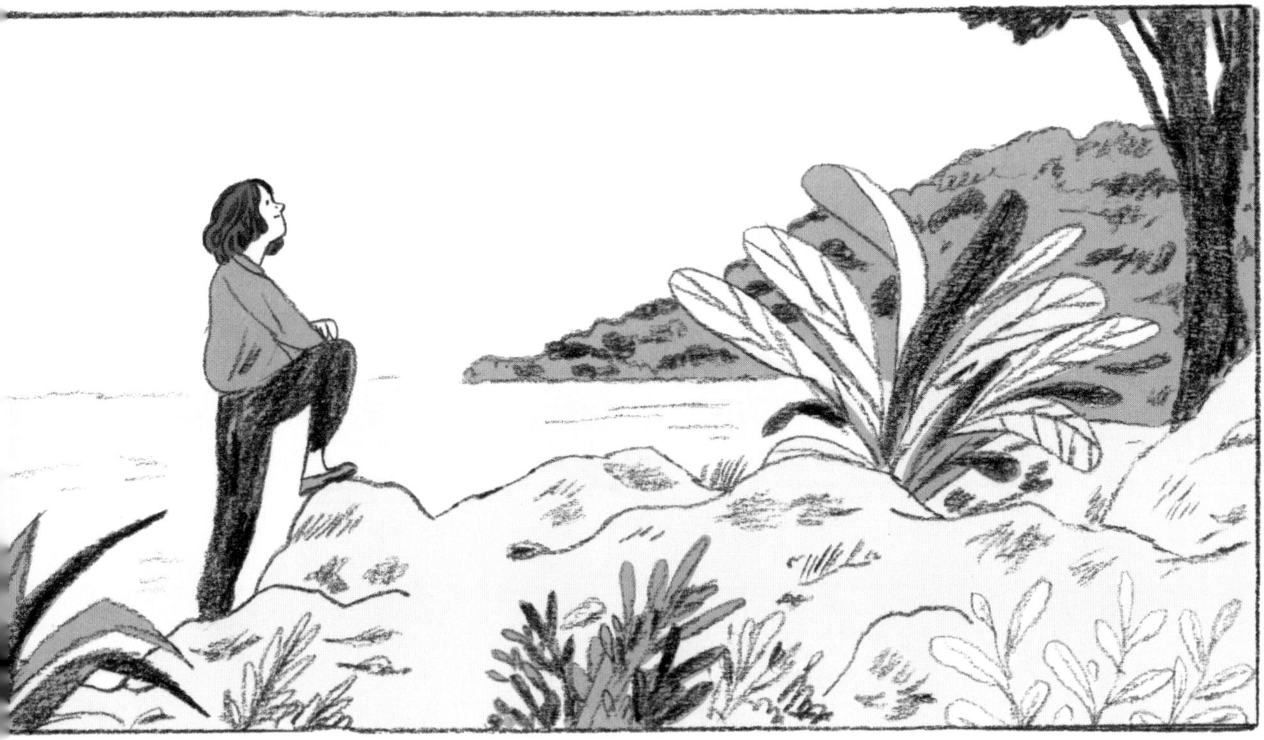

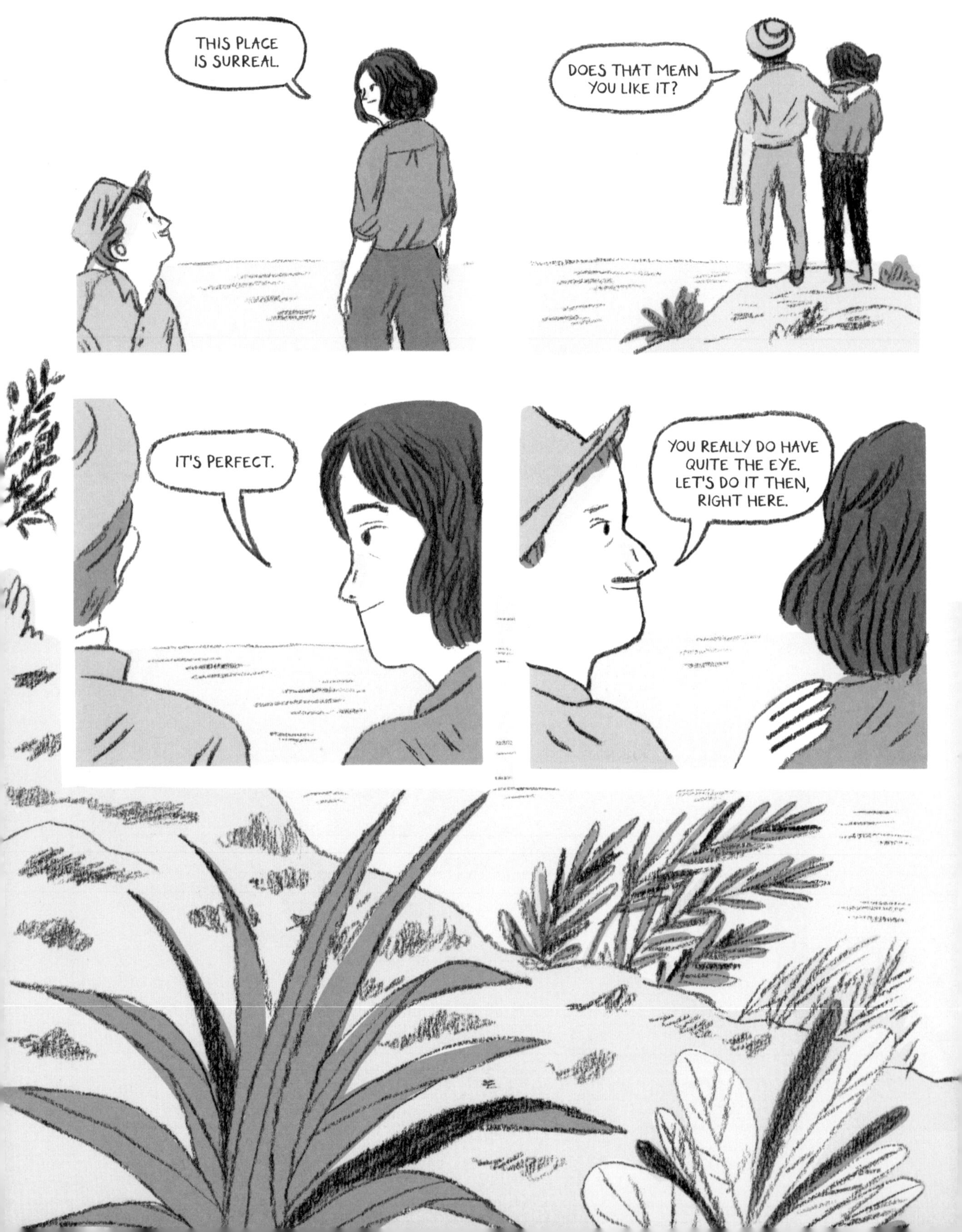
THIS PLACE IS SURREAL.
DOES THAT MEAN YOU LIKE IT?
IT'S PERFECT.
YOU REALLY DO HAVE QUITE THE EYE. LET'S DO IT THEN, RIGHT HERE.

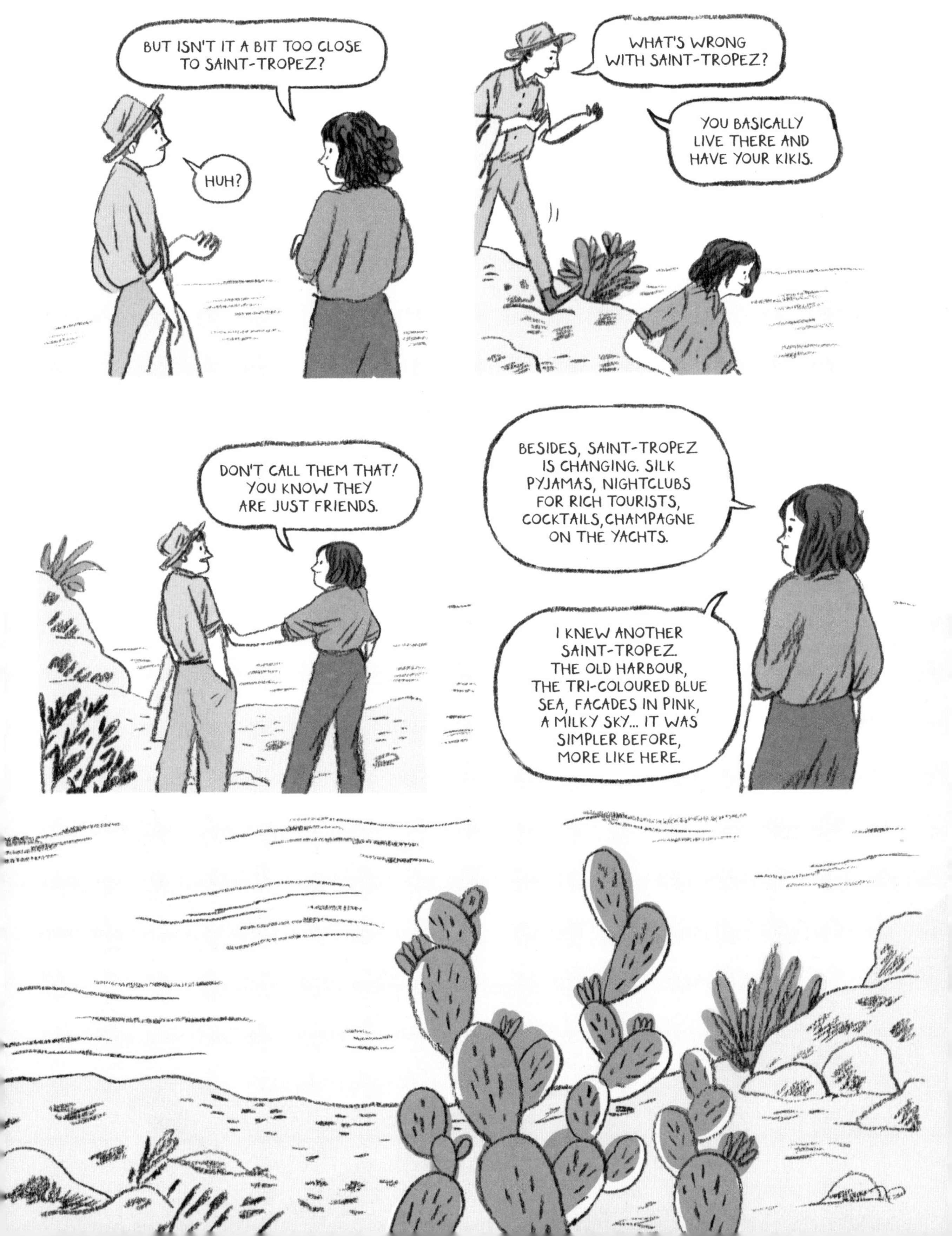
BUT ISN'T IT A BIT TOO CLOSE TO SAINT-TROPEZ?
HUH?
WHAT'S WRONG WITH SAINT-TROPEZ?
YOU BASICALLY LIVE THERE AND HAVE YOUR KIKIS.
DON'T CALL THEM THAT! YOU KNOW THEY ARE JUST FRIENDS.
BESIDES, SAINT-TROPEZ IS CHANGING. SILK PYJAMAS, NIGHTCLUBS FOR RICH TOURISTS, COCKTAILS, CHAMPAGNE ON THE YACHTS.
I KNEW ANOTHER SAINT-TROPEZ. THE OLD HARBOUR, THE TRI-COLOURED BLUE SEA, FACADES IN PINK, A MILKY SKY... IT WAS SIMPLER BEFORE, MORE LIKE HERE.

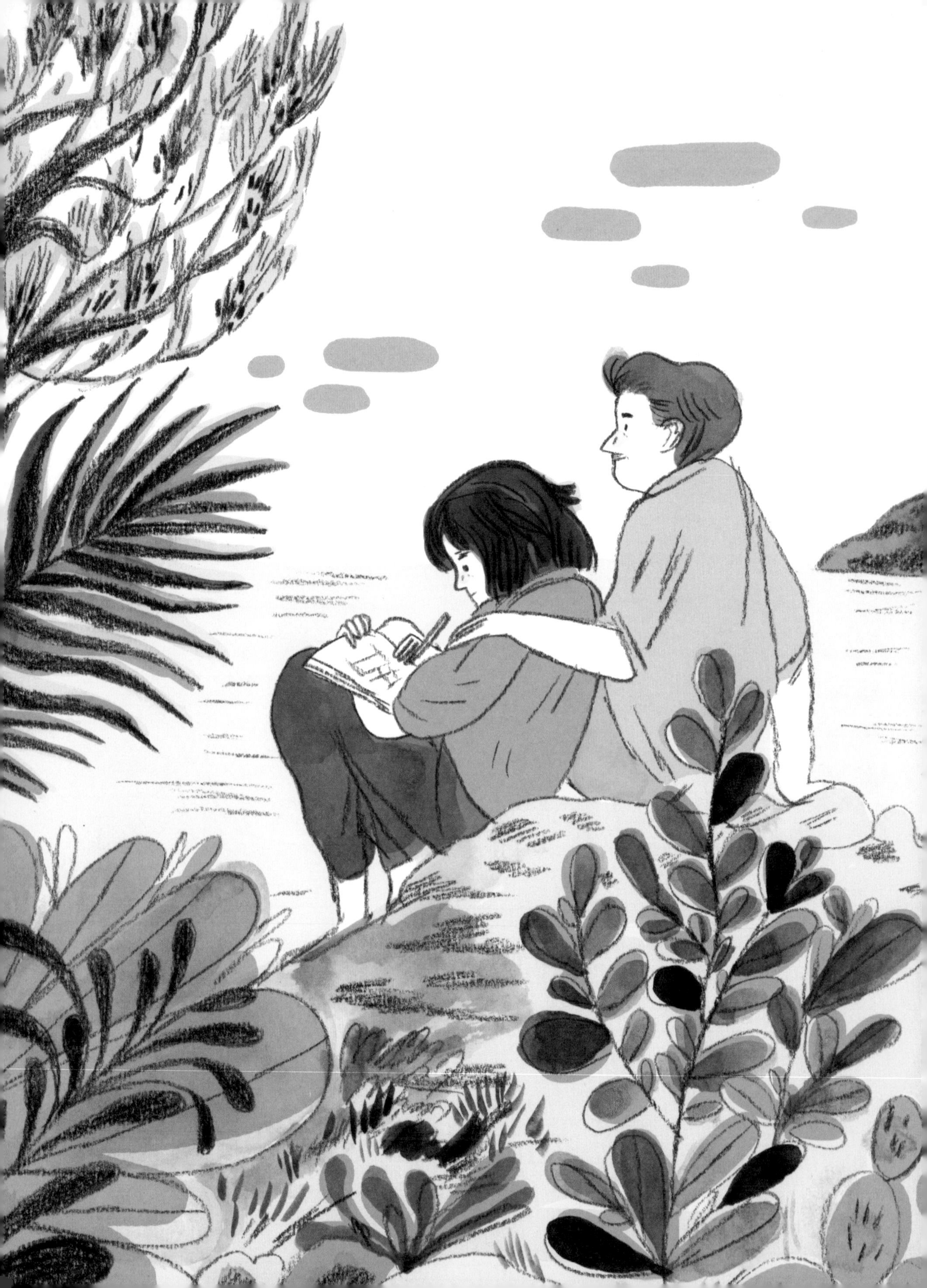

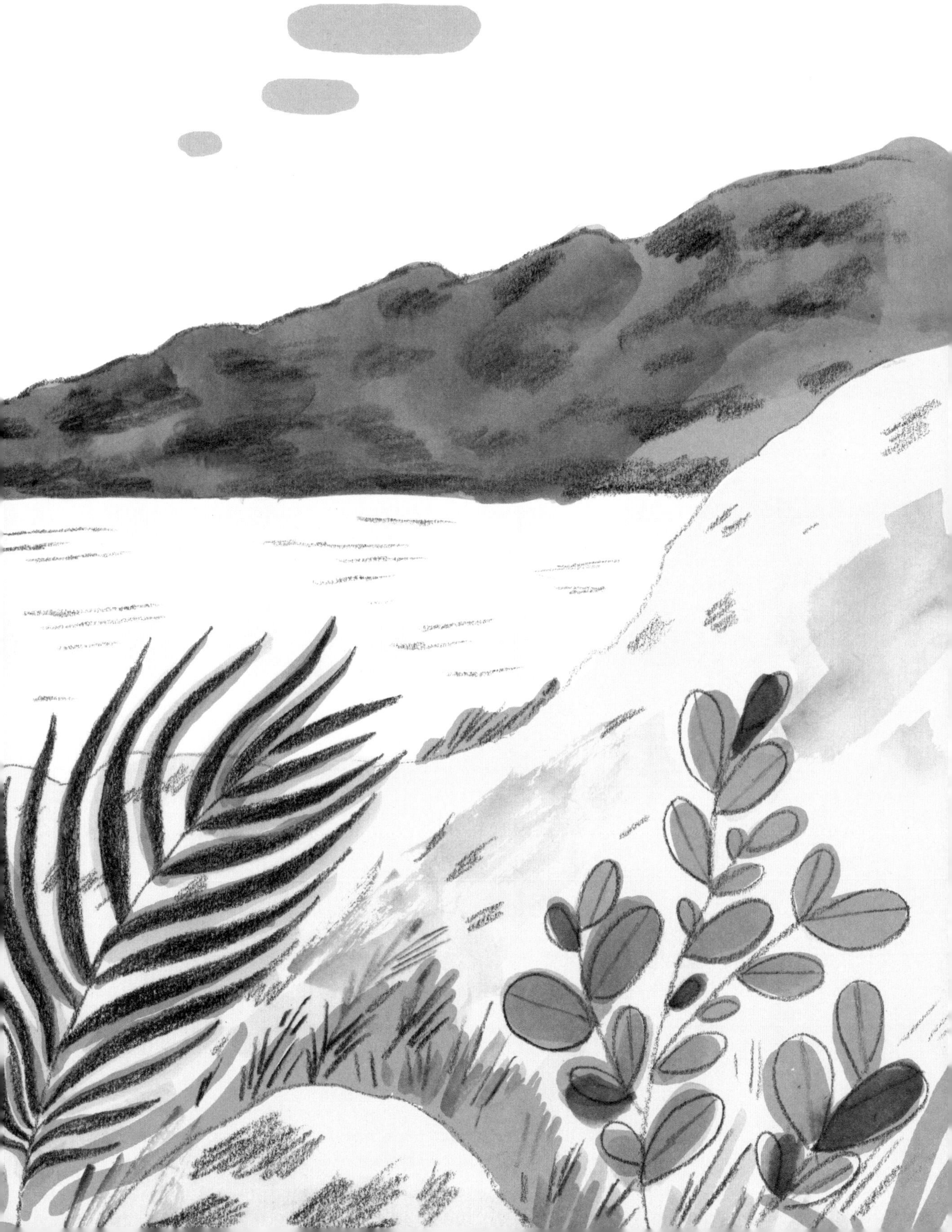

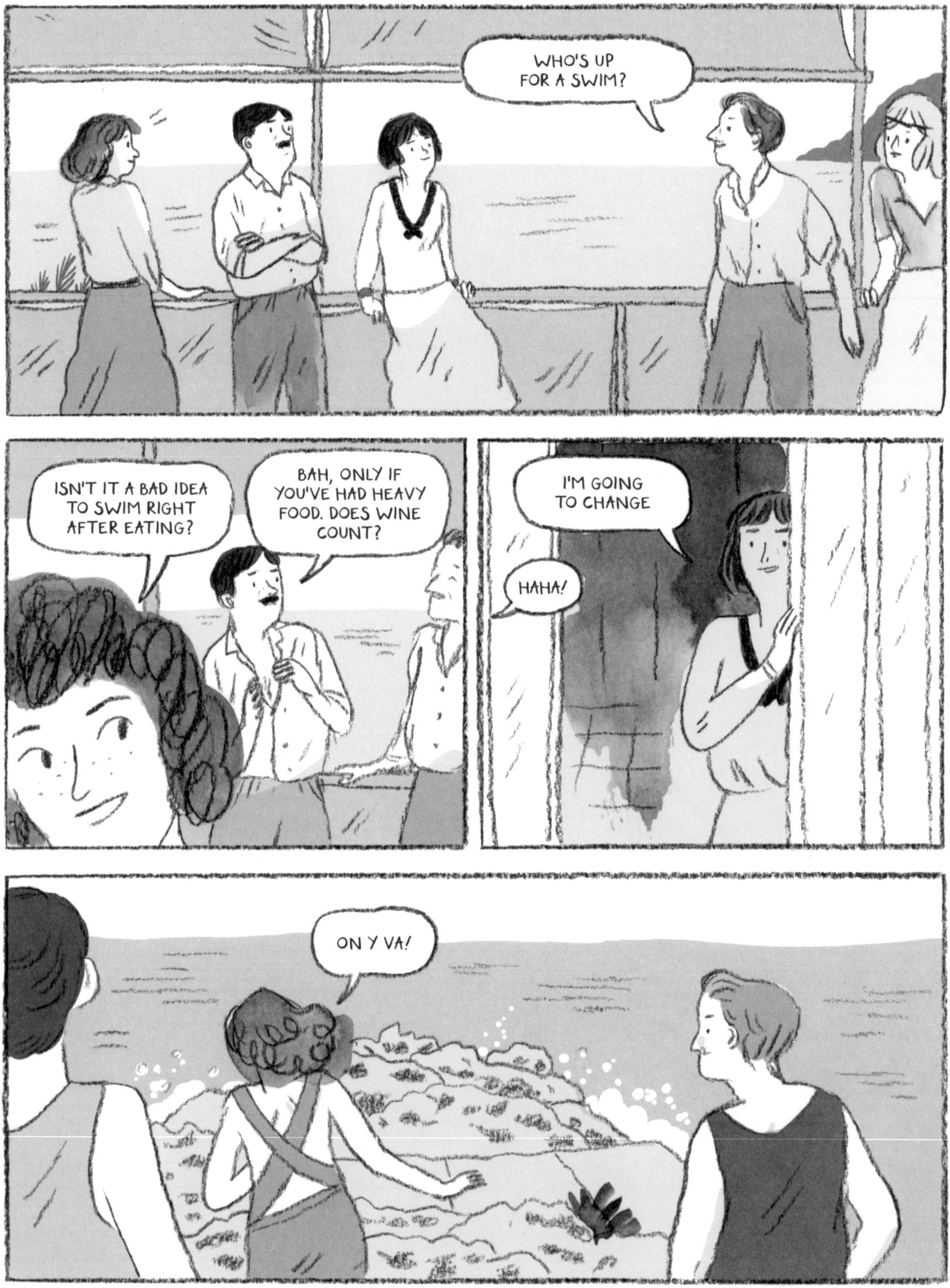
WHO'S UP FOR A SWIM?
ISN'T IT A BAD IDEA TO SWIM RIGHT AFTER EATING?
BAH, ONLY IF YOU'VE HAD HEAVY FOOD. DOES WINE COUNT?
I'M GOING TO CHANGE
HAHA!
ON Y VA!

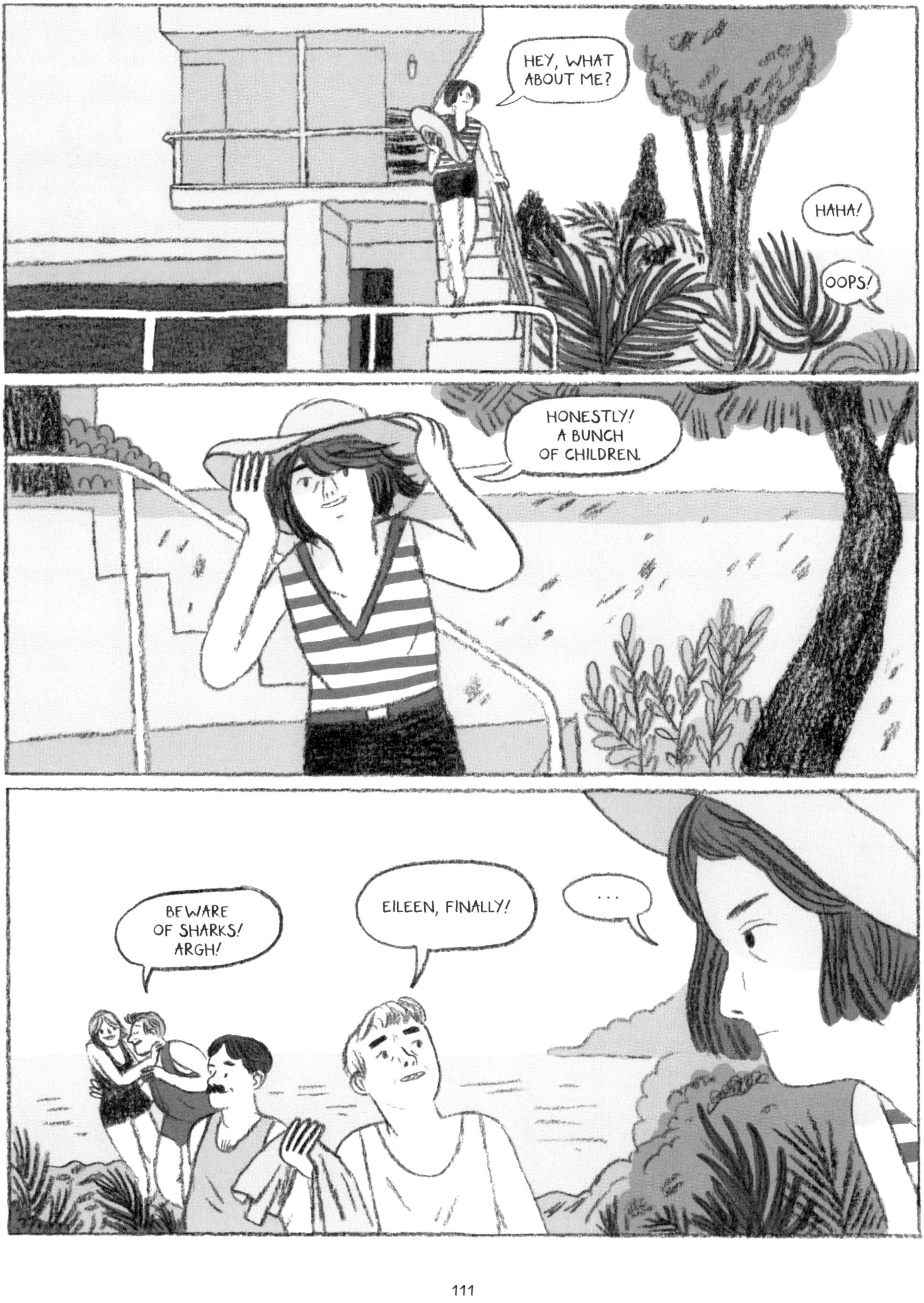
HEY, WHAT ABOUT ME?
HAHA!
OOPS!
HONESTLY! A BUNCH OF CHILDREN.
BEWARE OF SHARKS! ARGH!
EILEEN, FINALLY!
...

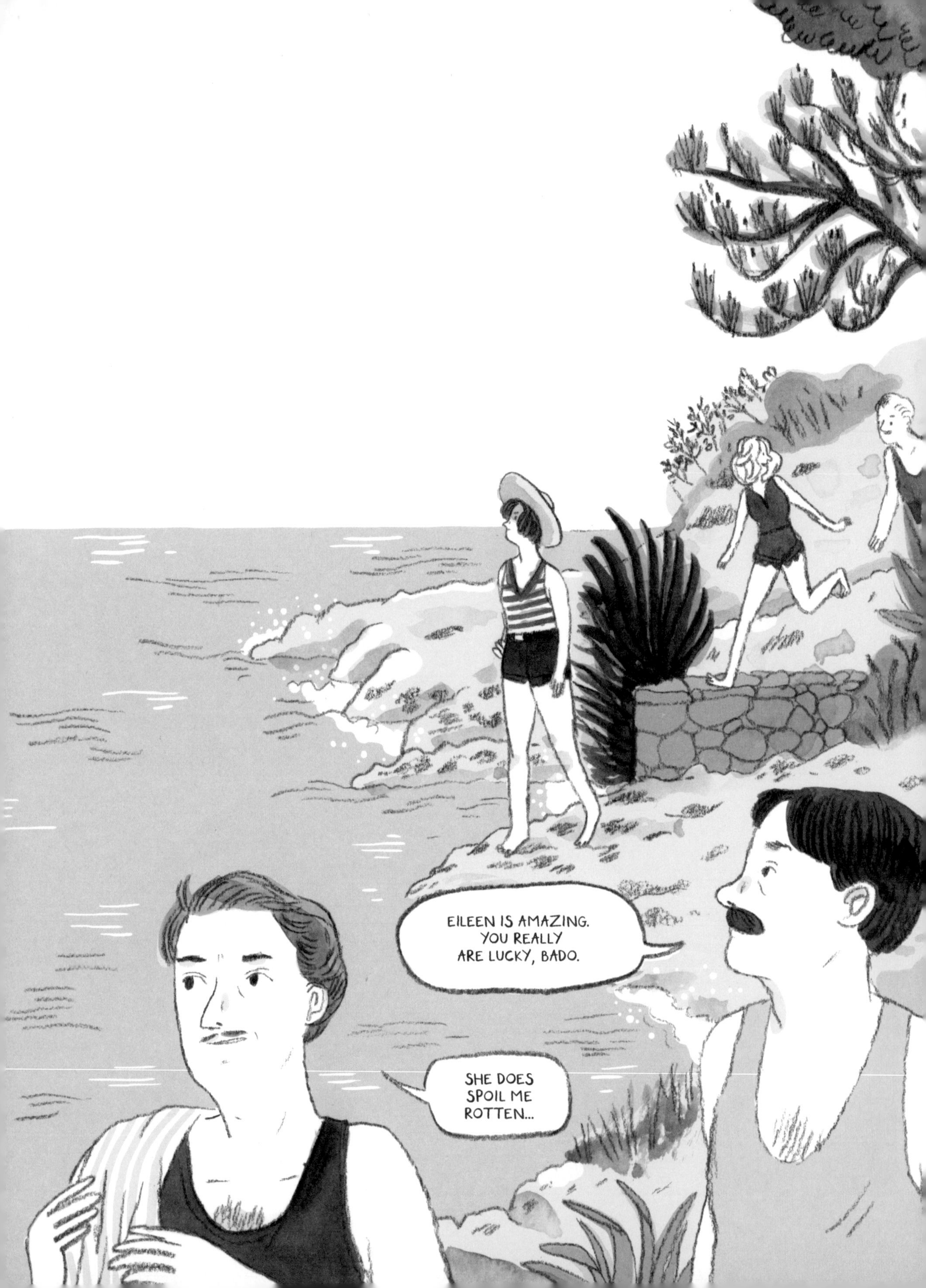
EILEEN IS AMAZING. YOU REALLY ARE LUCKY, BADO.
SHE DOES SPOIL ME ROTTEN...

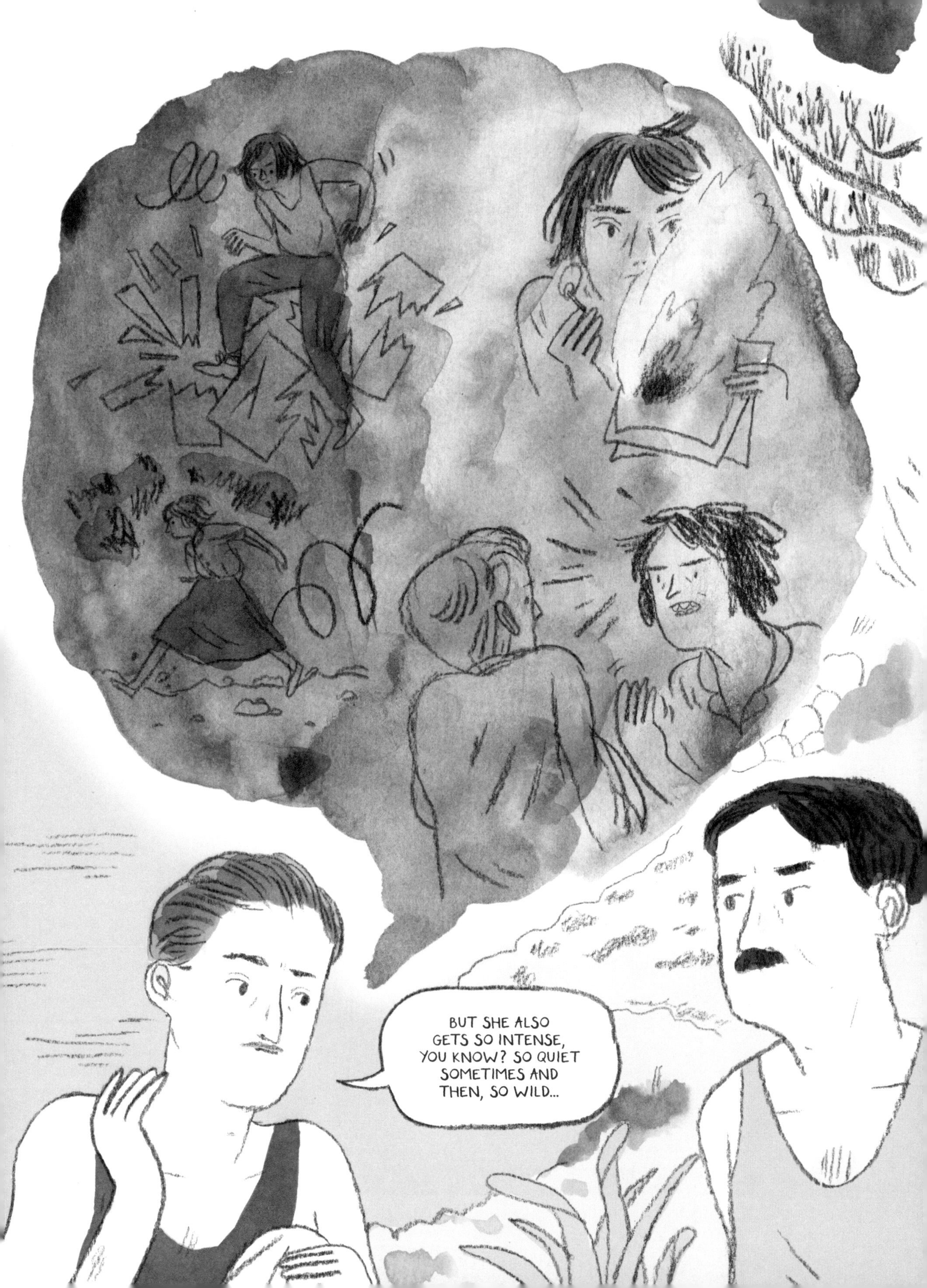
BUT SHE ALSO GETS SO INTENSE, YOU KNOW? SO QUIET SOMETIMES AND THEN, SO WILD...

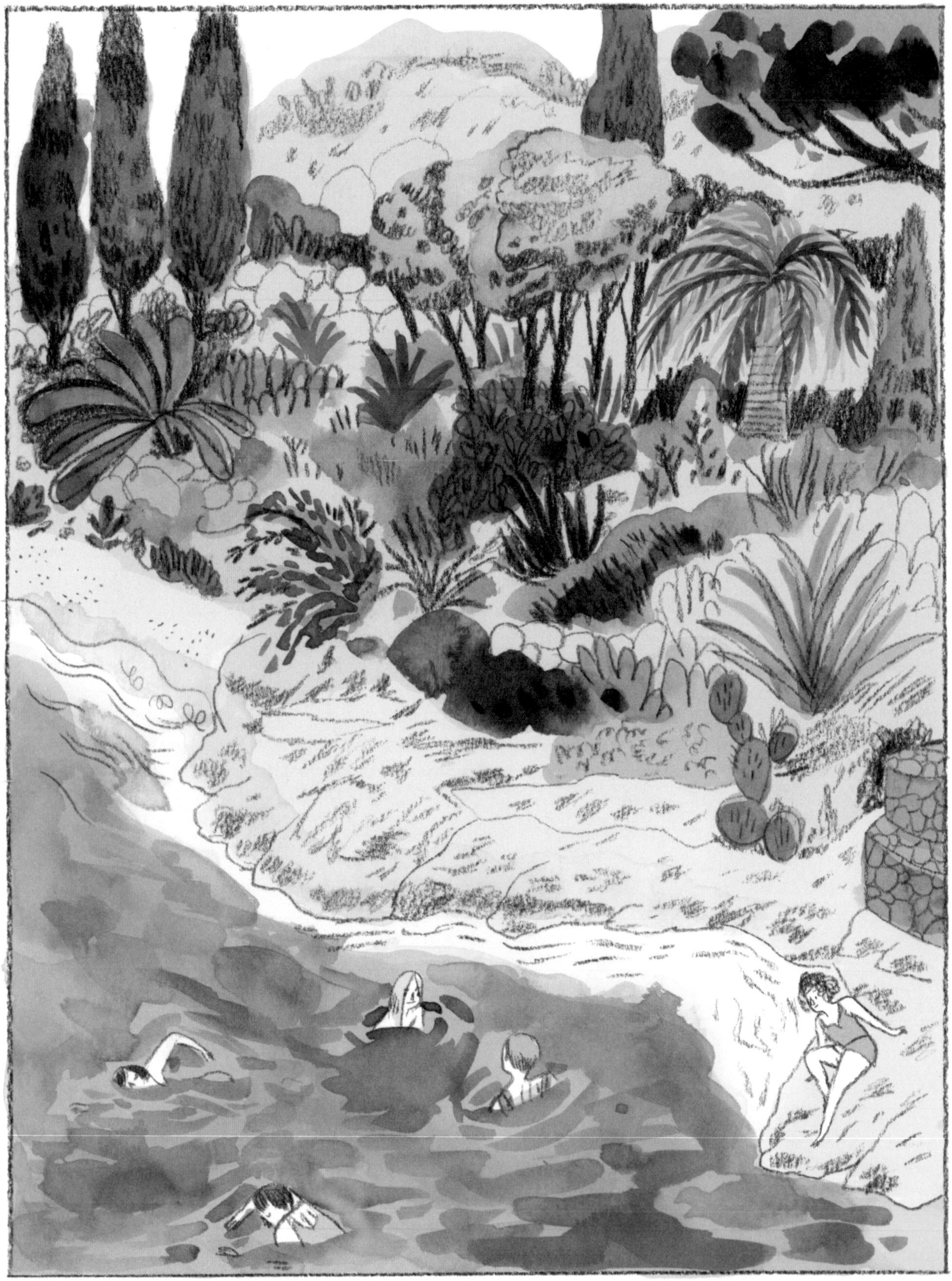

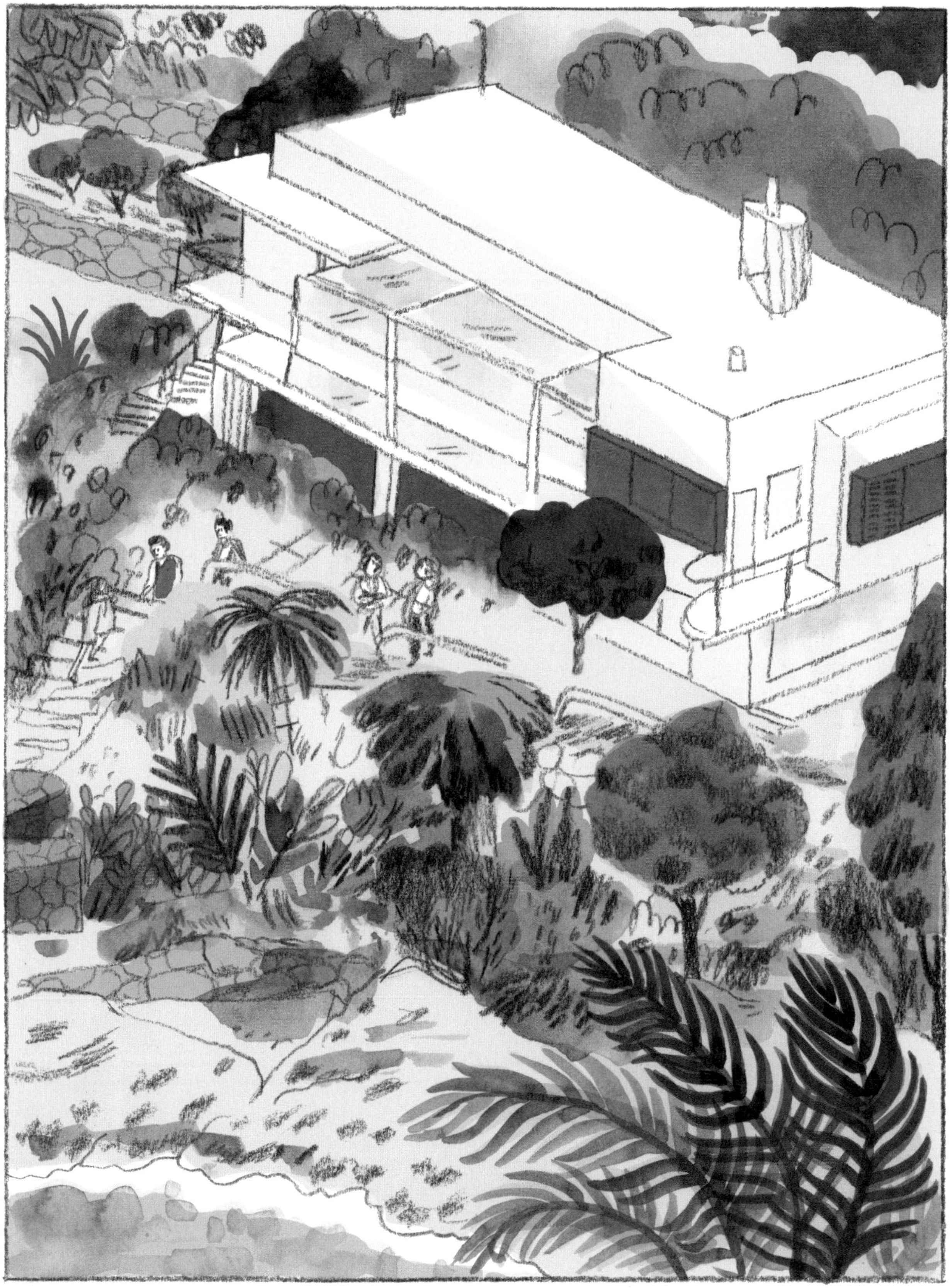

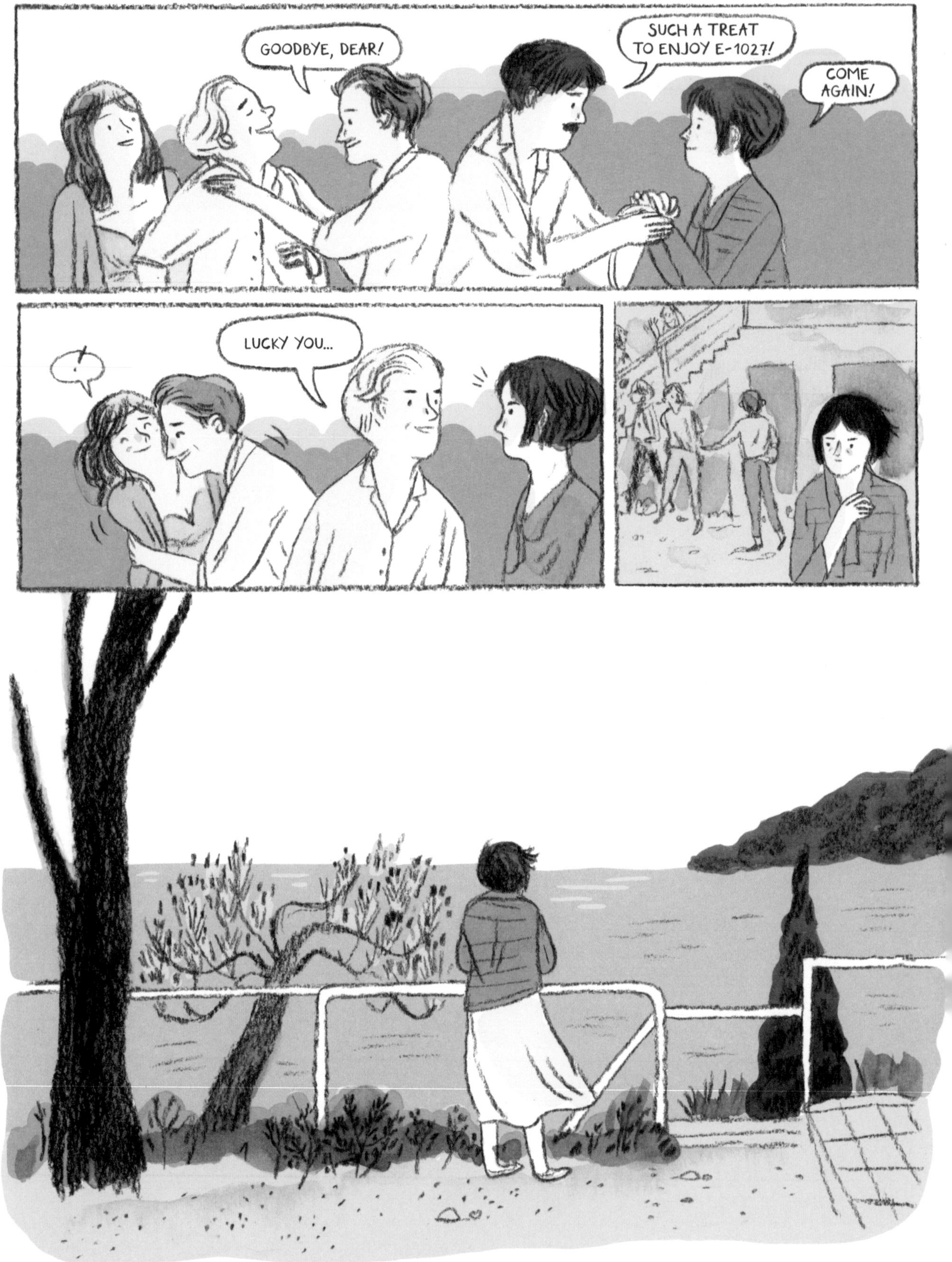
GOODBYE, DEAR!
SUCH A TREAT TO ENJOY E-1027!
COME AGAIN!
LUCKY YOU...

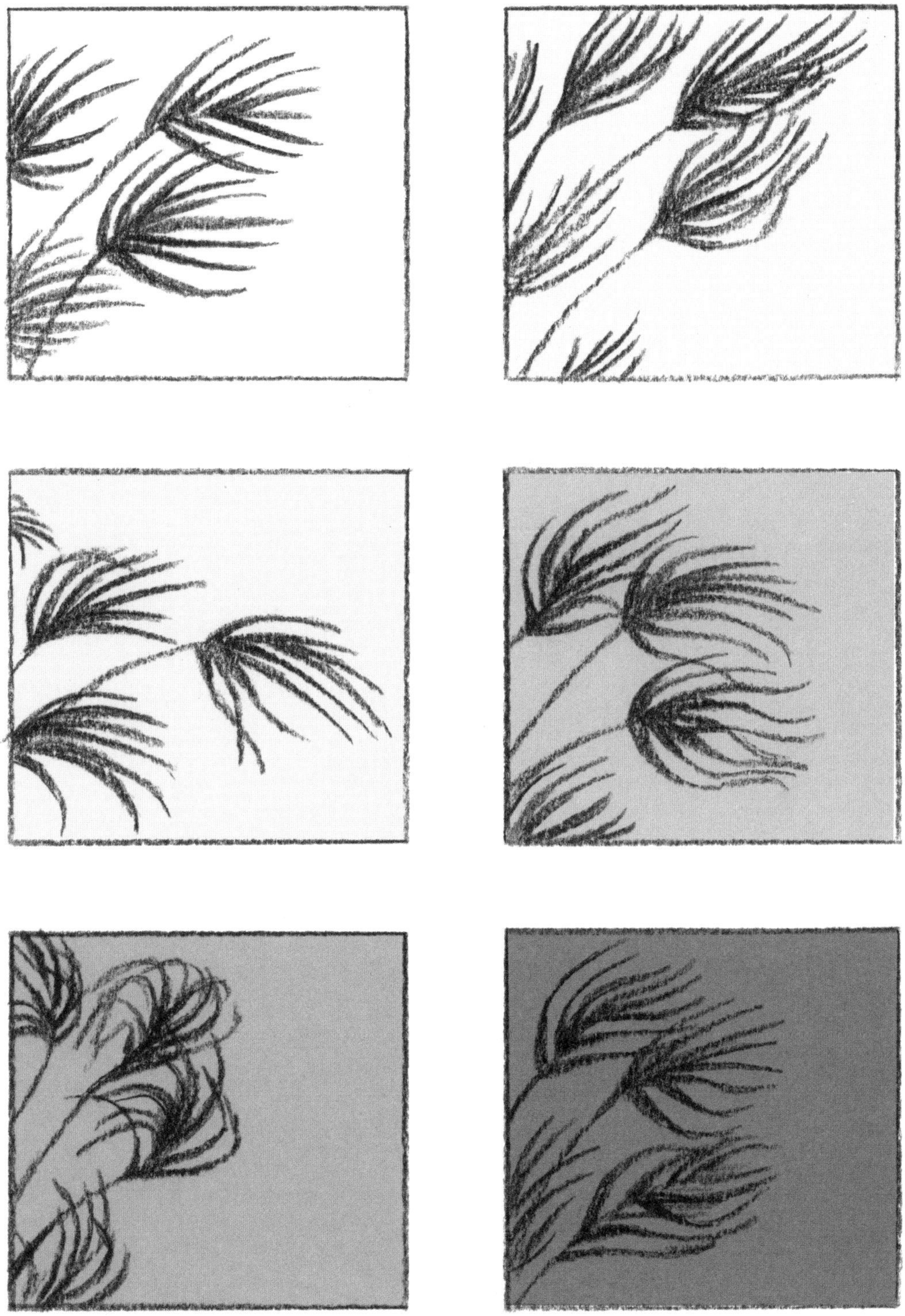

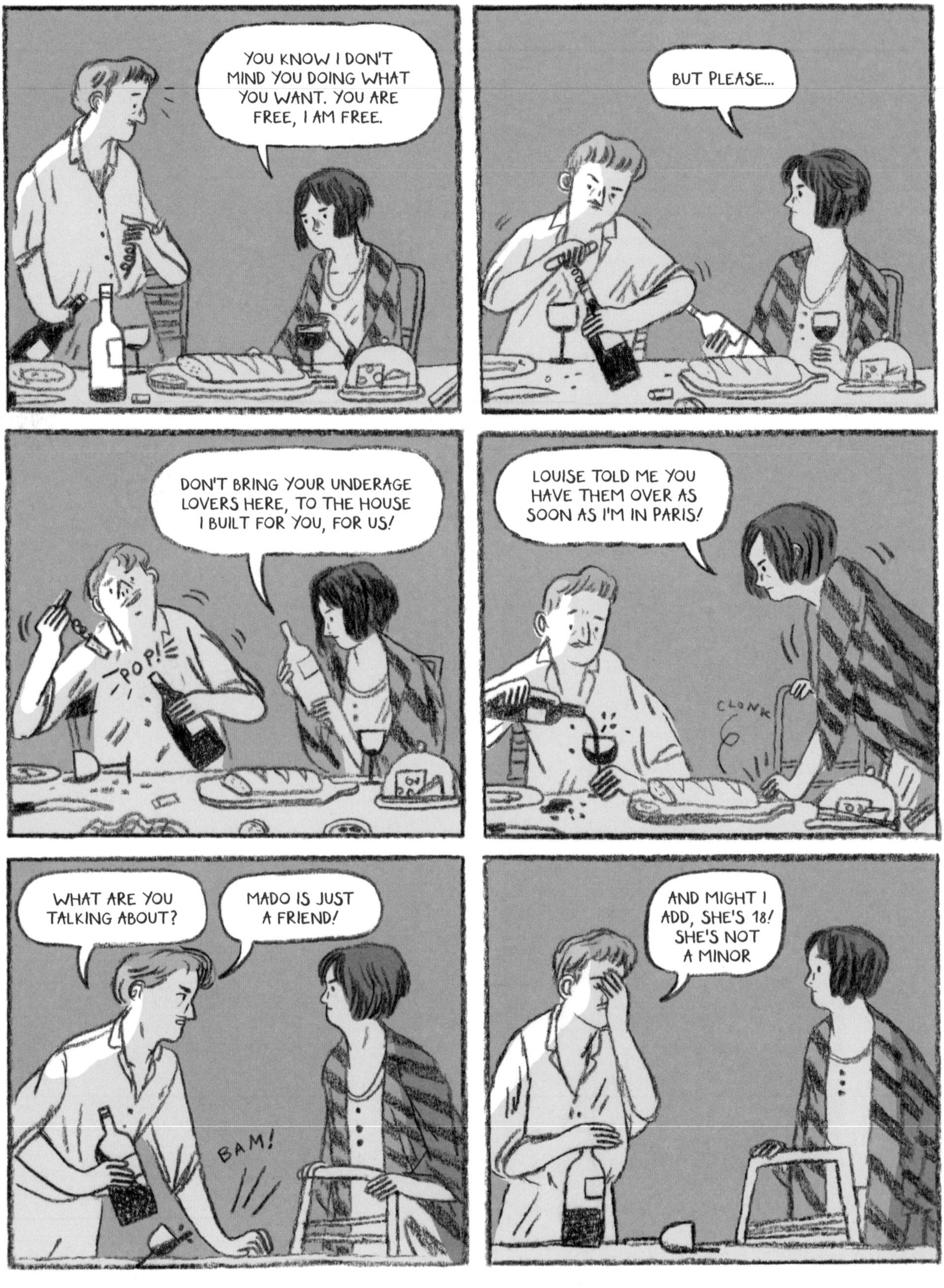

YOU KNOW I DON'T MIND YOU DOING WHAT YOU WANT. YOU ARE FREE, I AM FREE.
BUT PLEASE...
DON'T BRING YOUR UNDERAGE LOVERS HERE, TO THE HOUSE I BUILT FOR YOU, FOR US!
POP!
LOUISE TOLD ME YOU HAVE THEM OVER AS SOON AS I'M IN PARIS!
CLONK
WHAT ARE YOU TALKING ABOUT?
MADO IS JUST A FRIEND!
BAM!
AND MIGHT I ADD, SHE'S 18! SHE'S NOT A MINOR

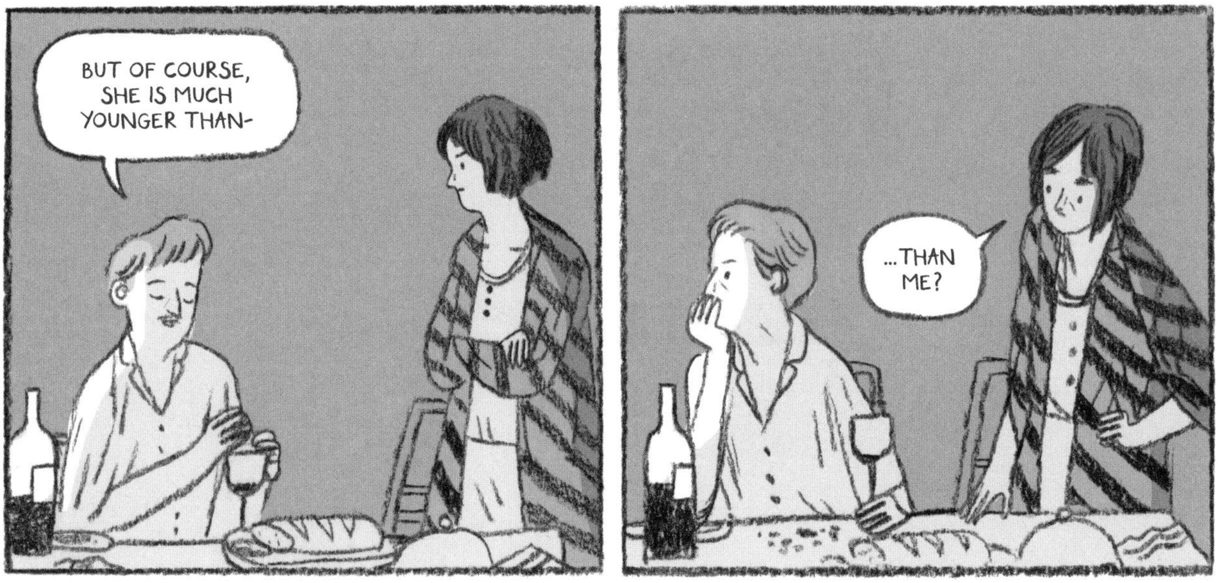
BUT OF COURSE, SHE IS MUCH YOUNGER THAN-
...THAN ME?

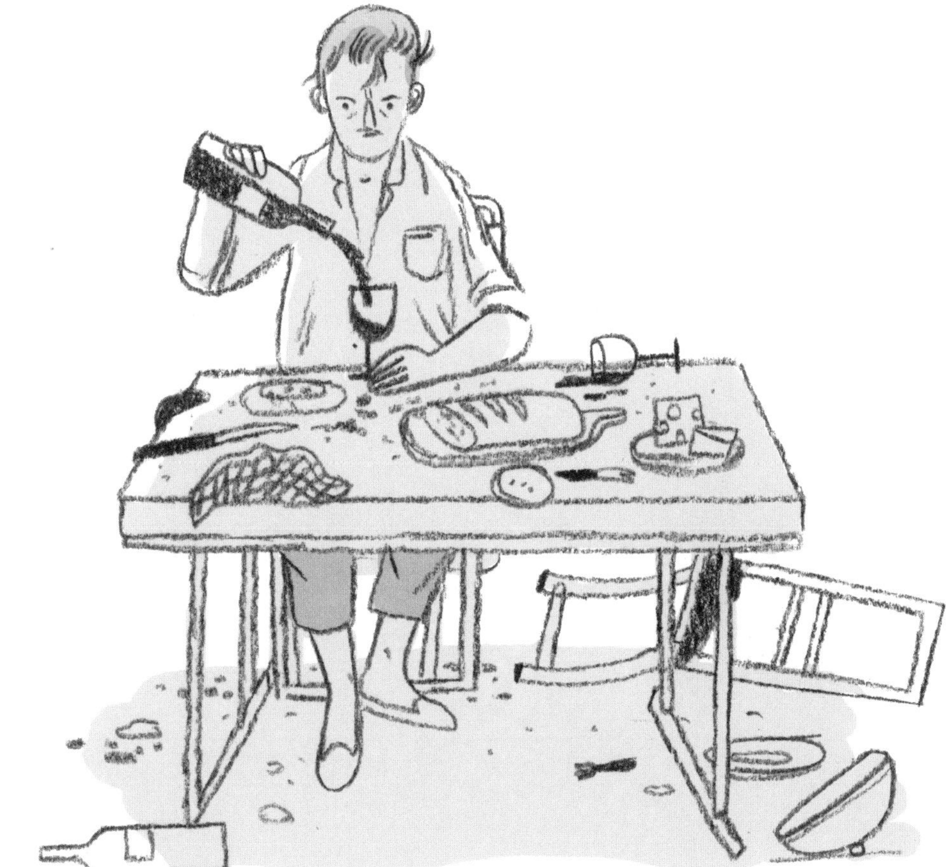

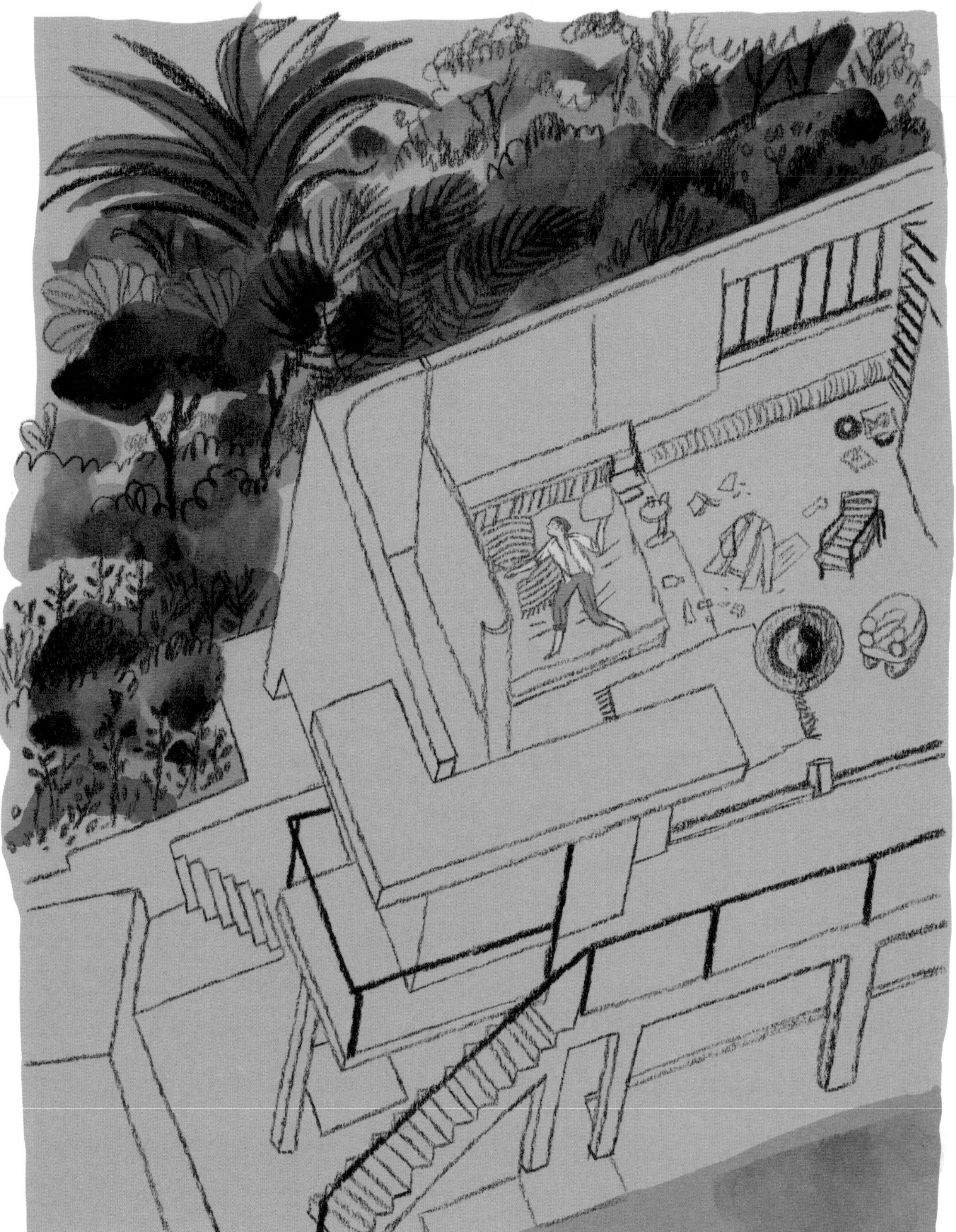

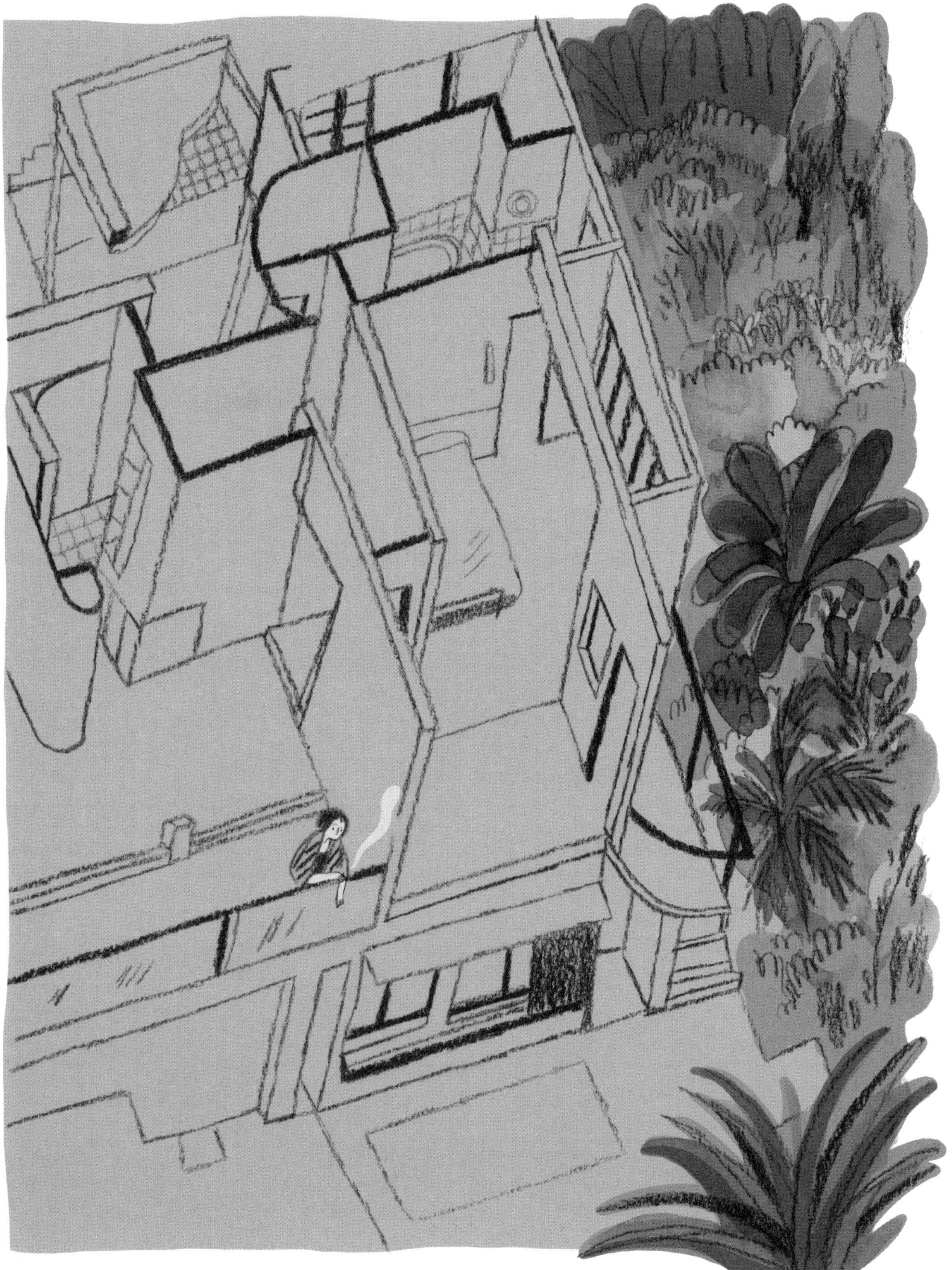

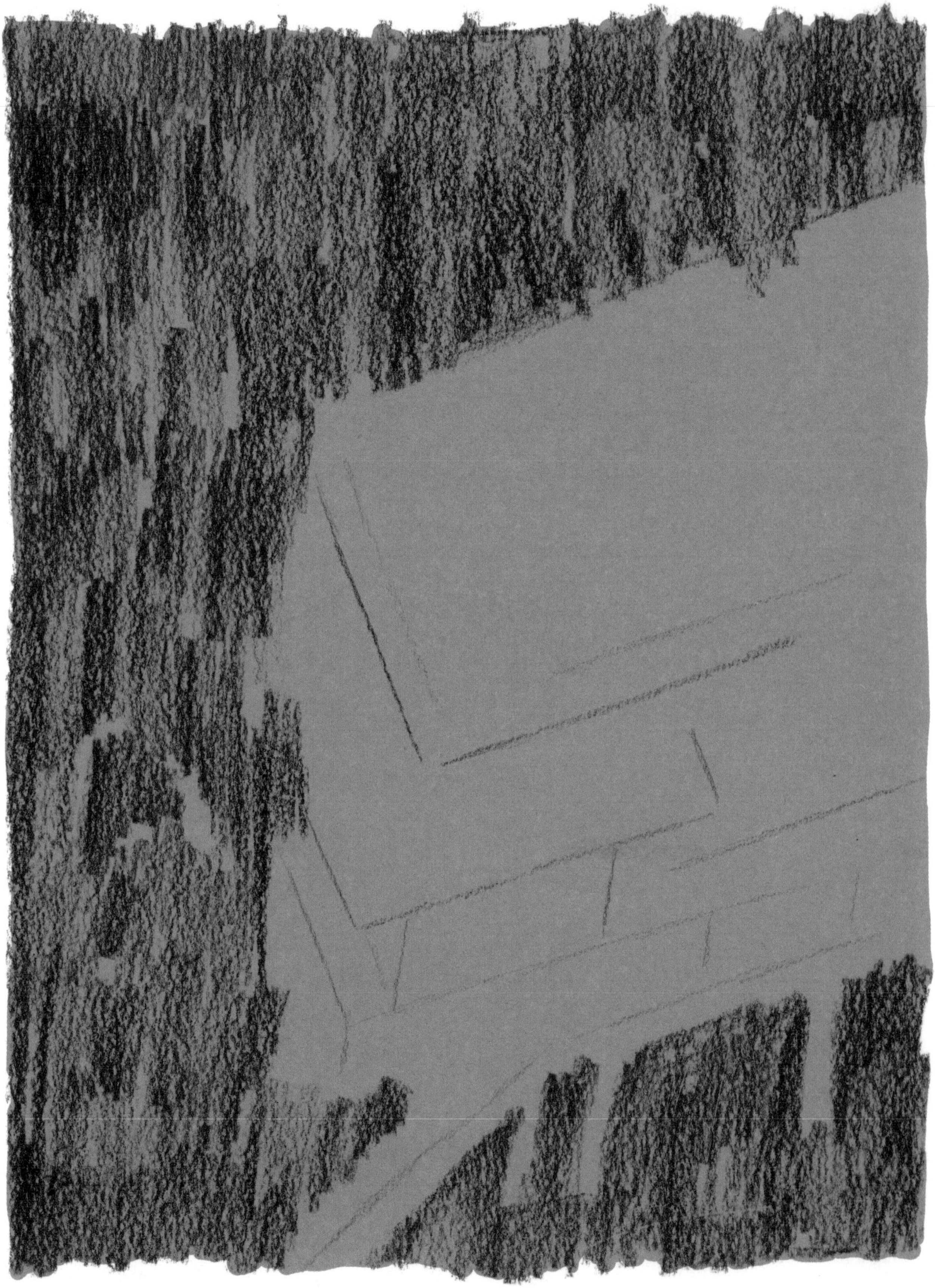

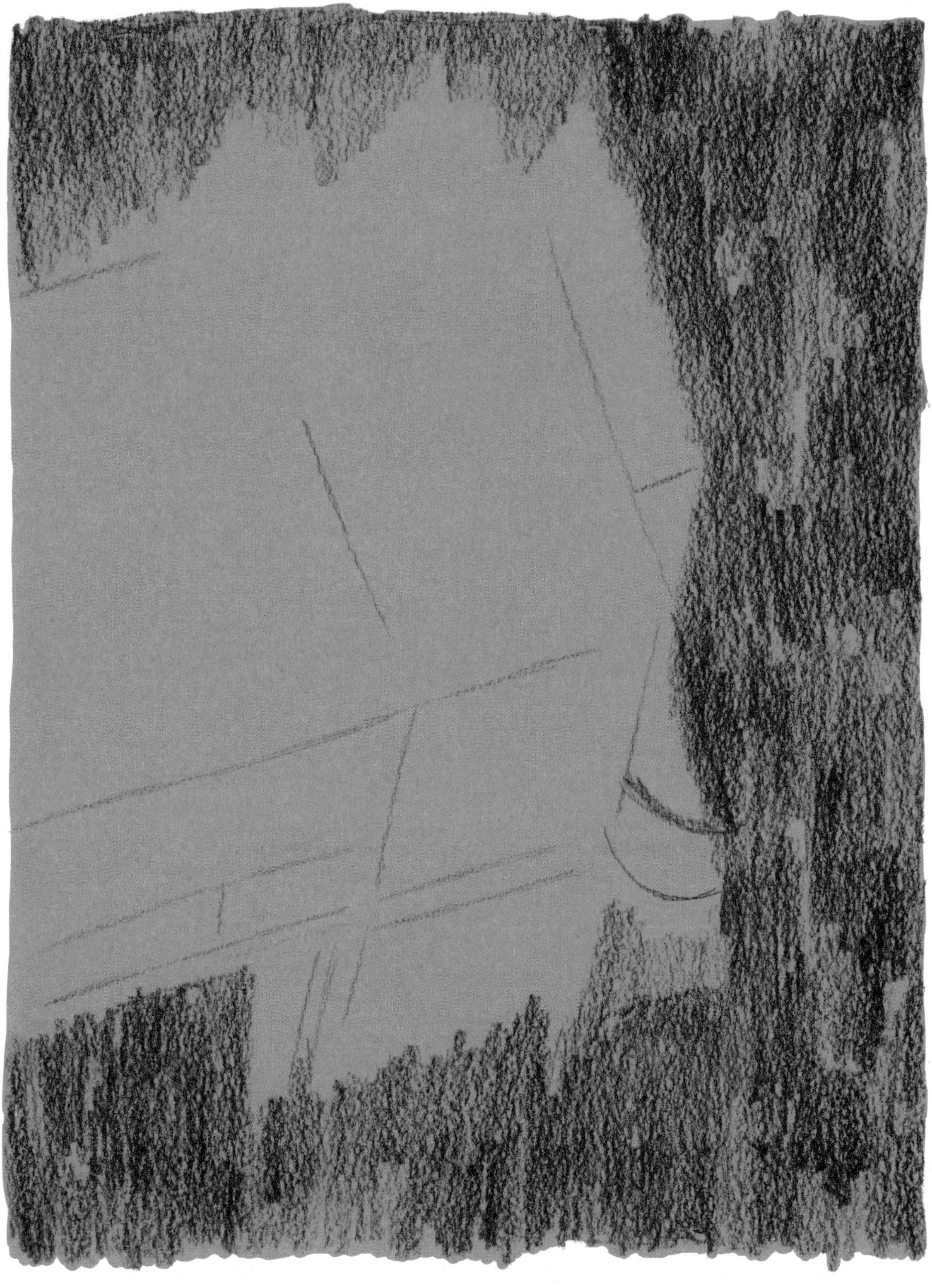

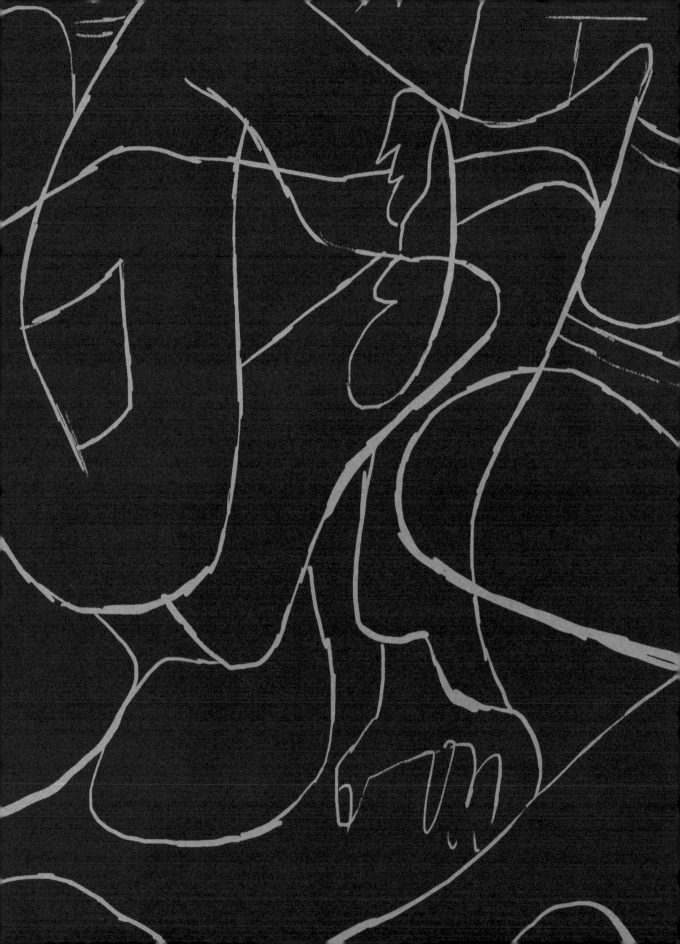

THE MURALS

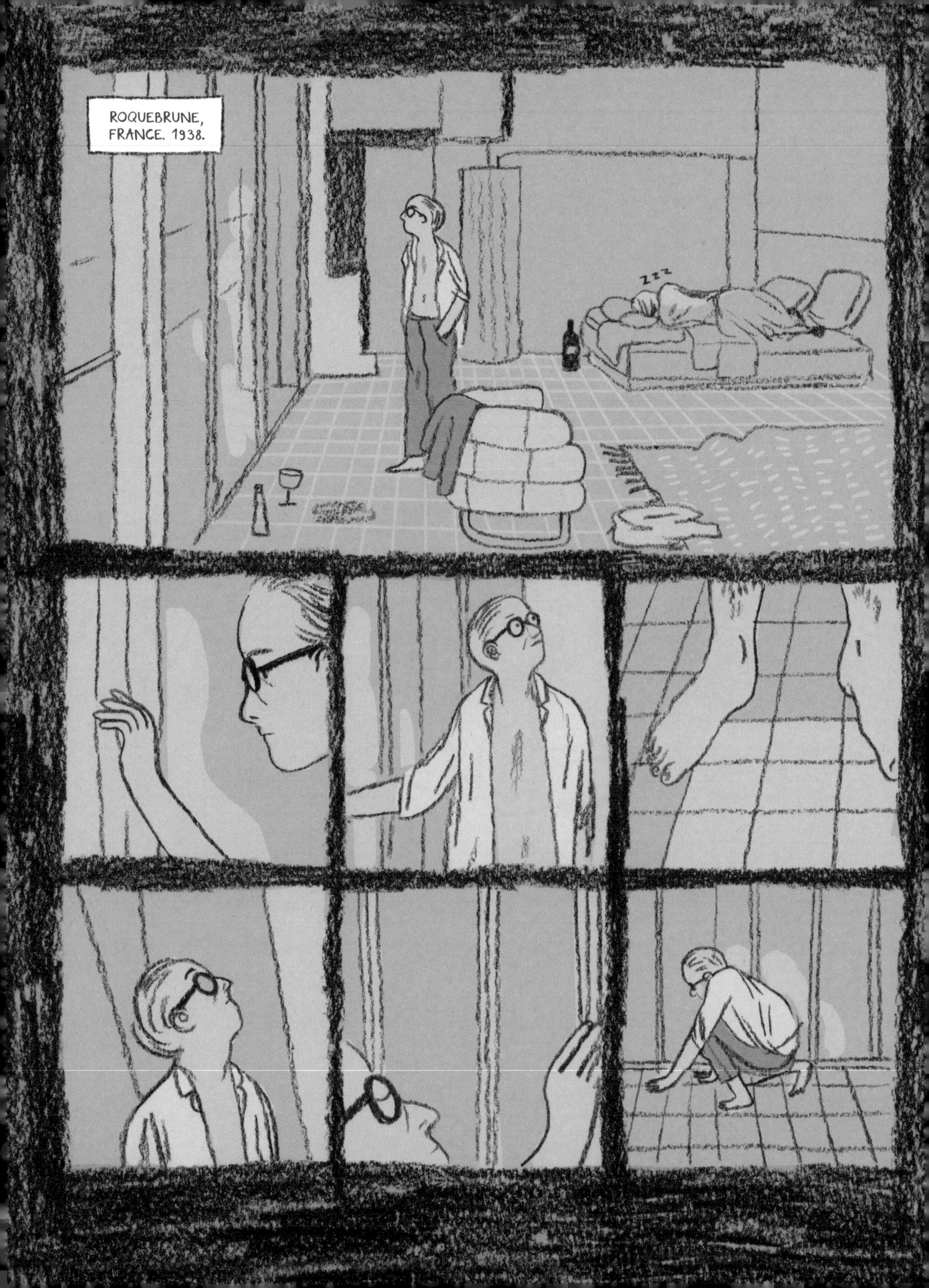
ROQUEBRUNE, FRANCE. 1938.
Z Z Z

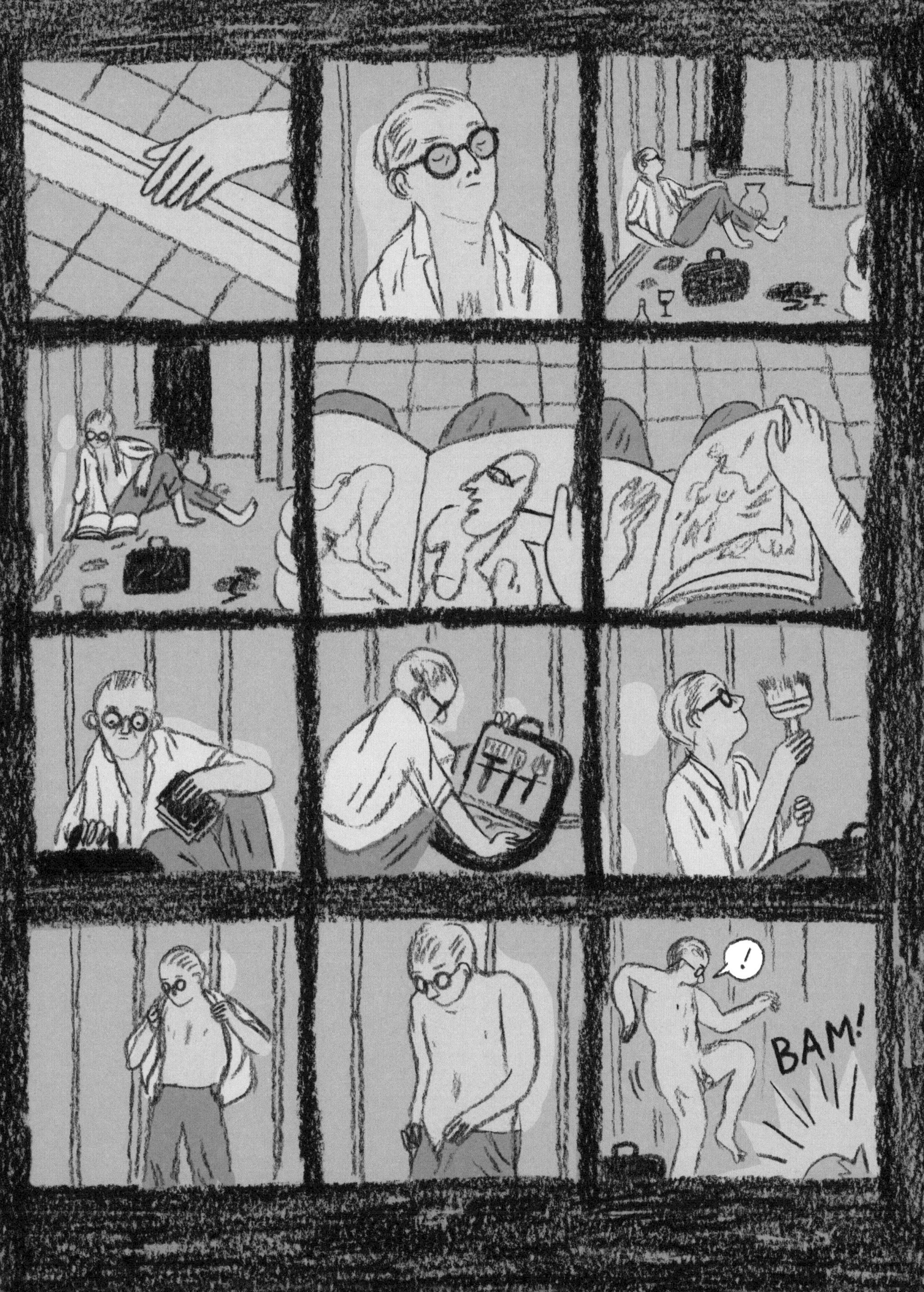
!
BAM!

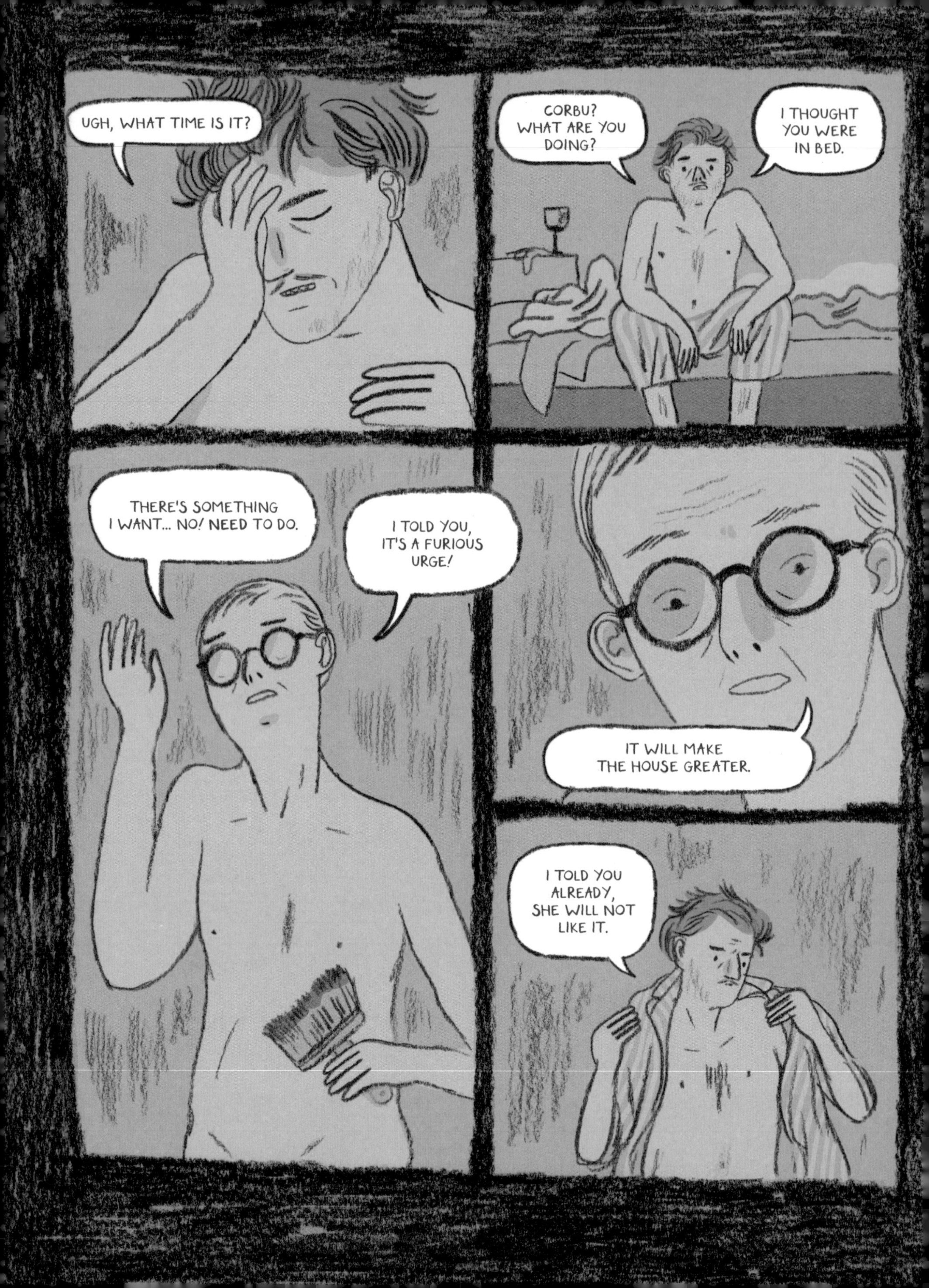
UGH, WHAT TIME IS IT?
CORBU? WHAT ARE YOU DOING?
I THOUGHT YOU WERE IN BED.
THERE'S SOMETHING I WANT... NO! NEED TO DO.
I TOLD YOU, IT'S A FURIOUS URGE!
IT WILL MAKE THE HOUSE GREATER.
I TOLD YOU ALREADY, SHE WILL NOT LIKE IT.

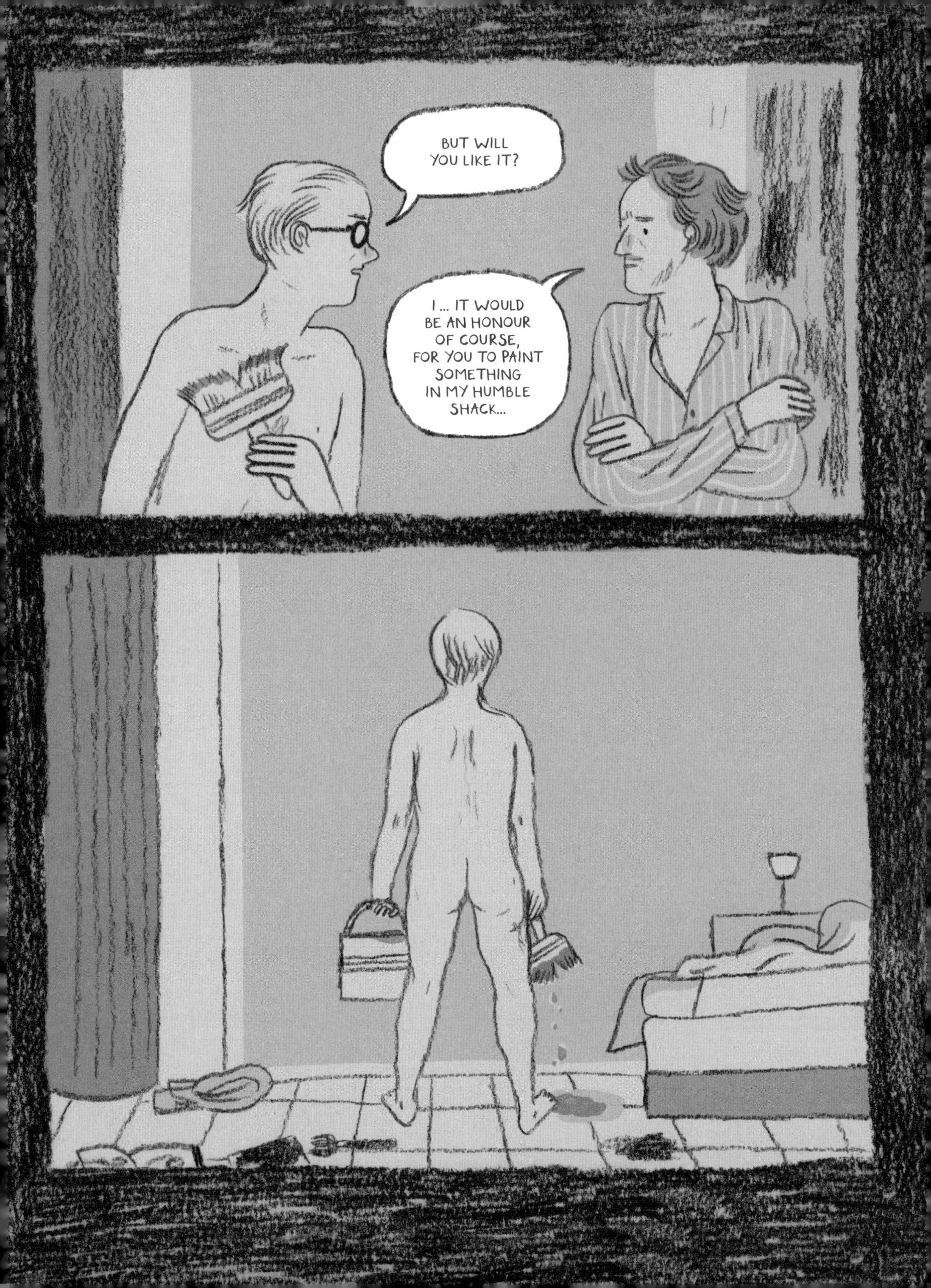
BUT WILL YOU LIKE IT?
I... IT WOULD BE AN HONOUR OF COURSE, FOR YOU TO PAINT SOMETHING IN MY HUMBLE SHACK...

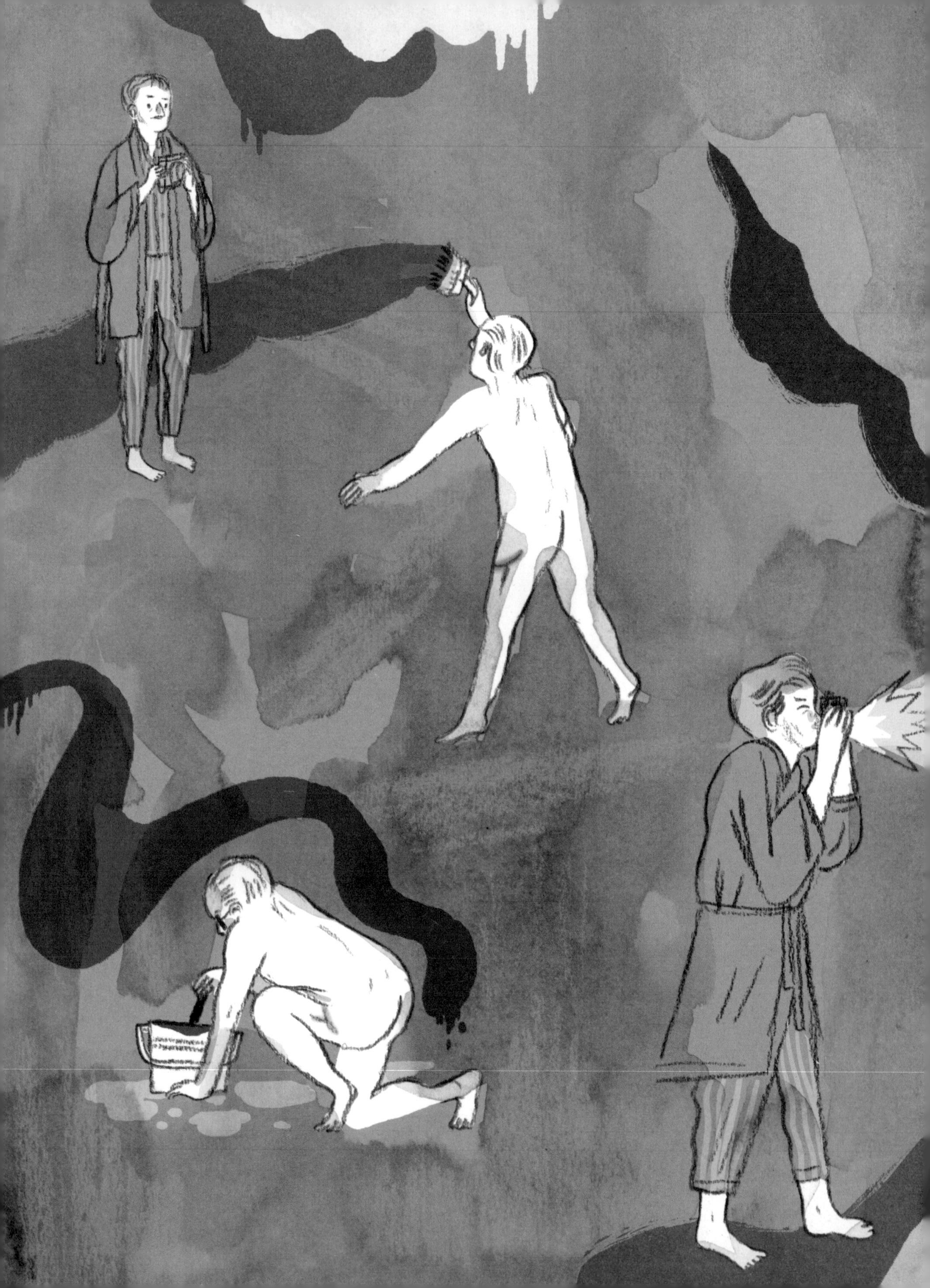

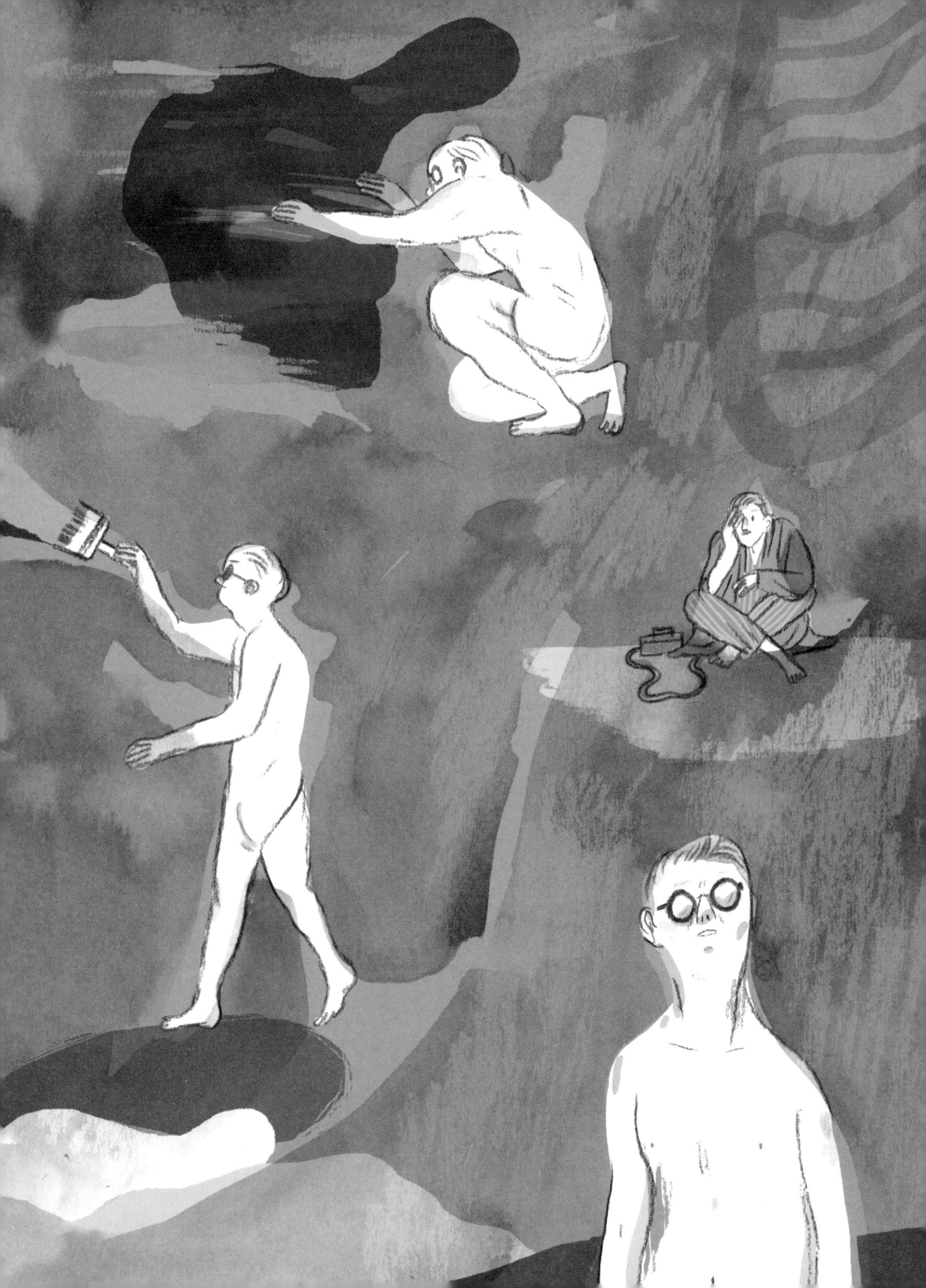

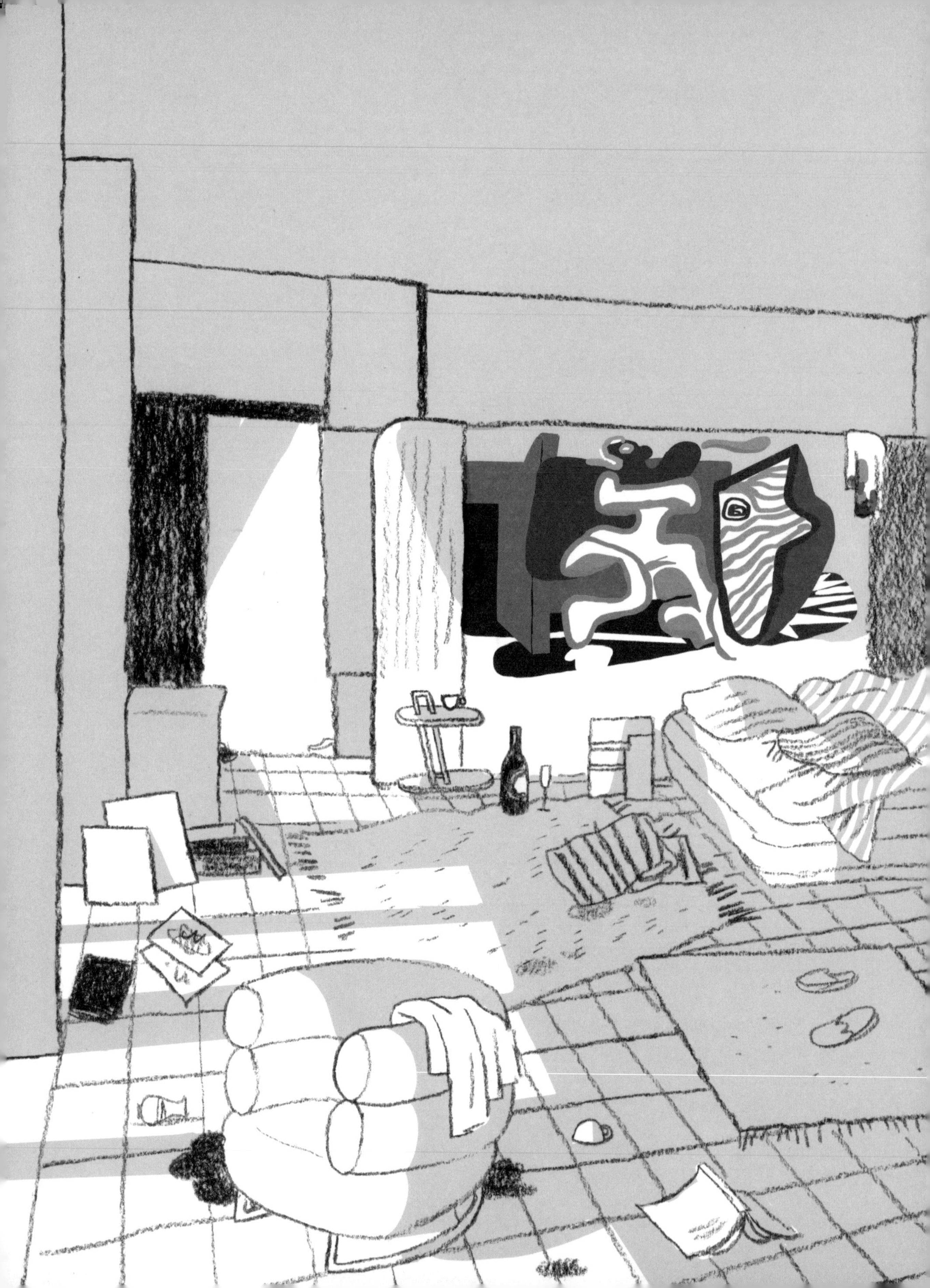

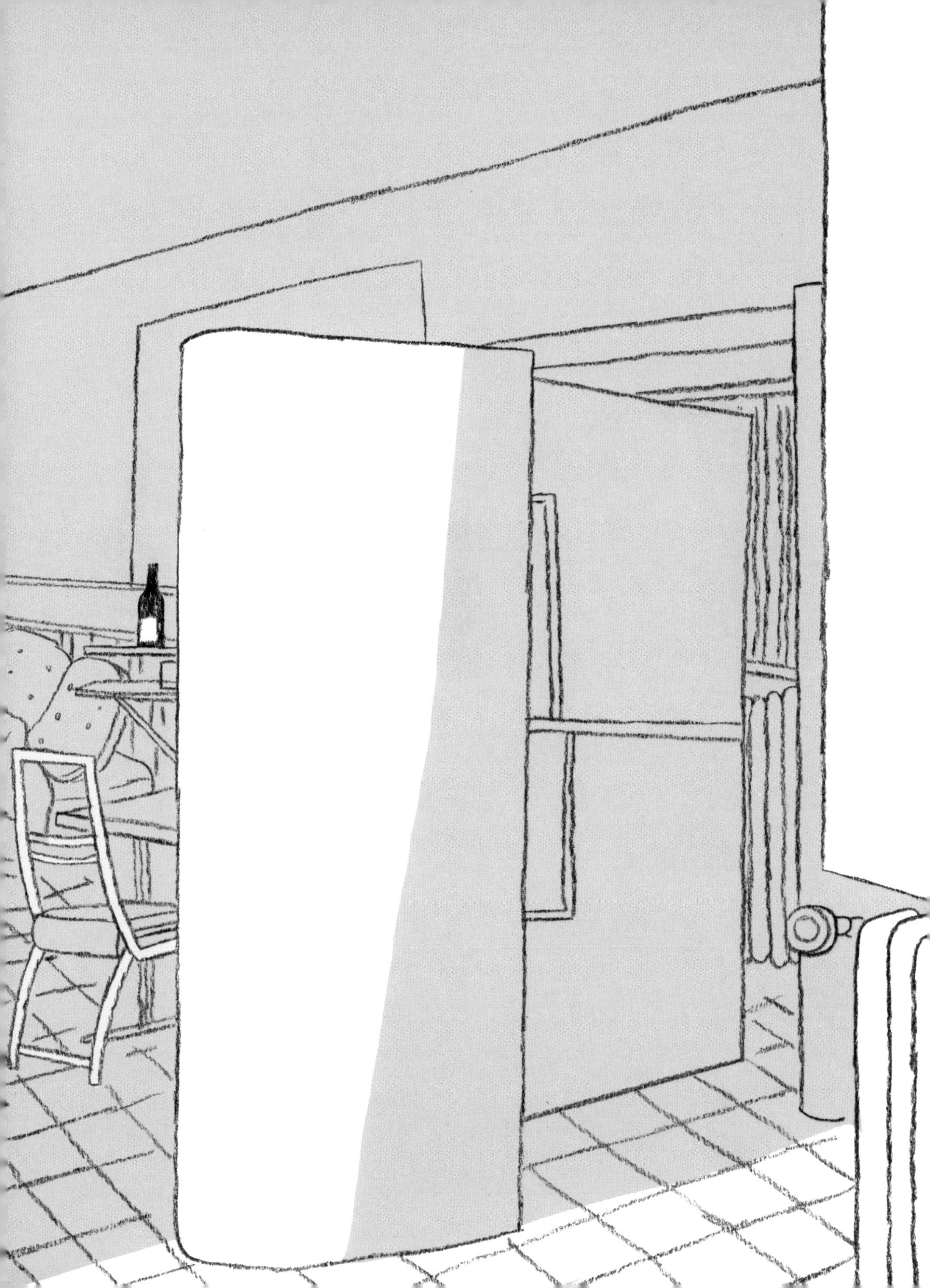

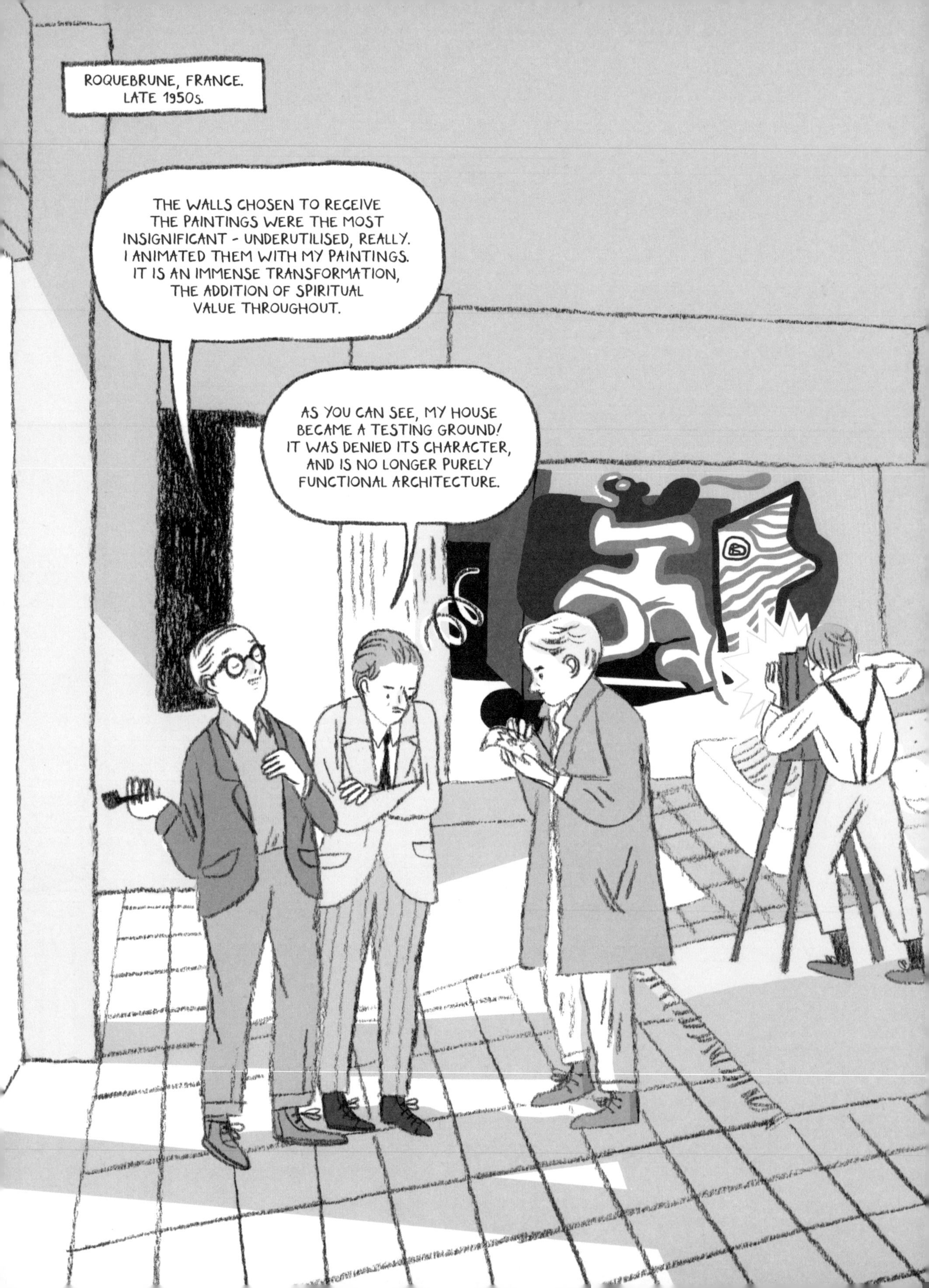
ROQUEBRUNE, FRANCE. LATE 1950s.
THE WALLS CHOSEN TO RECEIVE THE PAINTINGS WERE THE MOST INSIGNIFICANT - UNDERUTILISED, REALLY. I ANIMATED THEM WITH MY PAINTINGS. IT IS AN IMMENSE TRANSFORMATION, THE ADDITION OF SPIRITUAL VALUE THROUGHOUT.
AS YOU CAN SEE, MY HOUSE BECAME A TESTING GROUND! IT WAS DENIED ITS CHARACTER, AND IS NO LONGER PURELY FUNCTIONAL ARCHITECTURE.

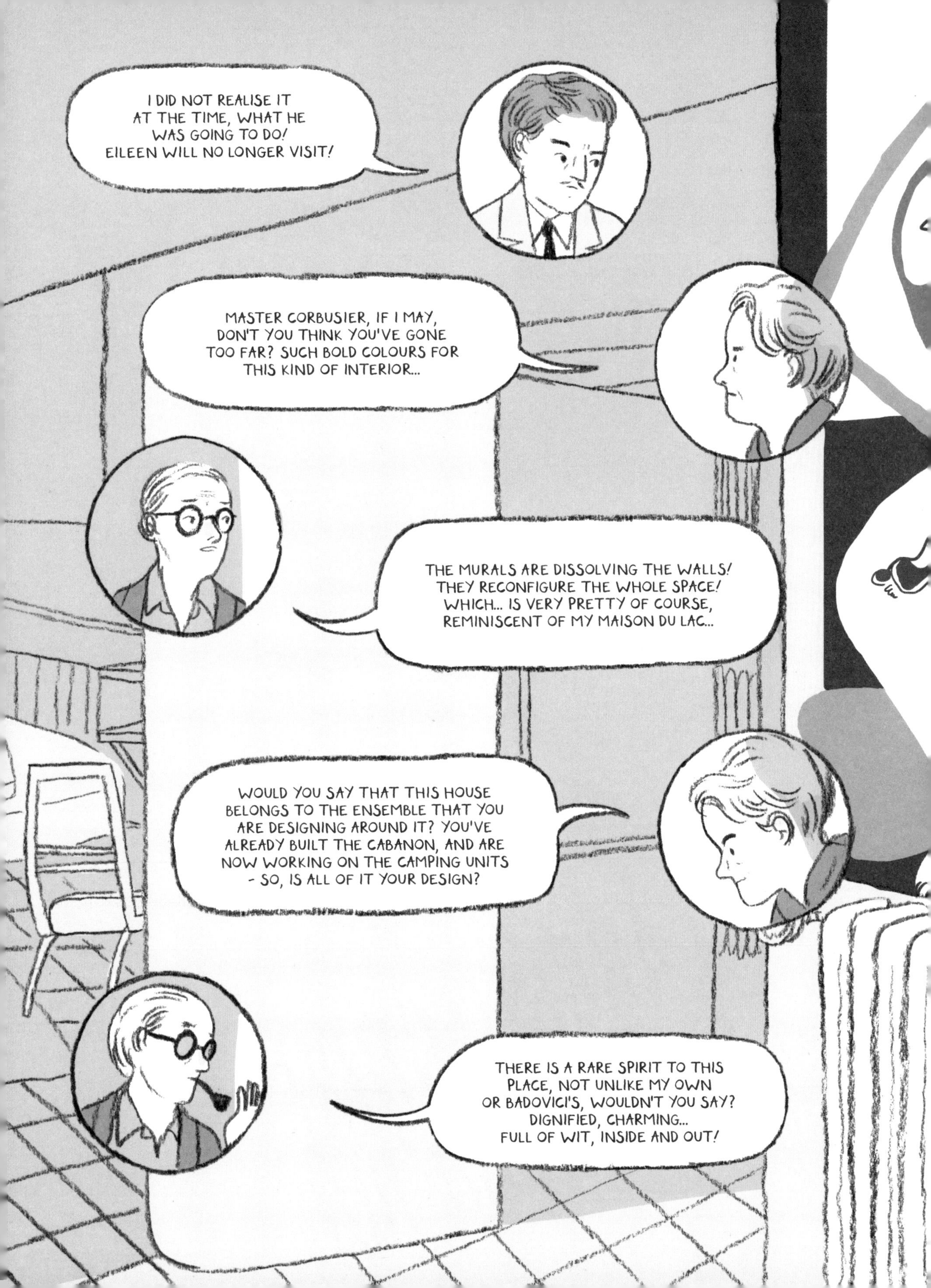
I DID NOT REALISE IT AT THE TIME, WHAT HE WAS GOING TO DO! EILEEN WILL NO LONGER VISIT!
MASTER CORBUSIER, IF I MAY, DON'T YOU THINK YOU'VE GONE TOO FAR? SUCH BOLD COLOURS FOR THIS KIND OF INTERIOR...
THE MURALS ARE DISSOLVING THE WALLS! THEY RECONFIGURE THE WHOLE SPACE! WHICH... IS VERY PRETTY OF COURSE, REMINISCENT OF MY MAISON DU LAC...
WOULD YOU SAY THAT THIS HOUSE BELONGS TO THE ENSEMBLE THAT YOU ARE DESIGNING AROUND IT? YOU'VE ALREADY BUILT THE CABANON, AND ARE NOW WORKING ON THE CAMPING UNITS - SO, IS ALL OF IT YOUR DESIGN?
THERE IS A RARE SPIRIT TO THIS PLACE, NOT UNLIKE MY OWN OR BADOVICI'S, WOULDN'T YOU SAY? DIGNIFIED, CHARMING... FULL OF WIT, INSIDE AND OUT!

HOUSE BADOVICI

While it is not without charm, the exterior architecture seems to ...itects more than the interior. As if the house was designed ...e eyes more than for the welfare of the inhabitants. ... appear in the playfulness of balanced masses ...eet the needs of man and the requirements ... ...t and intimacy. Theory is not enough ... ...ould have been imperative to f... ...ce failures are obvious, ar... ...the refinements o... ...ilities of the ... ...constru... ...wa... ...ro... ...e p...

L'ARCHITECTURE D'AUJOURD'HUI

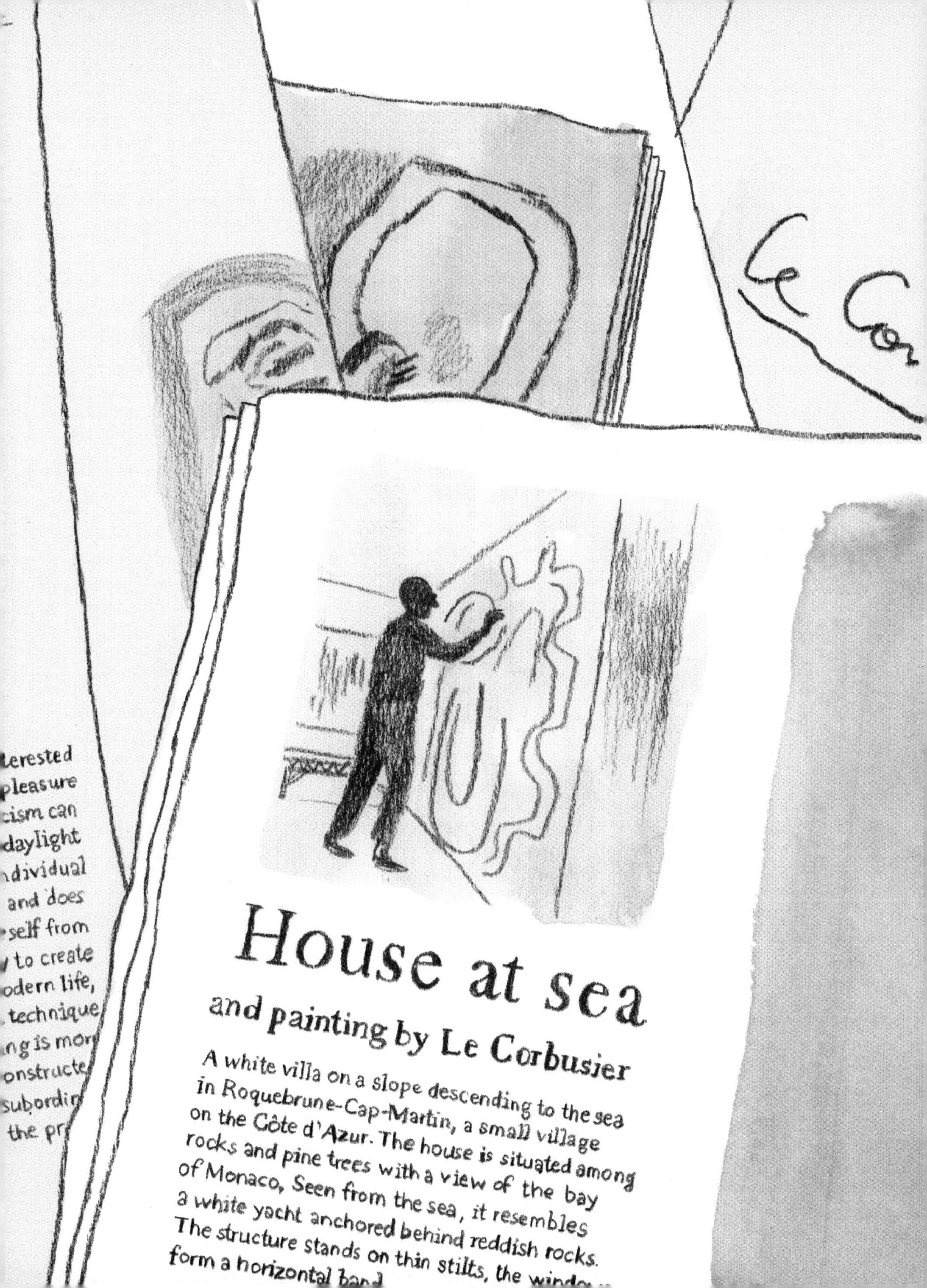
Le Cor
terested
pleasure
cism can
daylight
ndividual
and does
self from
to create
odern life,
technique
ng is mor
onstructe
subordin
the pr
House at sea
and painting by Le Corbusier
A white villa on a slope descending to the sea
in Roquebrune-Cap-Martin, a small village
on the Côte d'Azur. The house is situated among
rocks and pine trees with a view of the bay
of Monaco. Seen from the sea, it resembles
a white yacht anchored behind reddish rocks.
The structure stands on thin stilts, the windo
form a horizontal ban

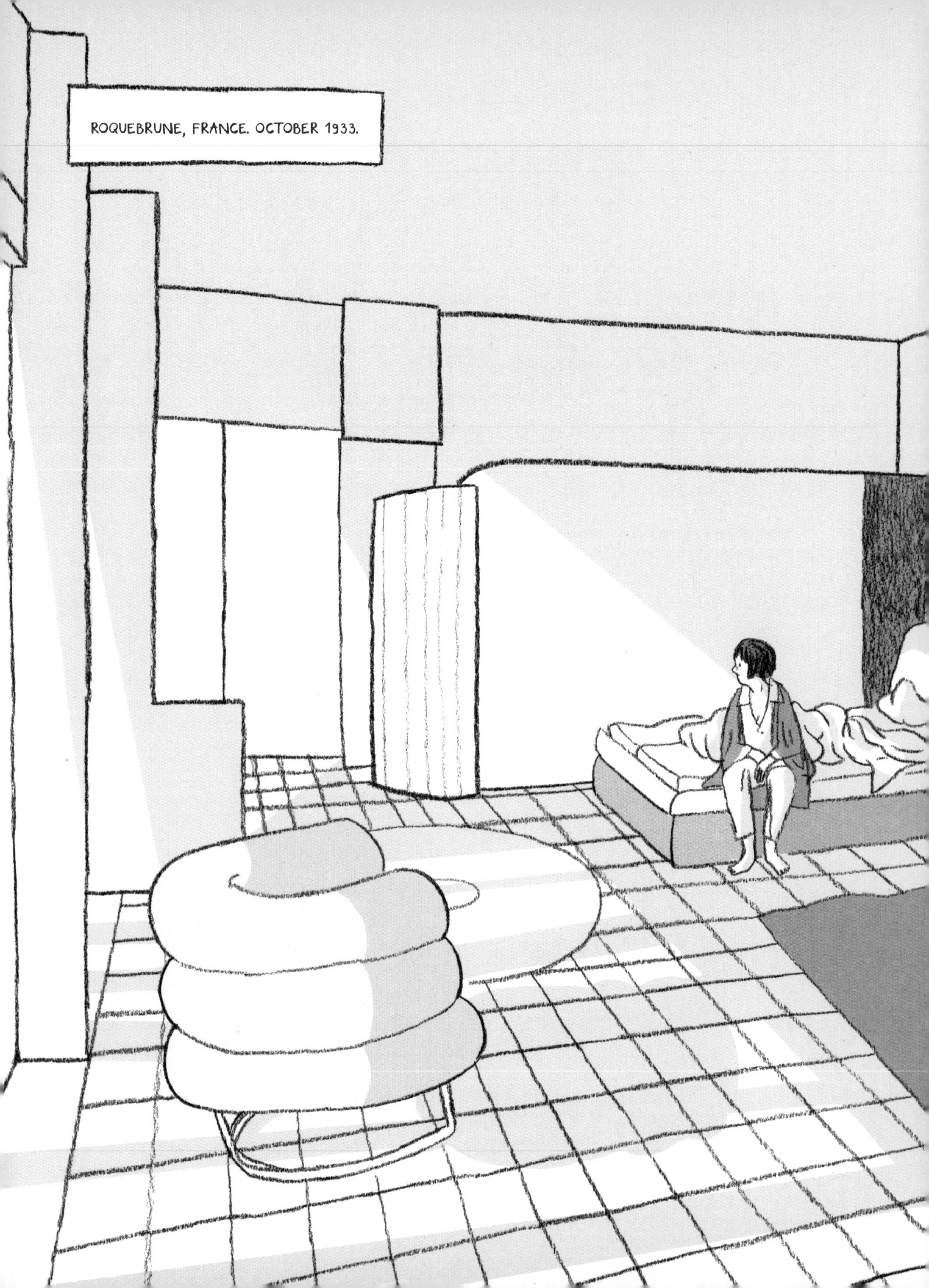
ROQUEBRUNE, FRANCE. OCTOBER 1933.

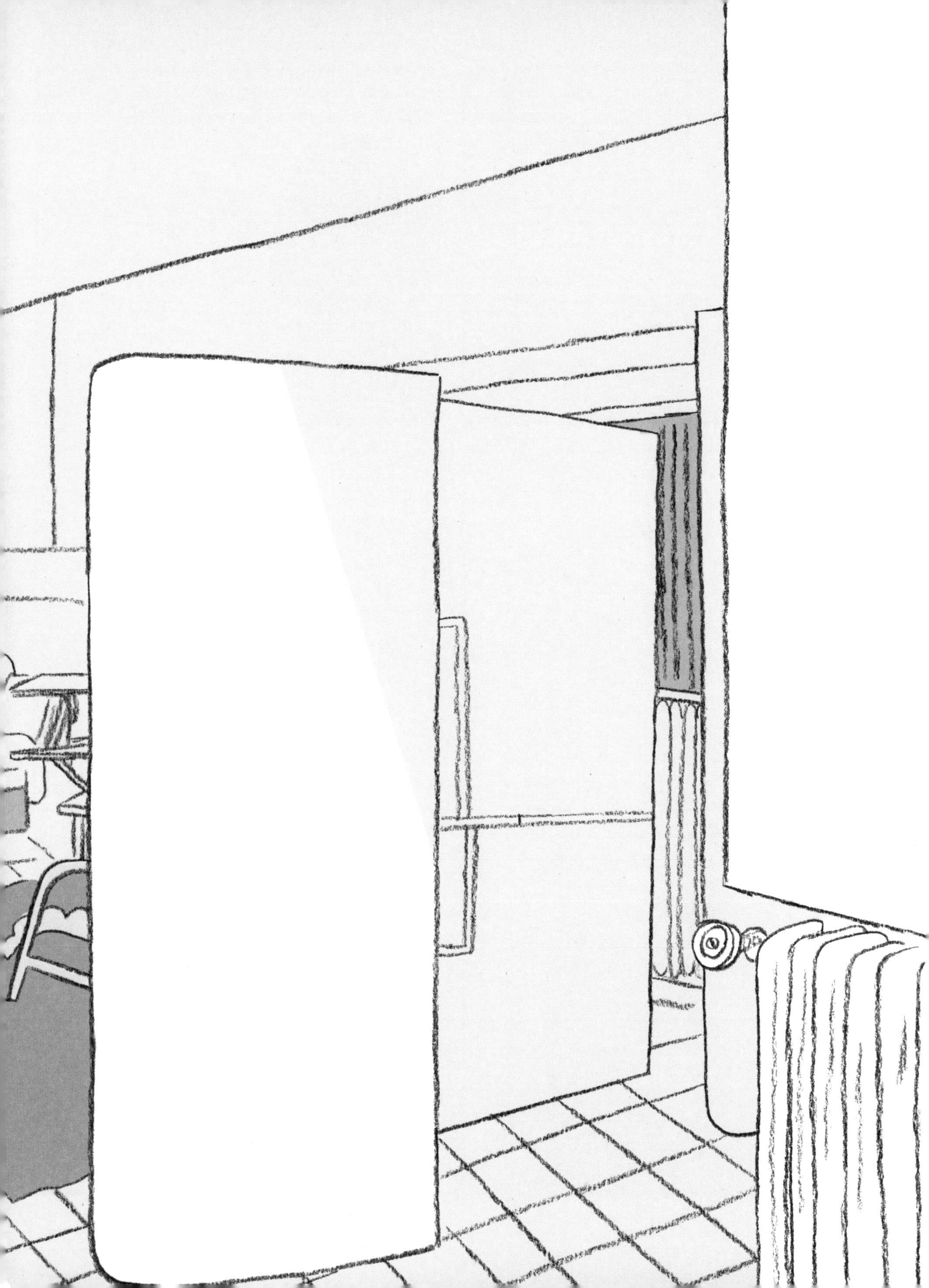

VALIS

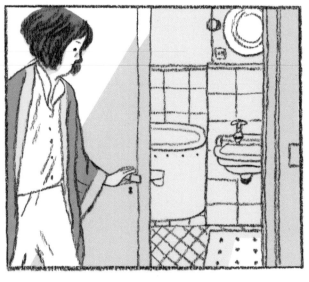

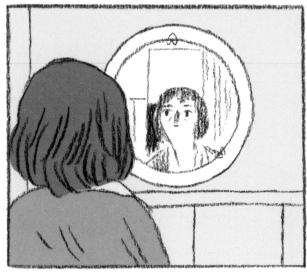

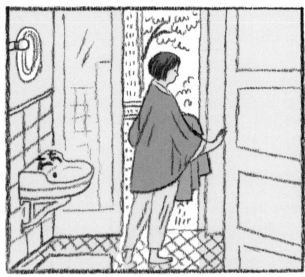

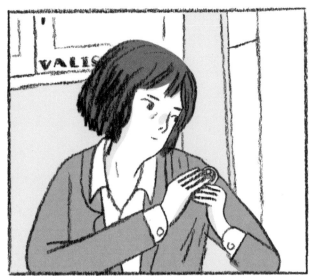

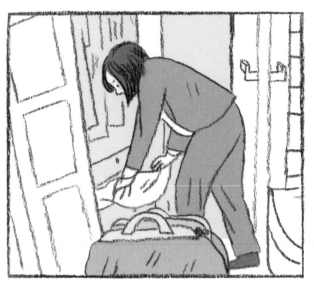

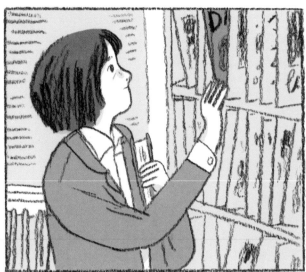

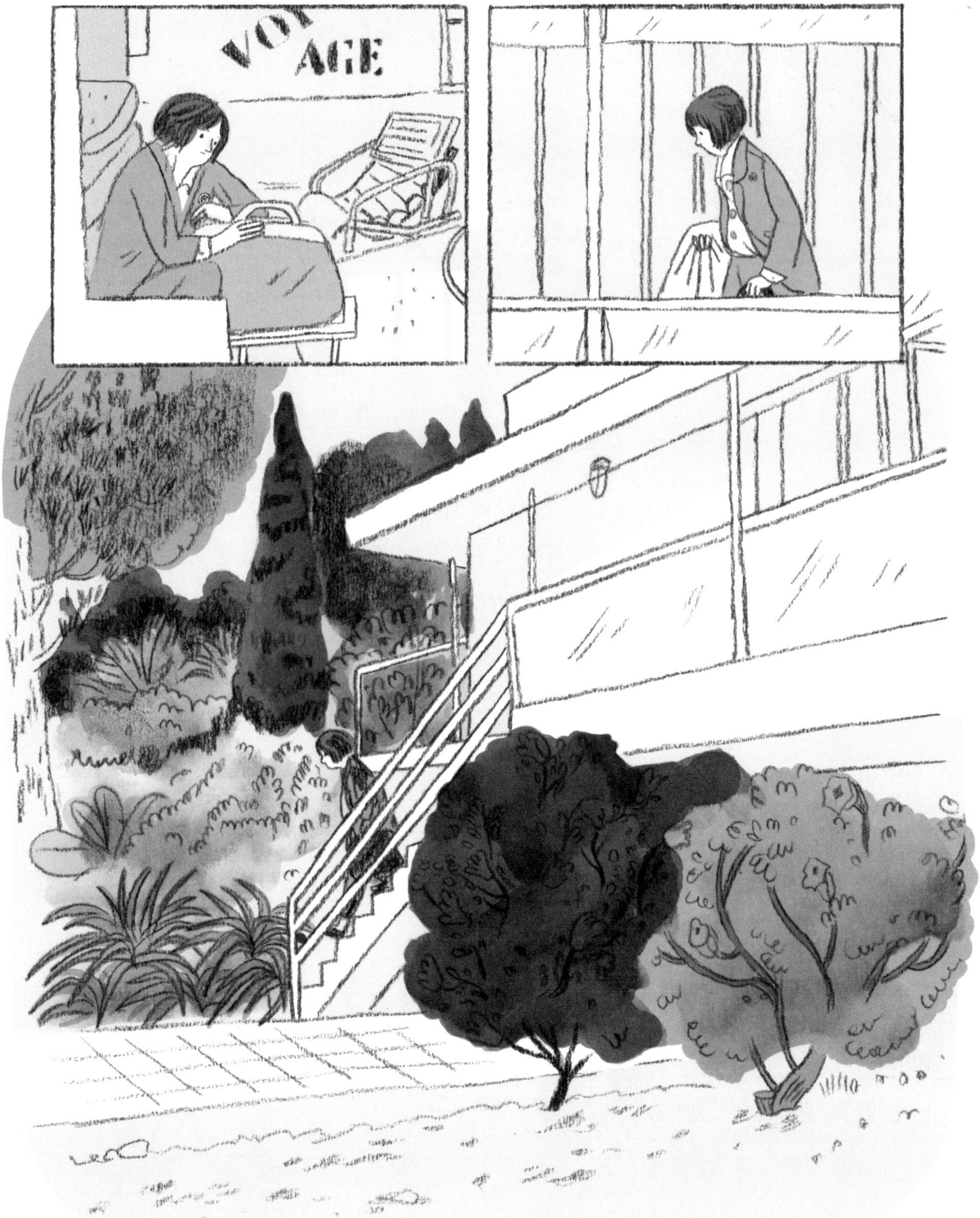
VOY
AGE

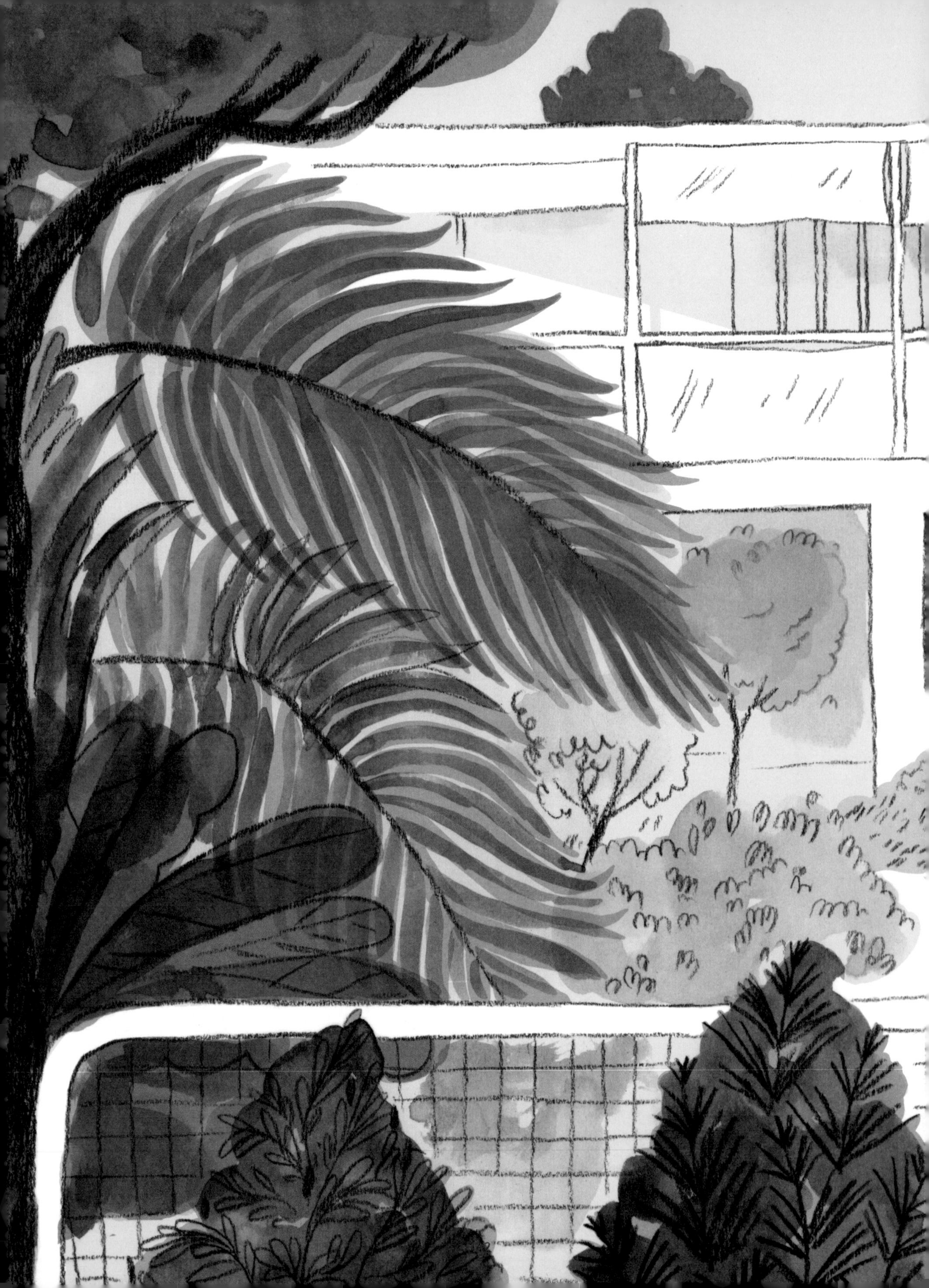

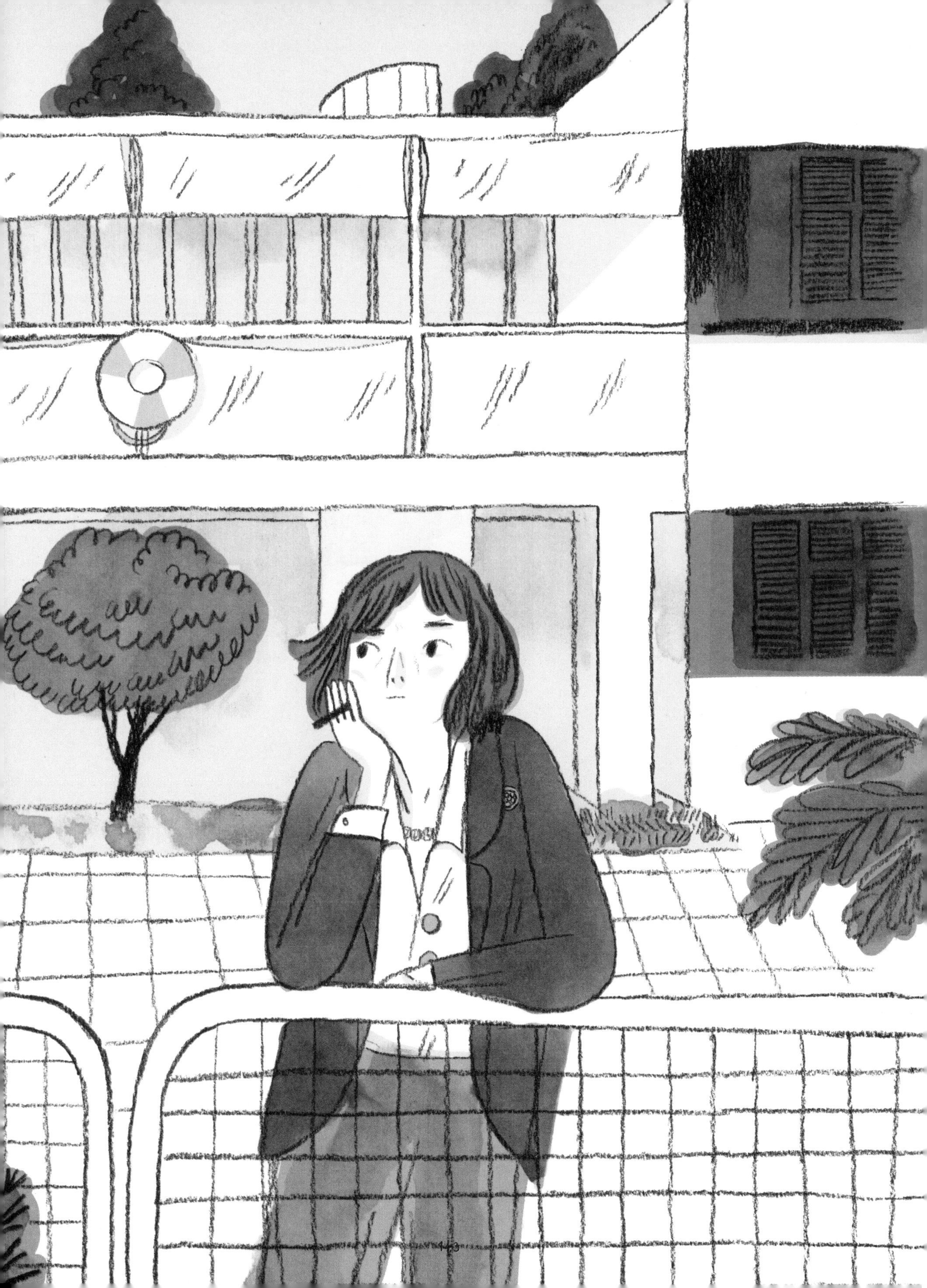

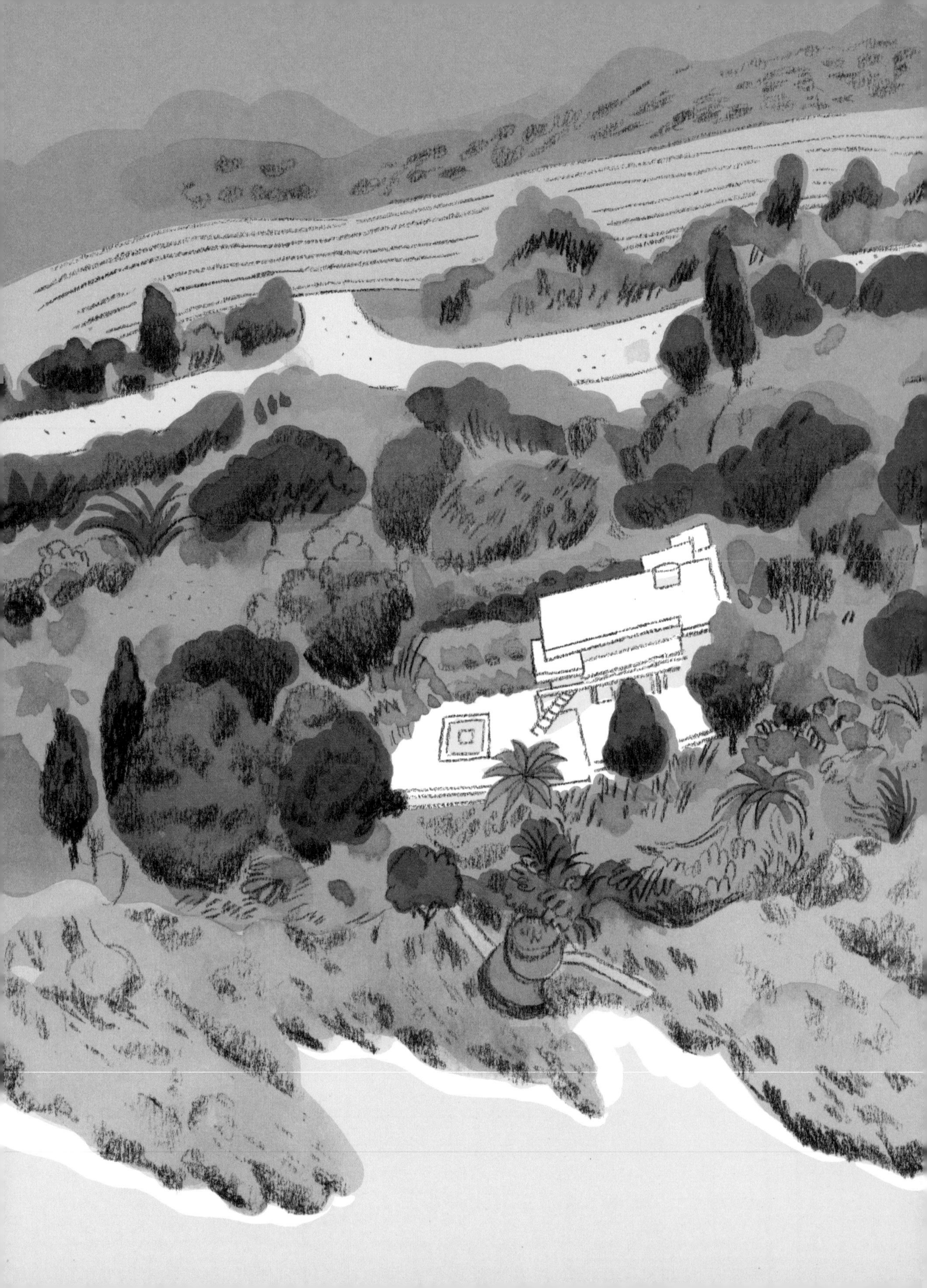

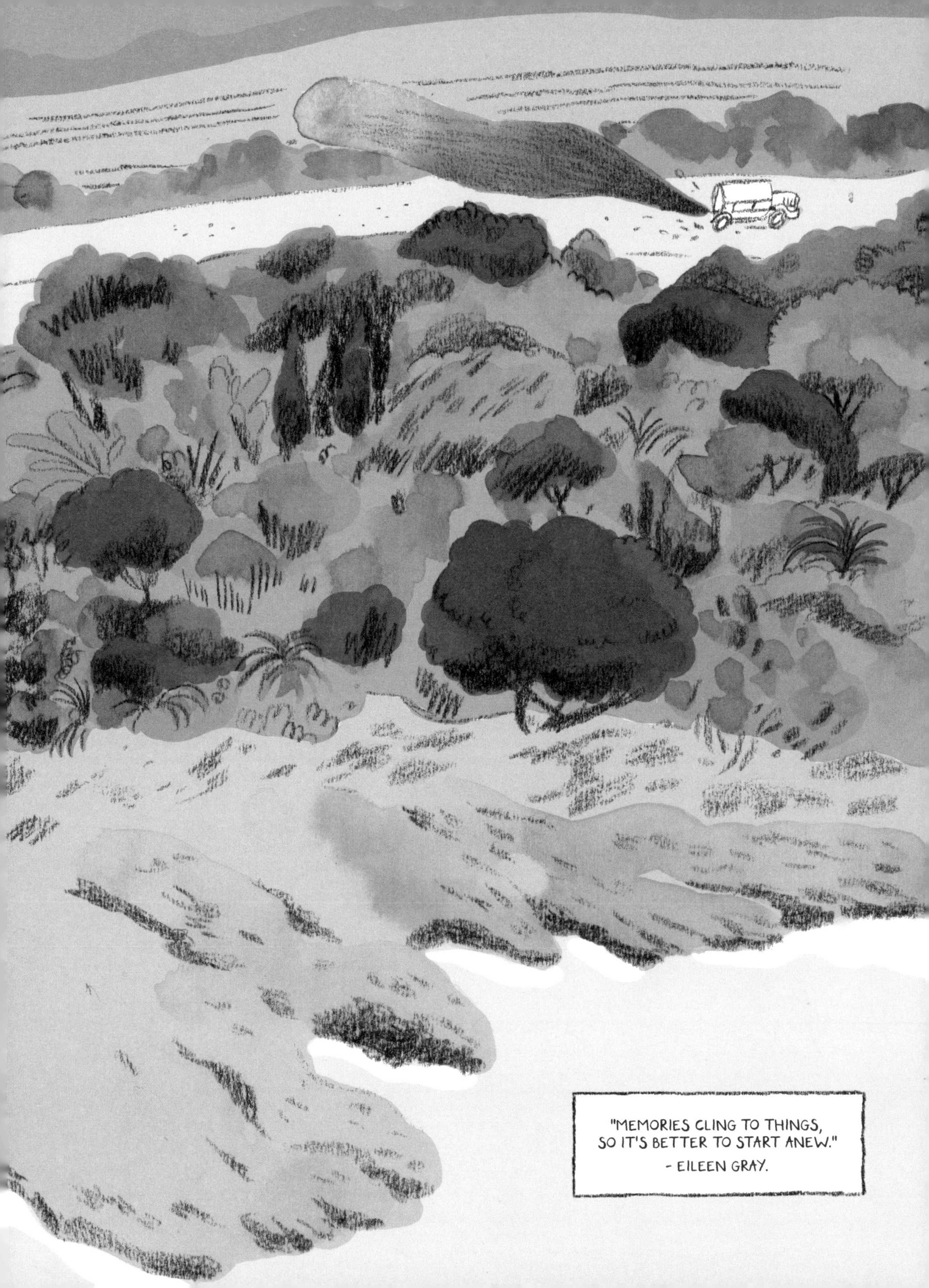
"MEMORIES CLING TO THINGS,
SO IT'S BETTER TO START ANEW."
- EILEEN GRAY.

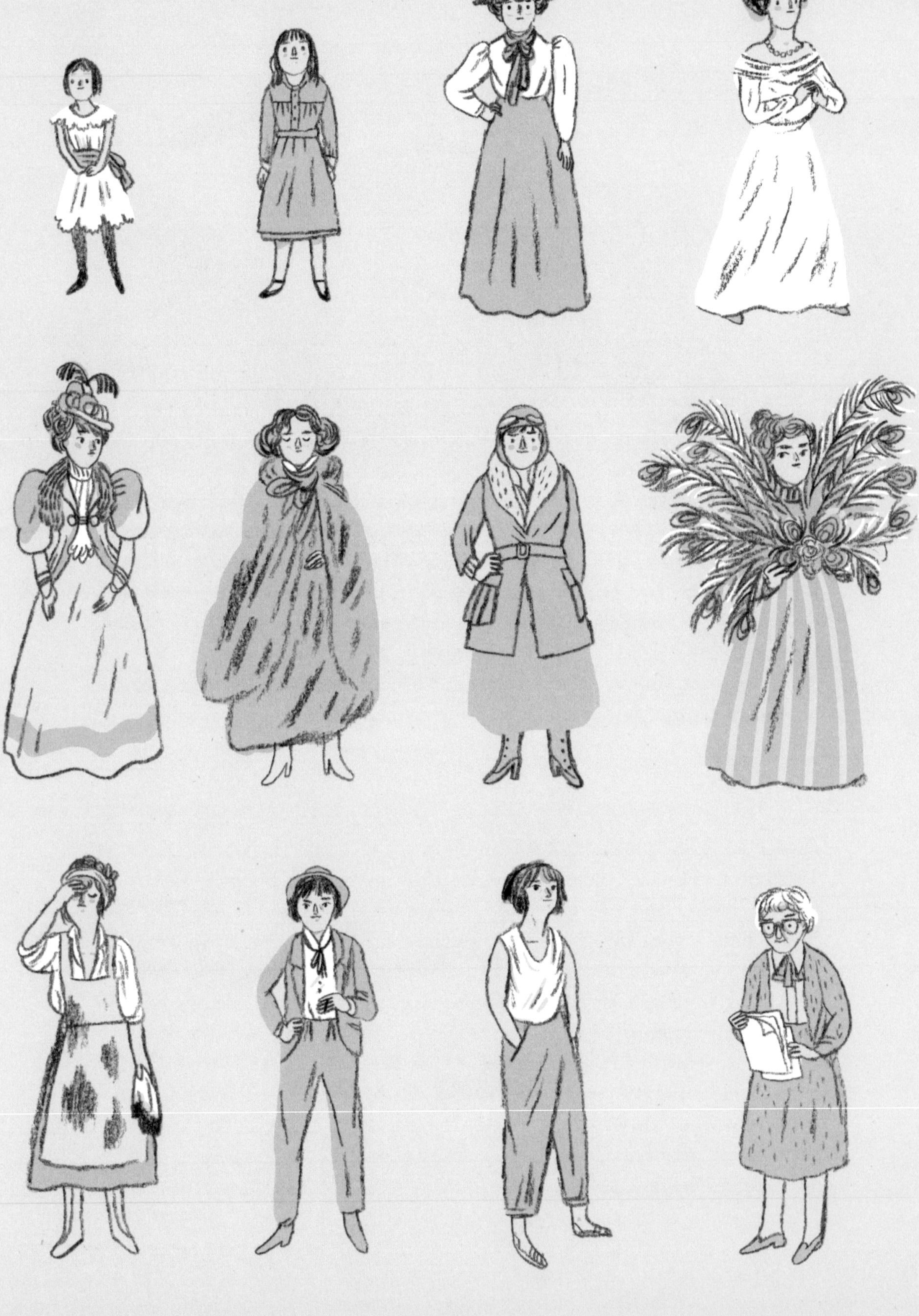

AFTERWORD

"THE BUILDING HAS BECOME SURROUNDED
BY MYTHS AND ANECDOTES."

Katarina Bonnevier, *A Queer Analysis of Eileen Gray's E-1027.*

EILEEN GRAY AFTER E-1027:

As their relationship disintegrated, Gray moved out of E-1027 in 1933, while Badovici remained and spent his summers there until his death in 1956. Even before completing E-1027, Gray had purchased a plot of land on the hills above Menton. There, between 1932 and 1934, she designed and built an entirely new home, a refuge that was just her own. The house, Tempe à Pailla, has been a listed building since 1990. Gray continued living between Paris and the South of France, designing a few other projects, such as a house in Lou Perou and apartments in Saint Tropez, but increasingly retreated from public life. Her groundbreaking work as an architect and designer was never fully acknowledged in her time as interest in her work only gained traction in the five years prior to her death in 1976. Today, Gray is fully, and rightfully, recognised as an innovative architect in her own right and a pioneer of modern design.

E-1027 AFTER EILEEN GRAY:

Throughout the 1940s and 50s, Le Corbusier's activities on the Côte d'Azur site intensified, as he constructed the cabanon in 1951 and the holiday cabins in 1956 around E-1027. After Badovici's death, perhaps to preserve the murals he had created, Le Corbusier made sure the house – called 'House Badovici' at the time – was bought by Marie-Louise Schelbert, one of his personal admirers, who was convinced for a time that E-1027 was Le Corbusier's design. Le Corbusier himself died in the waters of the Cabbé beach, right in front of the house, in 1965. A decade later, Mrs Schelbert sold the house to her doctor, Peter Kaegi, who moved in after her death in 1982. He sold most of the home's original furniture between 1991 and 1996 – coincidentally, the year he was murdered in the house. That same year, E-1027 was listed as a "historical monument". It is now almost restored to its original condition and open to the public.

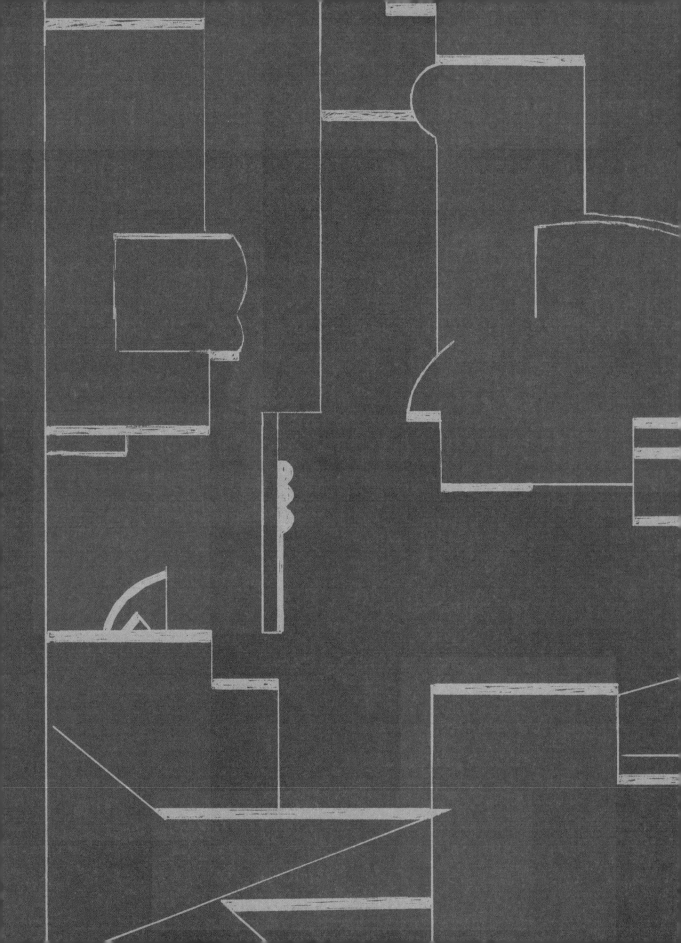

FURTHER
READING

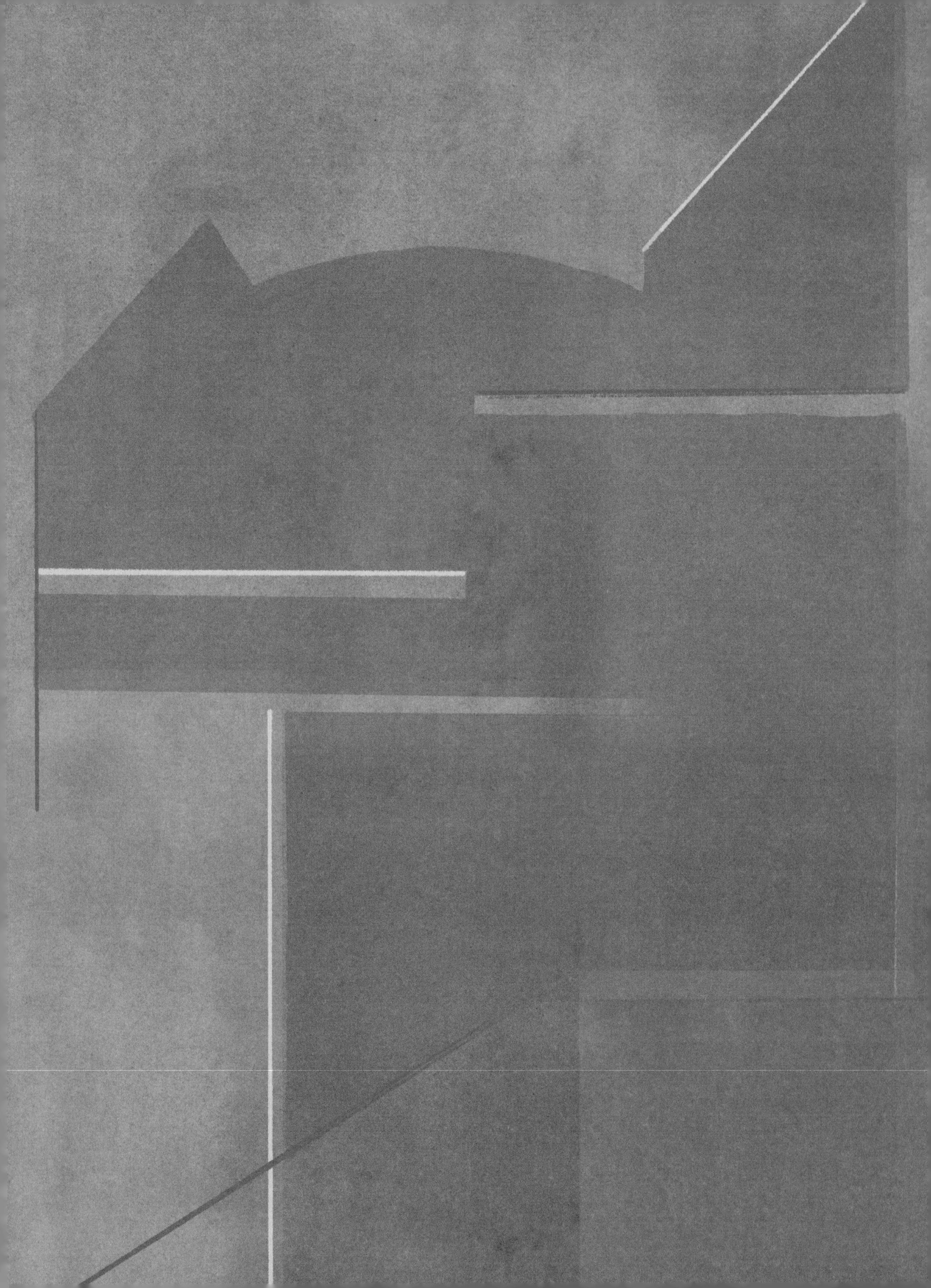

BIOGRAPHIES

EILEEN GRAY

Eileen Gray (1878–1976) was an Irish architect and interior designer. She questioned the "inhumanity" of the 'Machine-à-Habiter' concept popularised by Le Corbusier, as she saw homes to be more than shells to inhabit. After being ignored for decades, her works – often overshadowed or unjustly credited to male colleagues and partners – gained attention in the last years of her life, most notably, E-1027. She is now recognised as a major figure of early Modernism.

JEAN BADOVICI

Jean 'Bado' Badovici (1893–1956), was a Romanian-born architect. It was in his company, amongst the intellectual circles of 1920s Paris, that Gray developed her desire to design spaces in addition to objects. It was for Badovici, her brief lover and partner, that Gray designed and financed E-1027.

LE CORBUSIER

Charles-Édouard Jeaneret (1887–1965), known also as Le Corbusier, was a Swiss-born architect, designer and painter. Gray maintained a distant but deferential friendship with Le Corbusier until he defaced E-1027 with his murals in 1938. This, and the fact Le Corbusier never denied claims to him or Badovici being the designers of the house, saw Gray sever all contact with Corbusier.

FERNAND LÉGER

Fernand Léger (1881–1955) was a painter and good friend of Jean Badovici. Gray met Léger through Badovici, as Léger painted his first wall murals in Badovici's Vezelay home. Léger came to E-1027 several times and voiced his concerns to Le Corbusier about his defacing of Gray's design.

BARONESS GRAY AND MISTER SMITH-GRAY

Eileen Gray's parents were James Maclaren Smith (1833–1900), an Irish amateur artist, and Eveleen Pounden (1841–1918), the granddaughter of the 10th Earl of Moray. They eloped to Italy in 1863 but their marriage was not a happy one, with Smith moving definitely to Europe in 1989. Pounden formally became the 19th Baroness Gray in 1895, subsequently leading the entire family, including Smith, to change their name to Gray by Royal license.

D. CHARLES

D. Charles had a lacquer atelier at 92 Dean Street in London, near the Slade School where Gray was studying Drawing in 1898. It was with Charles that Gray began to learn the complicated process of manufacturing lacquer after spontaneously entering the store one day.

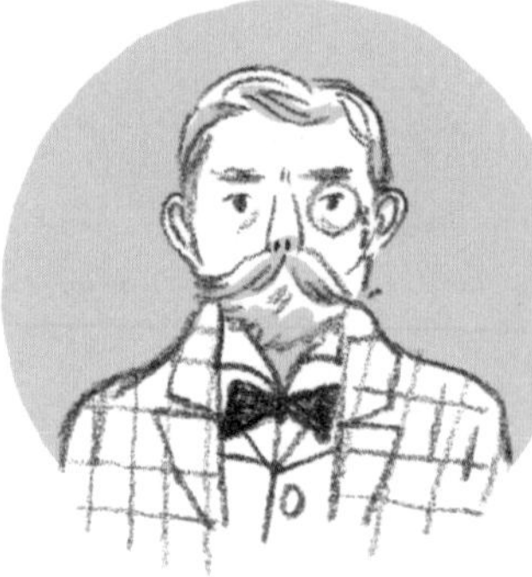

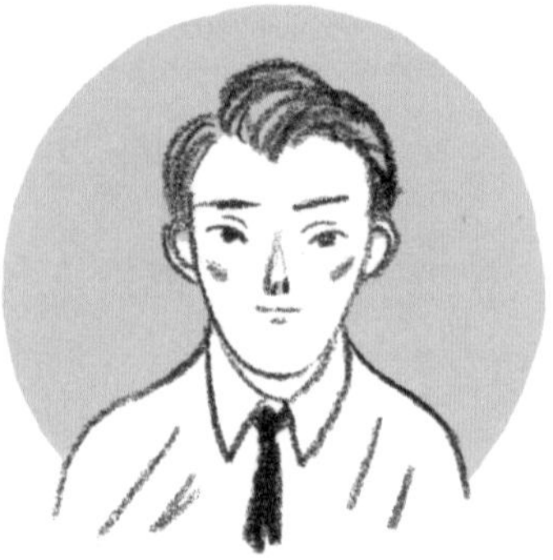

SEIZO SUGAWARA

Seizo Sugawara (1884–1937) was a Japanese artist and native of the city of Jahoji, where the craft of lacquer had been practised for centuries. Gray perfected the art of lacquer with Sugawara after her stay at D. Charles' shop in London. In 1900, Sugawara was sent by the Japanese emperor to represent Japan at the Exposition Universelle in Paris and never returned to his homeland.

LOUISE DANY

Eileen Gray's faithful housekeeper, Louise Dany, was a teenager when she joined the service of Gray in the 1920s and stayed with her all her life.

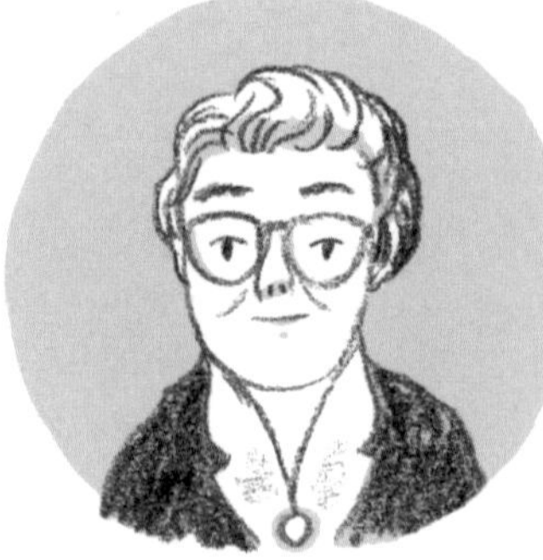

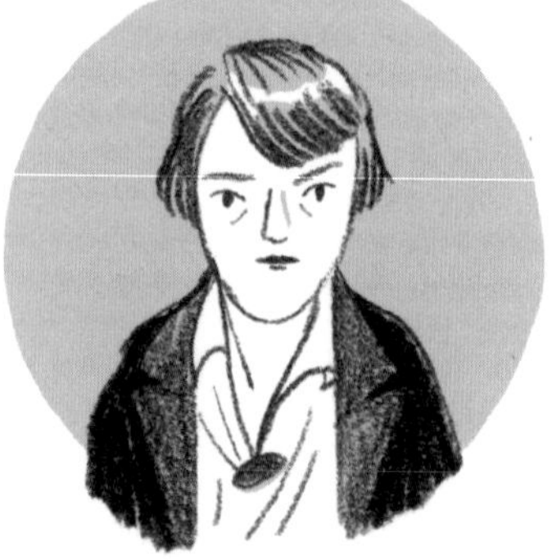

BERENICE ABBOTT

Berenice Abbott (1898–1991) was a photographer chronicling the artistic scene of 1920s Paris and notably the lesbian 'Left Bank' circles of which Gray was a part of. Gray commissioned Abbott for a set of now famous masculine-looking portraits. An assistant of Man Ray, Abbott developed her own practice and photographed Jean Cocteau, Djuna Barnes and André Gide, amongst others.

DAMIA

Marie-Louise Damien (1889–1978), also known by her stage name, Damia, was a renowned actor and singer. She became Gray's lover around 1922 and inspired furniture pieces and rugs created by Gray, who secretly named the pieces after Damia.

CHRISTIAN ZERVOS

Christian Zervos (1889–1970) was a Greek-French art critic and friend of Badovici's. Gray assisted Badovici in remodelling Zervos' house. Zervos founded the magazine *Cahiers d'Art* and wrote several articles on Gray's works in *La Revue de l'Art Ancient et Moderne* and *Les Arts de la Maison*.

GABRIELLE BLOCH

Gabrielle 'Gaby' Bloch (1878–1957), also known professionally as Gab Sorére, was an artist focused in filmmaking, choreography, set design and mechanics. She was one of Gray's lovers, a regular of Natalie Barney's lesbian salon and manager of Gray's interior design shop, Jean Désert, from its opening in 1922, until its closure in 1930.

DJUNA BARNES

Djuna Barnes (1892–1982) was an American writer and poet, best known for her novel, *Nightwood*. Barnes frequented the 'Left Bank' circles and was a close friend of Natalie Barney and a regular of her salon, where she met Gray.

NATALIE BARNEY

Natalie Barney (1876–1972) was an American novelist whose salon rue Jacob was frequented by Gray and other female artists and writers of the 1920s lesbian scene such as Gertrude Stein and her life partner, Alice B. Toklas. Barney's space allowed for critical discourse and dissent.

BIBLIOGRAPHY

Adam, Peter. *Eileen Gray, Her Life and Work.* Thames and Hudson. London, 2009.

Bonnevier, Katarina. "A Queer Analysis of Eileen Gray's E.1027," *Negotiating Domesticity: Spatial Productions of Gender in Modern Architecture.* Hilde Heyen and Gülsüm Baydar (eds). Routledge. London and New York, 2005.

Constant, Caroline. *Eileen Gray.* Phaidon. London, 2007.

Gatier, Pierre-Antoine. *"La restauration de la villa E-1027, un exemple d'intervention sur le patrimoine du XXe siècle".* Monumental, pp.14-19. 2009.

Gray, Eileen, and Badovici, Jean et. al., "E-1027 maison en bord de Mer", *L'Architecture Vivante,* 1929. Éditions Imbernon. Marseille, 2015.

Hubert, Marie-Odile. *"Les peintures murales de Le Corbusier ".* Massilia, pp.12-33. 2013.

ROQUEBRUNE
CAP MARTIN
Roquebrune
E1027
Plage du Buse
Pont l'Union
MENTON
Cabbé
Cap-Martin
THE
MEDITERRANEAN
MONACO
NICE
CANNES
ST TROPEZ
Pointe de la Veille

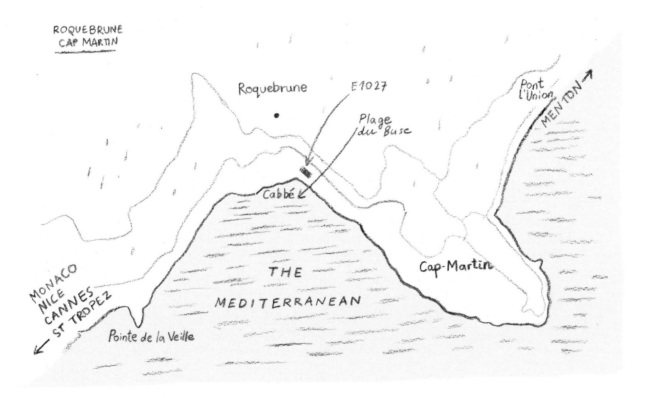

ABOUT THE CREATORS

CHARLOTTE MALTERRE-BARTHES

Charlotte Malterre-Barthes is an architect, urban designer and contemporary scholar. Principal of the urban design practice OMNIBUS, she teaches at the Architecture Department at the Swiss Institute of Technology (ETHZ), from where she holds a PhD. Co-curator of the XII Architecture Biennale of São Paulo, she co-authored *Housing Cairo: The Informal Response* and *Cairo Desert Cities*. She is a founding member of the Parity Group, a grassroots association committed to improving gender equality in architecture.

ZOSIA DZIERŻAWSKA

Zosia Dzierżawska is an illustrator and comics author with a passion for architecture, passed on to her by her urbanist dad. She's also one of the co-founders of Studio Armad'illo, an illustration and graphic design studio based in Milan. She works for a variety of international publishers, using her soft, expressive lines in children's books, comics and editorial illustration. Her works have been recognised twice at the Bologna Children's Book Fair Illustrators Exhibition, as well as at the Society of Illustrators in New York.

ACKNOWLEDGEMENTS

TO JEDREK, JUDYTA AND EWA, FOR MAKING ALL OF THIS POSSIBLE.
ADDITIONAL THANKS TO OLA CIESLAK FOR CHEERING ME ON, TO BRAM, WHOSE INFORMED
OPINION MEANS A LOT, AND TO THE ENTIRE STUDIO ARMAD'ILLO CREW FOR ITS GROUNDING
PRESENCE (AND THEIR BELIEF IN THE RESTORING POWER OF APERITIVI AND CENE).

ZOSIA

TO LORENZ, TO LOUIS, TO ANNE-MARIE MALTERRE-BARTHES,
TO MY FELLOW MILITANTS FROM THE PARITY GROUP AT ETHZ,
TO MY FEMINIST FRIENDS, EVERYWHERE.

CHARLOTTE

First published in 2019 by Nobrow Ltd.
27 Westgate Street, London E8 3RL.

1 3 5 7 9 10 8 6 4 2

Published in the US by Nobrow (US) Inc.
Printed in Latvia on FSC® certified paper.

MIX
Paper from responsible sources
FSC® C002795

ISBN: 978-1-910620-43-4
www.nobrow.net

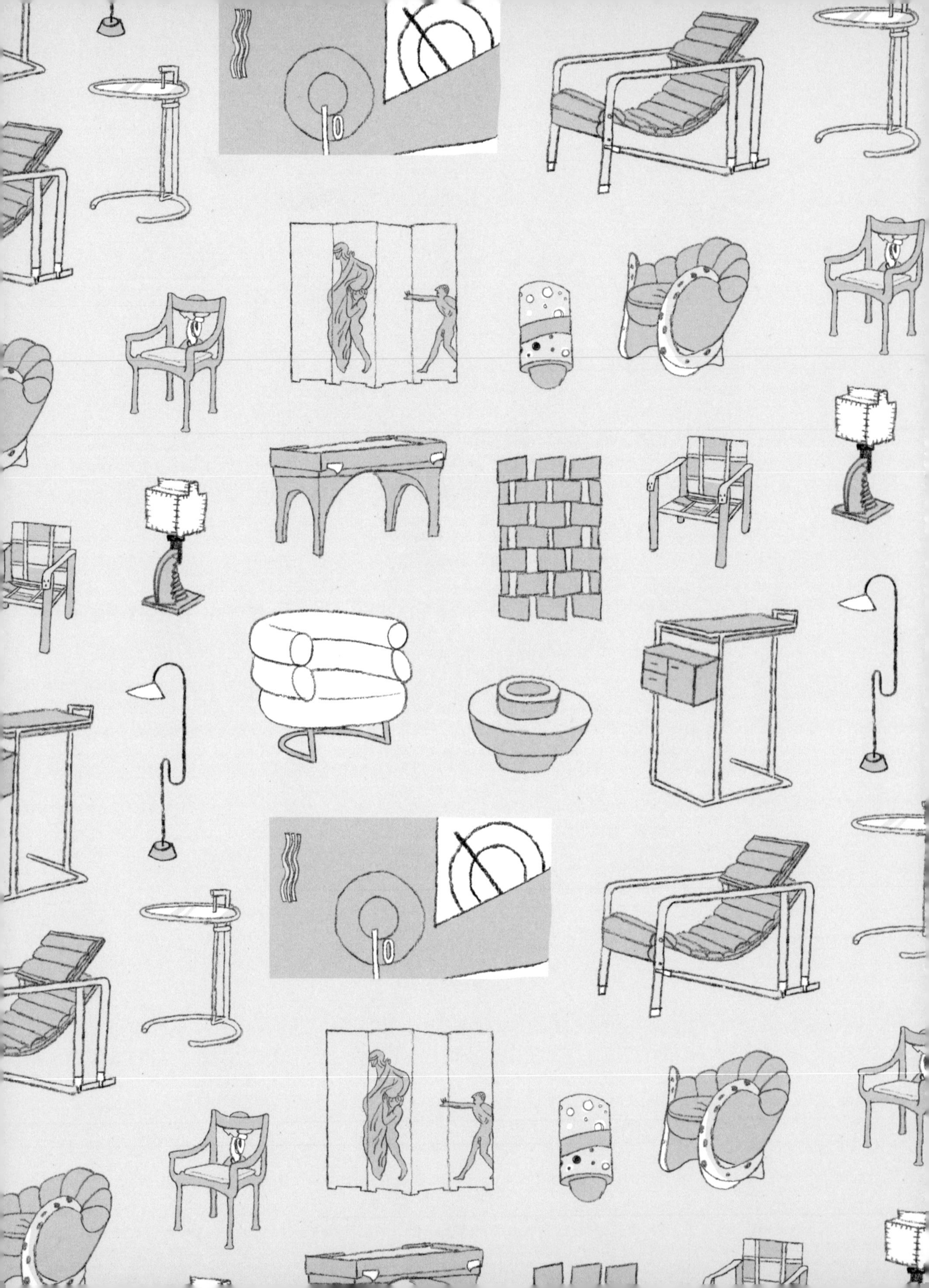